GERALDINE
OF THE
ALBANIANS

GWEN ROBYNS
GERALDINE
OF THE
ALBANIANS
The Authorised Biography

MBW

First published in Great Britain in 1987
by Muller, Blond & White Limited
62/65 Chandos Place,
London WC2N 4NW

British Library Cataloguing in Publication Data

Robyns, Gwen
  Geraldine, Queen of Albania : the
  authorised biography.
  1. Geraldine, *Queen, Consort of Zog,*
  King of Albania   2. Albania—Queens
  —Biography
  I. Title
  949.6'502'0924   DR971.25.G4

  ISBN 0–584–11133–9

Printed and bound in Great Britain by
Anchor Brendon Ltd, Tiptree, Essex.

INTRODUCTION

In telling the story of Her Majesty Queen Geraldine of the Albanians, it has been my most anxious endeavour to capture the flavour of her own thoughts and words. In my many conversations with her, I found it a constant astonishment that, after fifty years of being blown by the winds, she has such total recall. The images she conjures of people and incidents from so long ago remain diamond bright. The edges have not been blurred by age or time.

I am fortunate in having access not only to an uncompleted manuscript, begun by the Queen herself twenty years ago, but also to letters written from Tirana and Egypt to her governess Baroness Ruling. These were sold in a public auction in Switzerland just a few years ago and bought by a young Albanian royalist who recognised the people in an accompanying photograph album. The 200-odd letters were thrown in gratis with the album as being considered of very little value. They are now in Brussels and I have had access to these.

Although King Zog all his life deliberately refused to keep an official or personal diary, and forbade the Queen to do so, all the quotations accorded to him are taken from notes dictated by him at the time to the Queen, his Minister of Court, Colonel Sortir Martini, and his aide-de-camp, Colonel Salmani. In the maelstrom of Hitler's war this turbulent little country was overshadowed, and even shamefully neglected. Here at least I hope to correct some of the errors of the historians.

The Queen's life is not only a tender, enduring love story but a saga of courage and fortitude against overwhelming odds when a minority nation is used deliberately in the international game of war.

No biography is possible without friends — men and women — who share their experiences and give their time and patience to make the pages glow. This book has had many.

Firstly, Her Majesty Queen Geraldine herself for the trust she placed in me and a loving friendship that I hope will endure forever.

Then His Majesty King Leka I, who was not only determined that his mother's story should be told but encouraged me throughout the writing by telephone from South Africa where he is living now; and his wife Queen Susan, who confirmed my belief that Queen Geraldine emanates a special quality of immense spiritual beauty.

I will always remember those hours awash with laughter, with the Queen's bubbling, extrovert sister Virginia, Countess Apponyi, who brought to life their Hungarian childhood for me. Her friendship will be long treasured.

To Monsieur Skender de Zogu (nephew of King Zog) for arranging for me to see Baroness Ruling's letters.

To Barbara Cartland I owe so much, for it was she who initiated the first meeting between the Queen and myself.

I am also indebted to the Rt. Hon. Julian Amery, a man of many lives, for talking with me. 'King Zog was the most intelligent man I have ever met,' he said.

To Colonel Charles Inigo Jones who never failed in his encouragement, advice and practical help in the preparation of this book.

My gratitude to Colonel David Smiley for permission to quote from his book, *Albanian Assignment* (Chatto & Windus).

To Mr David J. Olson, State Archivist, the North Carolina Department of Cultural Resources, for his painstaking research.

FOREWORD

Albania is a strip of 11,000 square miles bordered on one side by Yugoslavia and by Greece on the other. Much of its awesome scenery is surrounded by soaring mountains where eagles fly free as protected birds. Most of the population of two and a quarter million live in the hinterland cities of the west, in a gentle climate where the temperature seldom falls below 40°F or rises above 81°F.

The country has a turbulent history. Albania was ruled by the Turks for 400 years, and after risings in the first decade of the twentieth century, Albanian independence was proclaimed in 1912. On 29th July 1913 an Albanian state was officially recognised; although the frontiers drawn did not nearly satisfy Albanian ethnic claims.

During the First World War, French, Italian and Serb troops occupied various parts of the country. Sovereignty status was not recognised until 1920 when the 1913 frontiers were confirmed.

It was Ahmed Zogu, a leading chieftain from the Mati tribe in the north, who forged the people into one nation, first as their President and later as their first elected King, Zog I.

King Zog established a special relationship between Albania and Italy achieving considerable progress and consolidation; but economically and financially Albania drifted into increased dependence on Italy. In April 1939 Italy occupied the country, Zog having refused further concessions. He and his Queen fled the country and a puppet government offered the crown to King Victor Emmanuel of Italy.

By 1942 the Allied Powers declared their intention of restoring Albanian independence. They tried to raise guerilla forces to drive out the Italians but were unsuccessful. Meanwhile, in Albania itself, a resistance movement had been formed in which left-wing elements, many of whom had been exiles, were prominent. Some fighting between the Left and Right followed until the former, having disposed of their rivals, formed a national independence front which took office in 1944 as the 'first democractic government of Albania.'

Diplomatic relations between Albania and Great Britain and the United States of America broke off in 1946 after the mining of two Royal Navy destroyers in the Corfu Channel off the coast of Albania. At the same time, Enver Hoxha was elected secretary-general of the Albanian Communist Party. His policy was characterised by close friendship with Russia and with Yugoslavia, but his links with the latter came to an abrupt end in 1948 when Marshal Tito broke with Stalin. As a fanatical admirer of Stalin, Hoxha threw in his lot with Russia. By 1960, however, the honeymoon was over. Hoxha accused Kruschev of revisionism and broke with the Soviet Union. Albania is the only officially atheist state in Europe.

Hoxha's next move was to exploit the growing conflict between Russia and China. China was delighted to have Albanian support for they had gained a vital foothold in Europe but it was not destined to last and in 1978 relations with China came to an end.

Since then Albania has remained remote, sinister and apart — the poorest and most oppressed country in Western Europe. During his reign of forty-one years, Hoxha succeeded in making Albania one of the most isolated countries in the world; only a few foreigners in later years were permitted to enter the country. In the last year tourists in strictly conducted parties have been permitted.

The view is bleak. Armed patrol boats police the shorelines and sharp-eyed observers can make out fortified trenches dug into the hillsides and beaches laced with barbed wire. Reports tell of food shortages and extensive rationing; milk is so scarce that it is on sale for only half an hour each day, soap and basic medicaments are unavailable. Apparently, many factories now work a two-day week because of the lack of electricity. Transport is limited to collapsed lorries struggling along dirt tracks and a small rail network; private cars are banned.

With the death of Enver Hoxha in March 1985, hopes were raised that there might come a thaw in international relations. Would the new leader, Ramiz Alia, succumb to outside pressure to open their borders and, most important, to liberate their minds? The new régime may already have produced signs of relaxation; Albania has expressed an interest in extending trade with the West, and has agreed to open the railway line which now

4

links Albania with Yugoslavia. Some prisoners have been freed, some people are allowed to travel abroad – but the legacy of the old Stalinist influence is dominant everywhere; the deification of Hoxha continues.

Once it was the dream of Queen Geraldine, Albania's first and only Queen, to open her country not only to become a development economist's dream (with its wealth of high grade chromium, oil, abundant hydro-electric power, fertile valleys and spectacular scenery) but to become a major European tourist resort.

Only time will tell.

A LAMENT FROM BEHIND THE IRON CURTAIN

Starlight, a ray of sunshine, a ray of blessed light
Is all that remains to us of life's light,
We wait for you midday and evening
In our hole with hope
But, even this has been taken from us.
The first window is being sealed with iron.

With wide open eyes we see branches moving,
People going down to a river laughing
Their faces seeming to shine.
Volcanos tremble with their hidden smoke,
The fire of our souls in hell.
Blind we stare into the night,
The window has been completely sealed with iron.

Ten men huddled in a hole
Who breathe in and out air which is no more
Air, air we smell of rotting fish.
Strength, strength to resist the filth
It is more than super human, oh poor flesh!
The window has been sealed with iron.

The alpine pine, winds from the west,
Caress us purely, freely
Fresh as white snowflakes,
Blow across our burning souls,
Take our message of supplication
To you, to the heights of the West.
Only symbolically alas, oh wind,
As the window has been sealed with iron.

The sirens of the ships, the laughter of youth,
The blessed sound of the organ,
Imagination, disillusion all is silence
Since each window is now sealed with iron.

Oh blue sky that we can no longer see,
Oh velvet, oh silk that we cannot touch,
Already each finger bleeds at their tips.
The rats of the night have bitten them.
Our senses bleed for
You, oh light of liberty,
Today all the windows were sealed with iron.

There is no tomorrow.
Let our sacrifice be not in vain
West, remember us, long live Liberty!

Written by Queen Geraldine on Christmas Day, 1956, in Cannes.

CHAPTER 1

The time was six o'clock in the evening on 11th April, 1985. Queen Geraldine of the Albanians walked slowly from the telephone in the library of her Madrid apartment. Her face as usual was serenely beautiful but she was obviously nervous and her azure blue eyes had a strange misty light in them.

"Hoxha is dead," she said quietly.

Without any more sign of emotion she sat down opposite me at the card table in the salon where we had worked together for several weeks.

Poor Albania. What is going to happen now? Do you realise how beautiful that country is? Such mountains, such gorgeous lakes and miles and miles of unpolluted beaches. I so wanted to bring it into tourism and open up my country to the whole world.

There was so much to be done and so little time. Just one year. Oh the plans and dreams I had for that country which had opened its heart to me. Who knows what will happen? It is probably too late for me now but it is my son Leka I am thinking about. I only think of his future and the happiness and safety of my grandson, Little Leka.

We sat in silence as the Queen's eyes roamed the room alighting on the various pieces of royal memorabilia, precious items that she has collected since she fled from Albania forty-six years ago. If she noticed the large photograph of herself and King Zog, taken from the official portrait which was left behind in Tirana, her eyes did not linger. Queen Geraldine has no time for tears.

Then came a second telephone call, this time from South Africa informing her that King Leka had left his farm house at the end of a dusty road near Randberg, on the outskirts of Johannesburg, and was already on his way to the airport to fly to Washington. The King had planned to go to America in any case, but the death of Enver Hoxha brought immediacy to his trip. Free Albania has many friends in Washington with Senator Jesse Helms leading the list. It is in the Free World's strategic interest to help prevent a Soviet re-occupation of Albania and such men as Helms claim that it is "America's moral duty to help the Albanian people to rid themselves once and for all of communism in their country." From his home in South Africa King Leka maintains contact with the Albanian communities abroad and is fully conversant with the situation in Albania and its immediate surroundings. He also carries out official trips to a variety of countries to acquaint the leaders with the Albanian situation. He finances himself through business activities, mainly dealing in commodities and often using his political connections around the world to facilitate his business deals.

Though he spent only three days after his birth on Albanian soil, King Leka has been brought up totally surrounded by an Albanian household which included family members, Ministers of the Court, officers of the Royal Guard and office staff. Throughout his youth he was given a great deal of instruction by his father and on King Zog's death bed pledged that he would continue to fight to free the Albanian people from the most ruthless and rigid of all communist régimes. Having this kind of background, and living through a variety of political ups and downs, it would be surprising if he did not have the devotion he does to his country. As one observer who escaped recently reported: "My country is one vast labour camp."

To the many thousands of Free Albanians scattered around the world, whether they are Royalists or Republicans, Queen Geraldine remains as a symbol of their nation, almost as the flag. For the young Albanians she is very much the mother figure and they are proud to pay homage to her whenever she visits their country whether it be Australia, United States of America, France or Belgium for these countries are where the largest colonies are to be found.

At seventy-one years of age much of her legendary beauty remains. Her figure, her long slender legs, are an inheritance from her American grandmother but the tender magic of her personality could only be Hungarian, a country known for its beautiful women. Her hair is the same sable blonde, the colour it was in her twenties when she became the second youngest Queen in the world; only Queen Farida of Egypt was younger. Queen Geraldine's azure blue eyes, the size of periwinkles, have the engaging habit of suddenly opening wide like a flower when she becomes animated. She speaks seven languages with equal ease, flipping from one to the other seemingly without being conscious of the change.

On meeting her, one senses that underneath this irresistible aura of romanticism there is a steel-bright political brain and an acute awareness of life in all its aspects. It was Queen Geraldine who spent a feverish four days visiting all the Muslim embassies in Madrid, seeking asylum for her son when he was ordered out of Spain in 1979 with only six days notice.

As King Leka described his mother to me: "She is very flexible. She is not hard, not brittle, there is no way you can break her. She bends with the circumstances but she does not change. I have never known my mother not know exactly what she is doing. There are times when she has not been exposed to certain things, but when she finally is, she then realises immediately why they happened. There is very little that I can teach my mother."

Queen Geraldine and her son have known forty-six years of exile – forty-six years in which hope has never failed them. King Leka tells of the very last conversation he had with his father before he died in the hospital Foch Suresnes in Paris on 11th April 1961.

"As I sat by his bed he woke from a deep sleep and looking directly at me said, 'I have had a dream. I saw your mother standing on the prow of a ship. She was a very old woman but still very beautiful and her hair was blowing in the breeze. The ship was edging into the quay at Durazzo . . .'

"My father then went on to describe in exact detail the scene he had just experienced in his dream. He told me that he had seen me and I was leading a column of troops and that we were in combat gear looking pretty bedraggled as though we had come through the mill. What was interesting about that conversation is that he had never seen a picture of the port as it is today, which was totally unrecognisable from my father's time nearly fifty years ago, yet his description was totally accurate when I later checked it with recent photographs. Another point was that it is only very recently that Albanian Freedom Fighters have gone into camouflage clothes. He described us in camouflage which was not Albanian gear as we only switched from greens two years ago, before that, in his time, the troops wore grey-green.

"All Albanians have a tendency to interpret dreams. It is part

11

of our character. In this case either my father had a pre-vision or an hallucination. I hope that it was the first. It's quite crazy but it is interesting that having told me about his dream, my father closed his eyes and slipped into a coma from which he never recovered."

If Queen Geraldine has any secret hopes that King Zog's dream will ever come to fruition she is keeping them to herself.

One must of course ask the pertinent question of age. Would she now wish to uproot herself and begin a new life? It was King Zog's wish that his remains should be taken back to lie in Albanian soil. One of the Queen's last gestures before she left Albania in 1939 was to collect a small bag of earth. This she kept with her through her travels and it was buried with the King in France.

> I have asked in my testament to be cremated so that my ashes may be put in a urn and buried with the King where we belong – in Albanian soil. Albania will remain in my heart forever and I belong there.

That changes will come in Albania over the next few years both Queen Geraldine and King Leka have no doubt. It is just a question of time.

CHAPTER 2

It was the morning of 31st January, 1938 when the reed slim figure of a young woman dressed in navy blue, trimmed with white, appeared on the balcony of a villa in Tirana, capital of Albania. She stood there, the wintry sun glinting on her blonde hair as she saluted in the Albanian fashion, right hand turned down horizontally across the heart, the interpretation being, "I carry you in my heart".

It was the first time that the ordinary citizens of Tirana realised for certain that at last their forty-two year old bachelor King Zog had chosen a bride and clearly they liked what they saw.

It was known that for political reasons Mussolini would have preferred the King to have chosen an Italian bride, thus linking the two countries through the House of Savoy, but the King would not agree to this. It was rumoured in America that King Zog would settle on an American heiress if she brought a dowry of $5,000,000. This was untrue. Known as a charmer to all women the King made no secret of his women friends, but none had been suitable to be his Queen.

Several mid-European beauties accepted the King's invitation to visit Albania with a view to marriage. Being a strict Muslim, one of the considerations was that his future Queen must be a virgin, and sadly the beauties had to return to their families having not been able to satisfy this request.

The twenty-two year old Countess Geraldine Apponyi came from a distinguished Hungarian family and was considered one of the most charming young women in European nobility. Because of her beauty she was known as the White Rose of Hungary and had the same beguiling look of innocence as the present Princess of Wales. She shone with health, a valuable asset for the continuation of the Zogu dynasty.

By her side was General Geregi, the King's aide-de-camp. Two Albanian flags in red silk emblazoned with black eagles and the helmet of Skanderbeg, the national hero of Albania in days gone by, fluttered behind her. Suddenly a breeze came up and whipped the flags around the young woman, completely enveloping her like the wings of a giant butterfly. There was a spontaneous cry from the people below who took this to be a good omen for the marriage.

Thousands of ordinary citizens of Tirana and from the surrounding mountain villages, who had flocked to the small capital when the news of the King's impending engagement leaked out, broke into wild cheering and clapping as they realised with the firing of cannon shots that the engagement was now official.

Again and again they cheered as she waved and threw pieces of bread and silver coins, an old Albanian custom, among the crowd. Many years afterwards little bits of bread, by then hard as stone, were to be found on hand-carved stands in the dwellings of loyalist Albanian families. The bread was treated with the reverence of a religious icon and carried the message "A gift from the King's bride". The silver coins were pierced and joined the other amulets on the fine long silver chains of the women.

Earlier that morning there had been a special session of Parliament. According to the Albanian constitution, the King's engagement request was first submitted for the consent of the two Chambers. Sitting in the principal gallery were his six sisters, the Princesses, while diplomats and dignitaries filled the other galleries. All the seats on the floor of the house were occupied. The president announced the House's approval and immediately thunderous applause filled the Chamber as cries of *Rroft-Mbreti* – Long Live the King – broke out. Four Deputies made speeches to celebrate the significance of the event, saluting the renewal of the Albanian-Hungarian links which had been so strong during the fifteenth century under John Hunyady and Skanderbeg.

The night before, there had been a gala dinner in the King's palace for members of the Apponyi family, who had come from Budapest and Vienna. There was Geraldine's American grandmother, Mrs Virginia de Strale d'Ekna, her aunts, Countess Muriel Scherr Thoss and Countess Adele Apponyi, and her sister, Countess Virginia Apponyi with her husband André de Baghy. Her mother who had remarried, was unable to be present. It was a night of glitter and grandeur as members of the Government, heads of the Army and the Diplomatic Corps joined in sitting down to a dinner table gleaming with silver-gilt services and covered with flowers. Geraldine wore a filmy silk dress, the

14

colour of deep sapphires, which the King had chosen for her from Worth in Paris as a surprise. On her engagement finger was a magnificent fourteen-carat solitaire diamond of purest blue-white. For the first and only time in his life, the King wore a gold, ruby and sapphire Hungarian engagement ring which had belonged to Geraldine's father, Count Gyula Apponyi, who died when she was a child. The King's six sisters, a bevy of dark haired princesses, represented his side of the family.

Before dinner the King had requested that the family gather in an ante-room where Princess Geraldine, as she was now styled, appeared on the arm of the King.

"I am very happy and hope that my fiancée is also happy." Spoken in German with an engaging foreign lilt these were the only words that the King said about the engagement. Continuing in his soft voice he added:

"I would be grateful if on this day of joy in my life, in this festival hour of my country, you would give a few moments of silent prayer to the memory of a woman who was dear and beloved to both myself and my people – more than anybody else. I know the spirit of my mother is among us at this moment. Blessed be her memory."

For a few moments there was silence in the room. The love of the King for his remarkable mother was legendary. Sadije, as she is called in Albania, was a daughter of the Toptani family who were the ruling family in the centre of Albania, and, to bring a durable peace with the leaders of the Mati province, a marriage was arranged between the fourteen-year-old girl and the near forty Djemal Zogu. Despite the difference in their ages it was a marriage of great happiness and fulfilment.

Ahmed Zogu's father was a widower when he married in 1891, and he already had a son. An elder brother died in infancy, so it is understandable why Ahmed was so precious to his parents. They had seven living children – six daughters and one son, Ahmed. Sadije was a woman of great heart, brilliantly sharp brain and a deep knowledge of her country. Though she had not had a formal education she had an instinctive wisdom and acquired a great deal of experience from life itself. She knew how to command and she even led troops on horseback when necessary.

A fearless matriarch, she brought up her children under an iron

15

discipline, but with affectionate care. Into her young son Ahmed she instilled national pride, courage and initiative; these same virtues were to make him worthy, later in life, of being called *Mbret i Squitarvet* – Bird of the First, King of all the Sons of the Eagle. When her husband Djemal Pasha died in 1901, Sadije Zogu had become head of the Zogolli clan in their fortress castle in the Mati province and had set about running the vast estate single-handed on behalf of her son, who was then only six years old.

Sadije died in 1935 and the King's grief was so devastating that he immediately banished the doctor who had attended her. He then erected an imposing mausoleum on a hill overlooking Tirana and arranged that the tomb was to be guarded day and night.

The engagement celebrations continued into the dusk when the people filed past the new princess's villa making music and singing. Time and time again they called for Geraldine who went out on to the balcony and, in the cascading flare of the fireworks that were exploding all over the city, she plucked blooms from bouquets that she had been receiving all day and threw them into the crowds. The dark brooding mountain men loved her fragile beauty and the women were entranced by her natural charm. It was a night of story-book romance and only to be compared in recent years to Princess Grace's arrival in the Principality of Monaco when she, too, was treated as a fairy princess.

A gypsy fortune teller two years before at a Magyar fair had predicted what life had in store for the young Geraldine. Wandering among the gaily coloured tents containing stalls bulging with fruits, handicrafts and the good things of the earth her Aunt Muriel had wanted to buy her a gingerbread heart iced in bright pink.

"Thank you Aunt Muriel but I have bought one already." Geraldine replied.

"Then give yours to someone else," the older woman laughed.

"Oh no, I haven't got anyone I want to give it to," Geraldine replied primly.

At that moment an old gypsy, typical of the soothsayers that were a feature of all Magyar fairs, accosted aunt and neice as they passed her tent. She coaxed Countess Scherr Thoss into her booth

16

while Geraldine waited outside. She was not only by nature as shy as a faun but fortune telling, or the art of divination, was against her religious beliefs, as she was a devout Roman Catholic.

Aunt Muriel had the full treatment with cards, crystal ball and the palm of her hand. When she finally emerged from the tent the gypsy woman turned to Geraldine and said, "As this young girl has brought the Spring into my house I would like to tell her future." No amount of protesting would stop her as she insisted that she would only read Geraldine's palm, and that she would not accept any money for it.

This was the gypsy's prophecy: "During the next year you will have three small accidents and you will receive three proposals of marriage. Be very careful. There will be two where the sea will have to be crossed. Choose that in which you will have to make the crossing and not your fiancé. You will achieve the highest station and will pass your life working for others. It will be necessary in some situations to think of yourself or otherwise you will suffer from your own selflessness.

"Great luck I see, lovely lady. A crown I see in your hand. A golden crown. Much joy and pride around the crown but also there will be suffering and anxiety. But the worry is pale and the crown shines. Nothing bad remains at the end, only happiness and fame. Just hold on to the crown."

The countess promised she would return and make good recompense should the gypsy's predictions come true. That evening she recorded them in her journal.

Geraldine did have three accidents within the same year. A carriage in which she was returning to the family chateau from a hunt overturned and she hit her head on a tree trunk. Another time the car in which she was returning to Budapest from a weekend in the country collided with a cart and killed the horse. The third accident was a motoring one too, when the car in which she was travelling overturned a taxi.

Also, just as the gypsy had prophesied, Geraldine received three proposals of marriage – from a German, an Englishman and a King. These last two involved a sea-crossing.

Many months later, when Geraldine had become Queen of Albania, the diligent Countess Scherr Thoss returned to the fair to look for the gypsy and so was able to recompense her.

At the time no one was more intrigued by the gypsy's prophecy than Geraldine's sister and her two closest girl friends. In a haze of teenage romanticism they had bought a thin ring with a blue-green shamrock on it and pledged to each other that whoever wore it would be married within a year. When Virginia Apponyi married the handsome young aristocrat André de Baghy, she passed the ring to Geraldine who now wore it on her fourth finger.

"Oh Gerrie," one of the girls had cried when she heard about the gypsy, "so you're going to marry the Prince after all." They were referring to a dark-haired young Duke who had been courting Geraldine that season. When they continued to tease her she quipped, "Why do you think that he is a Prince? Why don't you think that I may marry a King? The King of fairyland."

And like girls all over the world, they dissolved in giggles.

CHAPTER 3

Geraldine's mother, Gladys was an American heiress, and the daughter of the general counsellor of the United States in Amsterdam. A part of the wealthy social world of Europe before the First World War she attended many embassy balls and dinners, where often impoverished European noblemen were on the look-out for rich young brides. But her parents guarded her well.

It was in Paris in 1912 that Count Apponyi first met the attractive Gladys Virginia Stewart during a dinner party at the Austro-Hungarian Embassy. It was love at first sight as the handsome aristocrat set eyes on the flirtatious young American. Gladys Stewart had lived in Europe since the age of twelve and combined the insouciance of a typical American girl with the chic of a Parisian. The combination was irresistible.

A courtship immediately began, they discussed wedding plans and Gladys Stewart was even agreeable to changing her religion and becoming a Roman Catholic so that she could become part of the illustrious Apponyi family. It was to have been a spectacular society wedding as befitted such a union, but with the anouncement of war in 1914 all the plans had to be changed.

As Count Gyula Apponyi was forty-one years old, he had passed the age of being called-up for military service but volunteered as a liason officer and felt it his duty to return to Hungary and that marriage was out of the question. He carefully explained to his fiancée that he felt it unfair to take a young bride back to a country during wartime when she did not "know the language, nor the customs, nor even my family." However he had not reckoned with a free-spirited American girl.

The marriage between Gladys Stewart and Count Gyula Apponyi was celebrated in between trains in Geneva at St Joseph's Church on 29th July, 1914. On arrival in Budapest the bridal couple moved into the elegant sixteen-room apartment of the groom's mother, widow of Count Ludwig Apponyi, Grand Marshal of the Court of His Imperial and Royal Apostolic

Majesty of Hungary. Her husband had been left the immense task by his father, who had died heavily in debt, of disposing of the family palace in Budapest and houses in Vienna and Paris so as to maintain and modernise the family estate, Nagy Appony. The Hungarian State gave Countess Apponyi, the widow of their Grand Marshal, a magnificent apartment in Buda and it was here in her grandmother's home that Geraldine was born in 1916.

> A year after my birth the Central Empire crumbled and shortly afterwards the Bolshevik Revolution, under the guidance of Bela Kun, occupied Hungary and installed there a reign of terror and immense cruelty. By a miracle my father and mother managed to get passports to leave the country and took a train to Switzerland where they were able to join my maternal grandmother who helped them to live.
>
> My mother was an heiress but her money was held in trust in America until the day of her marriage when she gave over everything to my father to manage. He being a patriot put it all in bonds in Austria and Hungary from which he recovered nothing after the sinking of the two monarchies and the inflation that followed. My parents managed to exist through my grandmother's help.
>
> It was fortunate that my father went into exile as when the Bolsheviks pillaged the family house they also hung up an effigy of him as he was on the list of prominent aristocrats who were to be killed.

The origins of the Apponyi family go back to the conquest of Hungary by Arpad in the year 894 AD and the subsequent establishment of the Kingdom of Hungary under the Arpadian Dynasty.

> I can say without fear of mistake that there was no event in the thousand years of Hungarian history in which my ancestors did not take part.

It was before the end of the Arpadian Dynasty in 1280 that the name of a Chevalier d'Apponyi first appeared and the large estate called Nagy Appony became the family seat. It was situated on high ground dominating a huge expanse of forests and lakes and was to become the place that Geraldine was to love most in her whole life. The estate, where she spent most of her childhood, was to remain in the Apponyi family in an unbroken line until

1936 when it was taken over by a Slovak for debts incurred by her uncle and then bought back by King Zog in 1938.

After the war we lived for two years in Paris and Montreux before my father was at last able to go back to Hungary in 1921. He returned penniless so my paternal grandmother sold her court jewels and made three dowries for my sister Virginia, our cousin who was the daughter of Uncle Anthony Apponyi and myself. It was this uncle who had managed the Apponyi estates, but the difficulties with the new Slovak authorities obliged him to cede everything to the youngest of the brothers, Count Henry Apponyi. Although the family estate had been affected by the various reforms this still represented a handsome fortune in those days with its thousands of hectares of forests, the sugar refinery built by my father and a great deal of rich arable land.

My dowry enabled my parents to buy a lovely villa with a large garden in the suburbs of Budapest. I still remember the garden where we played and the comfortable drawing room where in front of a large fireplace my father used to take me on his knee and read me stories from *Bibliotèque Rose* by Countess Segur, a favourite children's author.

My mother used to be annoyed about this and chide my father: "You spend all day in town and in the evening you have Wee Wee (his pet name for me) on your knee." I shall never forget those hours so warm with love and tenderness before the leaping flames of the fire.

In the evenings before going to sleep he used to say the rosary with me. Many times, infuriated by this, I used to pretend to fall asleep.

My father had been suffering from a lung disease for some time and medical help in those days could do nothing to prevent his dying on the afternoon of 27th May, 1924.

Virginia and I were in the garden when my aunt Countess Adele Apponyi came to break the terrible news to us. At seven years of age one believes only what one wants to and it was not until about three weeks later that I first realised that I would never see my father again. There followed interminable days of nightmares and tears with my mother distraught, not knowing how to comfort me. It was not until I went to school for the first time that I began to forget my desperate anguish.

It seems that my father's love is still with me, even today, so many years after his death. Whenever I am in distress about something it is to my father that I send a plea. Sixty-three years later his memory is still fresh and imperishable.

21

Queen Geraldine's mother was only thirty-four years of age and by now had a son Gyula as well as her two daughters. She decided to sell the house in Budapest and return to France, the country she preferred. She was thirsty for sunshine and flowers and felt at ease with the French language. She chose Menton to be near her own mother who lived in Monte Carlo in the Boulevardes des Moulin.

Again tragedy struck this young mother, as the notary who sold the house in Budapest vanished and by the time he was found and charged he had gone through all her money. Another fortune had disappeared in the wind.

It was perfectly natural that such a vivacious young widow should wish to have a husband and when Colonel Contran Girault asked Countess Gladys Apponyi to marry him, she agreed. The house was filled with tension as Geraldine and Virginia sensed that something unusual was happening around them. There was even an estrangement between Countess Gladys Apponyi and her mother, who opposed the new marriage, so that they no longer spoke.

Though the sisters had been enrolled at the English school in Menton, and made life-long friends there, such as the Countess of Darnley (Rosemary Potter), their mother yielded to the wishes of the Apponyi family and agreed that the little girls should return to Hungary and be brought up there. Geraldine and Virginia were overjoyed as they remembered the sweet smell of Nagy Appony.

If they questioned at all why their mother, who was taking them back to Hungary, was accompanied by a French officer, Colonel Contran Girault, they were far too well brought up to question this anomaly. It was only when the train arrived at Ventimiglia, in Italy, the next station after Menton, that their mother announced, "My children this is your father." Without telling them Countess Apponyi had married the dashing Frenchman on an unknown date in a little chapel along the coast. In the fullness of time she was to produce a second family – Guy, Sylviane and Patricia Girault.

> The emotion we felt on returning at last to Nagy Appony and the loving welcome of our grandmother, aunts, uncles and cousins made us forget that a stranger had taken the place of the father whom we adored so much. It was to be a summer and autumn filled with golden memories. Our grandmother prepared us herself for our first communion which took place

with fifty members of the family present who had come from all over the world. This lovely family chapel today is a Marxist village school.

Childhood is full of inconsistency. It bends the rules without sense, relying on emotions and not reasoning. Happy as they were at Nagy Appony the two small sisters missed their fascinating mother and ached to return to Menton and be with her, even accepting the suspicious new father. Countess Adele Apponyi, their father's eldest sister, volunteered to take them back to Menton. On arrival they found that life had changed drastically at the Villa Iberia. There were no more Hungarian servants and instead of returning to the English school at Menton, they were now enrolled at the French Lycée, as the Girault family had moved to Nice. Geraldine's mother was preoccupied not only with the little Girault daughter she already had but a new baby she was expecting.

All this trauma was too much for chubby-cheeked little Virginia who suddenly became very ill as only small children can for no apparent reason. Even Geraldine, a sunny child by nature, became strangely quiet as she saw her mother in pain and even worse, her sister Virginia being sent back to Hungary. Madame Girault had persuaded her new husband to leave his army career and there was a general feeling of unrest within the newly created family.

It was Geraldine's Hungarian grandmother who saved the situation. On the pretext that she was eighty-five years old and feared she had not long to live, she asked that Geraldine return to Hungary to be with her. Accompanied by her American Aunt Muriel, the Countess of Scherr Thoss, she was once more shuttled across Europe to Hungary where she and Virginia were sent to the Sacred Heart School in Pressbaum, near Vienna. From then until 1936 she divided most of her time between her school at Pressbaum and holidays at the sixty-room castle, Nagy Appony.

The castle library was Geraldine's favourite haunt. Here she had found a small niche where she could spend hours undiscovered, given over to the delight of touching, smelling, looking at and reading the thousands of musty leather-bound rare books lining the shelves. She cajoled the carpenter to make her a set of her very own book shelves and persuaded everyone to give her some books. After the death of her grandmother, when she was sixteen, she had her very own library of more than six thousand books.

The grown-ups despaired of the shy, skinny child who preferred to read rather than join the hilarious parties for skiing, cycling, hunting and swimming. They feared for her health and she was ordered to spend three hours a day in outside activities. Never particularly keen on sports she became a gardener but refused adamantly to grow anything other than sweet peas and green beans.

One of the sisters' most exciting games was looking for the treasure that was supposed to be hidden in the grounds of Nagy Appony. They never found anything but many years later, when the Slovak Communists turned the chapel into a study centre, behind the altar the workmen found a small secret room where there were boxes of gold dubloons which had been hidden there during the thirty years' war between the Protestants and the Catholics many years before.

Childhood at Nagy Appony was filled with golden dreams, nights sleeping under the stars, days swimming in lakes, fishing for trout in the streams, catching fresh crayfish and roasting them over a fire of pine cones.

As the family was not rich, the servants did not wear uniforms but their own colourful national dress and the great dining room was never used for meals, which were taken in one of the small salons. An exception was the visit of the Maharaja of Patiala. Uncle Henry Apponyi, a great traveller and huntsman, had been in India many times and wished to repay the hospitality he had received in that country. The Maharaja arrived complete with one pretty young Hindu wife, his eldest son and a suite of secretaries and servants. 'Gerrie' and 'Ginnie' were mesmerised as they watched the Maharani transform her room into an Indian fantasy, the bed covered with sheets of silk, the furniture draped with rich brocades, the floor strewn with precious rugs and on the tables little boxes overflowing with jewels.

When the Maharaja appeared late one evening in the grand salon – and Grandmother Apponyi was a stickler for punctuality – she noticed with horror that instead of one wife he had three. Nor was she amused when her grand-daughters removed their fancy-dress veils and dissolved in giggles. Only Uncle Henry saved that situation from disaster, but as a reward the little girls were allowed to keep their saris and jewels as gifts.

They were very impressed by the respect the Maharani paid her husband. In the evening at a sign from him she would prostrate herself at his feet. She could not go out in the park unless accompanied by other women or the two girls. When the Maharaja teasingly invited Geraldine and Virginia to join his harem it was a subdued pair who made themselves scarce.

Though Albanian Muslims were much more emancipated than in other oriental countries it was the first taste of female subservience that young Geraldine had experienced and she was to remember it all her life.

After the death of her grandmother, Geraldine's stays at Nagy Appony became more rare and she spent most of her holidays at Zebegny with her aunt the Countess Fanny Karolyi.

A remarkably advanced woman in social work, Countess Karolyi had bought ten peasant cottages in a fishing village on the Danube not far from Estergom. These she painted in their original colours and furnished them in the greatest luxury, while keeping the essential character of the different regions of Hungary. Geraldine, Virginia, cousins and friends all lived there, each with her own apartment while Aunt Fanny was in charge in the main house where they all ate their meals.

I still remember Aunt Fanny's beautiful reddish blonde hair that fell to her ankles like a cloud. She was very alive and original and after the death of her husband she planned her life doing exactly what she wished. She had retired from the world, dividing her time between Zebegny and her palace in Budapest and spent much of her time doing charitable work. At her own cost Aunt Fanny founded an old people's home, medical centres and a hospital, but the village was her chief pride.

She organised and built a village for people badly disabled through the war. They not only had a house each but also two factories, one for women and one for men where they specialised in basket handicraft. Each house was the gift of a country and the tourists used to flock to see them with the flags of the various countries floating in the wind.

There were no lazy bones permitted in Zebegny. From nine o'clock to eleven o'clock in the morning the girls practised shorthand and typing and Queen Geraldine is still pretty efficient today.

Then we visited needy families in the surrounding areas. In the late afternoon, we gathered up young girls and boys and on the sportsground we played basketball, gymnastics, football and organised games. I had swum since I was five years of age but was not a very strong swimmer, tiring quickly. I remember one day when a group had decided to cross the Danube and I was left behind and got caught in a whirlpool. The others were too far away to hear my cries and when I was drowning a fisherman saw me and saved me by catching my hair and pulling me out of the river on to his boat.

In the winter, swimming and rowing were replaced by skiing, skating and riding. We skied on the hills that sloped gently down to the Danube and which were covered with forests. It was an extraordinarily productive childhood with a great deal of open-mindedness – a willingness to change a view in the light of new experiences, facts, information and argument. Aunt Fanny was building into us a sense of values and service that was to remain with me for all my life. Whenever in doubt I hear Aunt Fanny's voice and I know instinctively what is right or wrong. She gave us all a freedom of choice and the rest was up to us. I can never thank her sufficiently for what she gave me in life. It was almost as if she knew what lay ahead for me.

Although Hungary had been greatly weakened by the Trianon pact at the Treaty of Versailles in 1919, the country had made a courageous effort to recuperate. There was a feeling that for the first time in centuries Hungary was now completely independent. As a result the social life that season had never been gayer, especially if you were as pretty as Geraldine and an Apponyi. Though she was only seventeen, Geraldine made her debut at a magnificent ball given by the Hungarian Monarchists. Countess Adele Apponyi, the eldest sister of her father, who was unmarried, was chosen from among the aunts to chaperone her. Young ladies were still closely chaperoned and could only speak to those to whom they had been formally introduced. To Geraldine all this seemed perfectly natural as she had been brought up dropping curtsies to her elders and obeying their whims.

I still remember Aunt Fanny and Aunt Adele helping me to dress in front of a wood fire in my room which was hung with blue brocade in the Karolyi Palace in Budapest, from which I was to go to all the balls that season.

My first ball dress was apple-blossom pink tulle and the bodice was decorated with little fresh pink rose-buds. I wore a tiny tiara of light pink feathers on my curled hair. A slim necklace of pearls and a turquoise ring from my mother were my only jewels.

I was amazed on entering the salons blazing with light from huge chandeliers. I remember an immense feeling of pride as for the first time in my life all the men kissed my hand. I felt that I was being treated like a married lady though naturally it was not because of this but the name I bore.

The party lasted until early morning. After the dance orchestra had finished, gypsies appeared on the scene and stayed until dawn. I did not miss one dance but I have no romantic memories.

Countess Geraldine Apponyi could not possibly have known that one of the photographs taken that night would transform her life.

Her second ball, for a thousand guests, took place at the Opera at the time when Franz Lehar was visiting Budapest. Lehar, magnificent with a white beard, conducted the orchestra in one of his operettas in which the Hungarian opera singer Jeriza sang. Geraldine had been chosen to be *Mimi* from *La Bohème* in a selection of living tableaux taken from ten operas. Again her photograph appeared in the society columns.

From then on she never missed a ball. There were cotillion balls where at midnight the gentlemen gave the girl of his choice a gift, fancy dress balls, private fêtes and public gala ones.

During the day Geraldine studied and took care of herself. She began working as a librarian at the National Museum whose director was an Apponyi uncle. Here she was especially interested in the Egyptian part of the museum and spent many hours there every day.

Though still desperately shy, and delicate as a clematis, Geraldine had now grown up into an interesting young woman. She had an inquiring mind and a will of her own. She was invited by Aunt Muriel, Countess Scherr Thoss, to the winter Olympic Games at Garmisch-Partenkirchen. During a walk in the town Geraldine found a ravishing ski suit which she simply had to buy. On entering the shop she went up to the first saleswoman and asked her politely the price of the suit not forgetting to say '*Guten Tag.*' The woman replied in a sharp voice that she should say '*Heil Hitler*'. Thereupon Geraldine promptly told her that she was not German and would not do so. The saleswoman flew into a rage and insisted that she would not be served unless she said '*Heil Hitler*'. Geraldine left the shop in fury and without her ski suit.

As she bloomed and her beauty became known, Geraldine was surrounded by beaux but all these she rejected. The incident which was to influence these romantic years was the day she went into the library of her aunt's house and found a family album with a picture of her parents; her father in uniform and her mother apple blossom pretty. It had been taken on the day of their engagement.

> At the bottom of the picture I saw Father's handwriting. Only two words "For Ever". So theirs was a love that was destined to last for ever. My father died and then my mother remarried but I knew that when I did fall in love it would have to be for ever. I wanted to love the man whom I married eternally and knew that he must also love me for ever. Our love must be stronger than misery and death. Only then I realised that this is why I had rejected my suitors. I must wait for the right man to whom I did not doubt that I could remain faithful forever.

One day when she was just twenty-one years of age, Geraldine received a letter inviting her to Albania from one of the sisters of King Zog I. It ended by saying that General Cyczy, a friend of King Zog, who was also a trusted friend of the Princesses, would be visiting Geraldine and her family in Budapest to repeat the invitation to visit Albania. The King had deliberately chosen to select a bride from central Europe, where he had waltzed many hours away in Vienna as a young colonel in the Imperial Austrian Army and admired the beautiful women there. In his desperation to find a suitable bride the King had sent his sisters to Vienna and then on to Budapest. It was there that they had seen Countess Geraldine Apponyi and after securing copies of those early ball photographs had sent them to the King saying that they were good likenesses.

King Zog fell in love with a photograph. It was as simple as that. The gypsy's forecast was about to come true.

CHAPTER 4

The twenty-one year old Countess Geraldine Apponyi was appalled when she heard of King Zog's request for her to visit Tirana. The thought of being a real Queen and not a make-believe one, had never seriously entered her head. Brought up in the sophisticated ambience of Hungary and Austria she was aware of the protocol surrounding the world of royalty, that cocooned them from everyday life and everyday things and all the simple pleasures that she enjoyed.

After meetings with the delegation from Tirana, that lasted over several weeks the Apponyi family decided that if the visit was arranged discreetly and Geraldine did not wish to become engaged, then she could return to Budapest and her work at the museum and the Press would never have to hear about it. As she had very delicate lungs the official explanation was that she was being sent to the mountains for three weeks to recuperate and this was accepted.

Aunt Fanny, Countess Laszlo Karolyi, recorded in her journal her conversation with her niece. By today's standards it is naive and honey-sweet but this was the innocent era before the holocaust of Hitler's war. Graceful living and heady romanticism still flourished in the hot-house climate of central Europe.

'"But I don't know him at all. The King is twenty years older than me. I've never even seen a picture of him. And now they expect me to go to Albania when I've just got this lovely job at the museum. I know it is possible to grow to love someone even if you don't love them in the beginning but this has to be *forever*."

"But Gerrie . . . nobody can force you to stay down there if you don't want to. If you like you can come back and I am sure that you will get your job back again."

'Now she laughed and I saw in her sparkling eyes that she would go to Albania.'

But this did not happen immediately. Geraldine still had to be convinced and was not totally impressed by the family's talks with the King's men. She wanted advice from a woman close to her. It was decided that her best friend Countess Katherine Teleki, who had also been invited, should go ahead. As Geraldine had obviously been chosen for a specific reason it was quaintly acceptable that Katherine should proceed her and personally thank the King on Geraldine's behalf for his invitation and at the same time "have a good look round".

The girls talked for days about their plan and even invented a hypothetical list of questions – points on which Geraldine expected Katherine's detailed reply.

After a couple of days in Tirana, Katherine wrote an airmail letter back to Geraldine. The news it contained encouraged the members of the pro-marriage party and strengthened the critisim of the contra people who, with some justification, argued that a romantic young girl was hardly the right person to judge such a delicate situation objectively.

Katherine returned from Tirana and the summary of her crisp and mature report was as follows.

"Albania is a country on the make. It is a strange state between old and new, tradition and modernity. The striking contrasts which are the consequence of this state, offer to the foreign eye a quite peculiar picture. Only the person who realises these contrasts can understand the heroism and brilliance of the King who wants to raise the country to European standards.

"He fulfils an immense role both in the political and cultural field, his attention covers all questions of economic and spiritual life. Of course the woman at his side would have a wonderful opportunity to share in this work.

"The King is a lonely man. He has to fight his battles alone and his success would be more complete if he had a wife with whom all this would be shared. She would be his inspiration and encouragement. The role of Queen of Albania is not that of a 'luxury lady' but that of a human being willing to make sacrifices, ready to work. To be Queen of Albania is a task which can only be mastered by a woman who possesses equal strength and self assurance to fulfil a mission. There would be enough difficulties; it is not easy to combat the prejudices of a people which was reared in the respect of traditions. It is not easy to teach a people which has always had to fight for its existence in every respect, the will to a new form of life. But the King is a man whom everybody would like even if one did not know that he was a King."

Though the words surely are an echo of King Zog's jingoistic voice, they were mulled over in every detail. The two girls spent several days together in intimate conversation and Geraldine was tactfully spared any family pressure.

Clearly this charismatic, cultured and charming man had won Katherine's own heart. Geraldine listened intently before telephoning Aunt Fanny: "I have decided. I'm going to Tirana. I have written to the Princesses and accepted their invitation. Now I shall be present at the court ball on 1st January. And . . . I'm coming back straight away if I don't like him."

White-haired, handsome Baroness Ruling, who had been known to the family for many years, bringing up various young cousins, was chosen to accompany Geraldine as her chaperone. As her guardian, Uncle Charles Albert promised that Geraldine would not be forced into anything she did not wish. He explained that she would have a wonderful trip and see a new country and return in three weeks if she wanted.

The Apponyis were not at all rich and accepted the funds sent by the King to meet all expenses during the journey. He also offered to pay for a small travelling trousseau but this the proud Hungarians refused. The whole family got together to provide a modest wardrobe so that Geraldine would not feel obliged to anyone, and certainly not to her host. It was always this or that aunt, or her sister Virginia, who had to fight against Geraldine's characteristic modesty when they considered still another dress or another pair of shoes were necessary. Two psychological factors may have contributed to this. First, since her mother had remarried and she had been sent back to Hungary she had realised how much she depended on the Apponyi relatives. She was well aware that she did not have money like many of her girl friends from the nobility, and wanted to face the consequences of this fact openly and honestly. She did not want to feel ashamed of her lack of money. On the other hand she was intelligent and bright and fully aware that she was considered desirable. The American blood flowing strongly in her veins gave her character an unexpected practical twist. She always has known, and still does, exactly what she is doing.

Every effort on the part of the Apponyi family to keep General Cyczy's visit a secret was thwarted when an alert newspaper reporter, who happened to be near the entrance of the leading hotel in Budapest, noticed a well-dressed gentleman with black eyes and a swarthy skin asking for the name of the leading florist and directions how to get there. To the reporter he looked a stranger, an Albanian. Curious, he followed at a discreet distance and when the courtier went into a fashionable florist in the Inner Town he also followed. While the young journalist took his time buying a modest posy he watched the stranger taking great trouble in choosing an immense bouquet of red and white roses which he asked to be sent to Countess Geraldine Apponyi.

The reporter took a gamble and that evening his newspaper carried the banner-heading: KING ZOG OF ALBANIA TO MARRY COUNTESS GERALDINE APPONYI.

Though the Apponyi family immediately disclaimed the statement the rumour persisted and was never officially denied.

Geraldine decided that she wanted to spend Christmas with her family and went to stay with Virginia on her estate. These were gay and happy days yet under the high spirits every hour that passed masked sadness. Virginia was intuitive. She *knew* that Geraldine would become Queen of Albania. Geraldine became more and more thoughtful as if she, too, realised that this would be her last Christmas on Hungarian soil.

On 26th December there was a tearful family farewell. Everyone was aware of the sensitive nature of this particular 'holiday'.

When we caught the train to Rome I was extremely unhappy. Arriving at this city which I loved I did not even want to eat the spaghetti and the marvellous Italian food that I adored. I ate nothing. I was too nervous. We travelled from Rome to Bari and embarked on a little ship. I was on deck early as I had not slept all night. Ahead of me lay Durazzo. I was already in love with the Adriatic which reminded me of the Mediterranean of my Riviera childhood. I looked at the ancient walls originally Roman then Venetian and now splattered with Turkish bullets, and behind the mountains, great cliffs of grey granite rising straight up from the sea. It was so different from anything I had ever seen before. So untamed.

We were asked to remain on board until all the other passengers had disembarked and when the quay was empty a black Mercedes appeared. I was greeted by Colonel Sortir Martini, a Minister of the Court, who was to remain with the King until he died in Paris in exile in 1950.

The main road from Durazzo to Tirana is a distance of thirty miles and the beauty of the countryside bathed in the luminous light of opaque sunshine gave courage to even the most failing heart. The closer the Baroness and Geraldine got to Tirana the better they could see the shadows of the towering Northern Mountains which dominate Albania.

The Albanian people are mountain people. Since the first tribes of homeless Aryans pushed towards Europe for refuge they have built their houses along the shores of the Adriatic, on mountain peaks and over stark dry rock where nothing grows but hope. From the majestic eagle, who still makes its nest on the highest peaks, they took the name *Shqipetars* – Children of the Eagle.

In 1934 Tirana was a small provincial capital. During the ten years of his reign, King Zog had paved the muddy streets but there was still a large part of it that consisted of small ramshackle wooden houses or stone buildings almost windowless on the street side. Secret worlds hidden behind high stone walls. One of the newest sections was a broad street where the ministries had been built standing like huge blocks of Neopolitan ice-cream. As Geraldine was to find out later, within these newly built institutions the equipment introduced by King Zog's régime was startlingly modern in a capital which was in many respects still a small town. Dominating the whole city was the mosque, old and mysterious, where the muezzin called the faithful to prayer during the day.

There was little traffic, only buses and a few smart motor cars that obviously belonged to foreign diplomats or high ranking officials. Mountain men, rifled and bandoliered or with large revolvers at their waists rode on donkeys with their head-scarved wives walking ahead, carrying various bundles of produce or sticks for firewood. Carts piled high with country produce rumbled through the main street. In a recent documentary, made by Austrian television, it is obvious that time has stood still in Tirana, for today it looks much the same as it did fifty years ago.

The car stopped at a pretty villa surrounded by a garden, on the outskirts of the town which belonged to a Toptani relative of Sadije Zogu. Though an old building, and certainly not luxurious, it had all the necessary comforts. A delicate detail was that it was filled with vases of red roses sent by the King.

It was 31st December and that evening there was to be, like every other year, a great reception followed by a ball to celebrate the New Year, which was an official feast day. Two thousand guests had been invited and because many important foreign visitors would be present it was thought that the young Countess's appearance would be less noticeable.

Baroness Ruling naturally wanted to make her young protégé look as beautiful as possible and took her to the Austrian hairdresser who did the hair of the Princesses. In her acute state of nerves Geraldine was rebellious, ashamed and embarrassed. It seemed to her that, as in the East, she was being taken to the slave market and she reacted accordingly. From her modest wardrobe she chose her most unbecoming dress, a drab brown crêpe which she had never liked. In fact the Cinderella dress produced the opposite effect. Aunt Fanny Apponyi wrote to friends in Budapest that she had never seen Geraldine look better and everyone was captivated by her soft beauty which was highlighted by the simple dress.

Eventually, with great difficulty, Baroness Ruling finished dressing the sulky Geraldine and at eleven o'clock they left for the King's palace in a black Mercedes with General Cyczy seated in front. Driving through gardens filled with roses they drew up to the portico of the palace which was in reality little more than a very large villa.

They entered through a series of salons furnished in the French style and continued into an extension which had been previously added for the celebrations of twenty-five years of independence and ten years of monarchy. It was an immense hall, the walls of which were decorated with a collection of precious arms all worked in gold and silver, richly embroidered coats, capes with sumptuous furs, colourful costumes from the various districts, prayer mats and hundreds of exquisite carpets chosen from the King's personal collection of four thousand. It was a blend of Graustarkian operetta and Kubla Khan.

My legs were trembling and I could see nothing. I was absolutely petrified. I kept telling myself that with all these people my presence would go unnoticed. It was not until afterwards that General Cyczy told me that my appearance caused a sensation and that he noted sympathy, interest and even hostility, especially in the eyes of the Italian guests.

All I remember was a young lady in a sparkling lamé dress coming up to me, and the Albanian officer who accompanied her told me that this was the Princess Senije, the eldest sister of the King. I made my little curtsy and she kissed me on the cheek before taking my arm and saying that she would present me to her brother.

The room was so long that it seemed endless and I only wanted to disappear. Suddenly I was face to face with a handsome, tall man impeccable in the white uniform of Colonel-in-Chief of the Army. It was his eyes that I noticed mostly – blue piercing eyes.

I had practised at Appony a curtsy like the ones we learned at dancing classes but in the confusion I forgot, and only made a slight bob. The King immediately raised me with a charming smile and thanked me for coming to his country, asking me if I had had a good journey.

By now the Princesses had formed a screen around us and he presented each of the six to me. I could not see the rest of the guests and in a strange way felt entirely alone with the King. He never took his eyes off me as he handed me a glass of champagne. Our fingers touched and at that moment the lights dimmed. It was just midnight and this was an Albanian custom. In my nervousness I let fall the glass which seemed to splinter into a thousand breaking crystals.

I felt I had become quite pale but the King laughed. "Splinters bring luck," he said in German, and spontaneously stroked my hand as if to reassure me. The echoes of the twelve strokes of midnight had not died out when an immense applause seemed to thunder around the room like surf breaking in a storm. From all sides and in all tongues came the cries of "Good luck." I felt quite different from anything I had ever experienced before.

I had fallen in love.

CHAPTER 5

Aware of the young Countess' nervousness and her dismay at dropping her champagne glass the King immediately suggested that she went to the buffet to have some food and that they would meet again later.

The table looked magnificent, set with a silver-gilt dinner service for three hundred which was engraved with the helmet of Skanderbeg, the symbol of the Crown of the new Monarchy. Years later, long after the rape of Albania by the Italians, a friend found a few pieces of this dinner service in an antique shop on the Riviera which he purchased and gave to the Queen. Today they are among the very few souvenirs she has of her three hundred and eighty-eight days as the first reigning Queen of Albania.

The massive table was laden with platters full of every kind of European banquet delicacy as well as several Albanian specialities which the King always ordered for his guests. These included *burek*, wafer thin pastries filled with layers of spinach and cheese, and *kabuni*, a delicious dessert made with rice, sugar, raisins, fried almonds, minute pieces of meat, spices and steaming butter, the whole dish coated with a layer of powdered sugar.

Geraldine had been escorted to the buffet by one of the King's Army adjutants. The King had retired to another salon and the princesses began distributing small gifts to the guests to celebrate the Eve of St. Sylvester. Soon the Court Chamberlain appeared at Geraldine's side and asked her to follow him.

When she arrived at the salon the King was waiting for her and, smiling, motioned her to sit down. Though she was still shy, the initial panic had disappeared and now she was only curious to know more about this man who had selected her as a possible bride.

The King began to talk and chose as his subject Vienna, a city which they both knew well. Just as Scott Fitzgerald took it upon himself to create a 'College-for-One' for his paramour Sheila Graham, so King Zog, there and then, began the Albanian education of Geraldine, the first of dozens, even hundreds of talks, which were to take place over the next three months of their courtship. It was a curious way to begin a romance but all Albanians are fine story tellers and the King was no exception. In his soft voice, speaking German, their only language in common, he told the history of his country and of his own exploits when he was simply Ahmed Zogu, the young leader of the Zogolli clan, in the province of Mati.

While the orchestra played Lehar waltzes and Albanian folk music in the background the King told Geraldine how in 1915 the Serb troops made their famous retreat across Albania, taking the sick King Peter I of Serbia with them lying on a chariot. They took a ship at the small port of Durazzo and crossed over to Corfu under the protection of the Allied Fleet. Hard on their heels were the victorious Austrian troops. Seizing his opportunity young Ahmed Zogu had then taken the chance to negotiate with the Austrians, ruthlessly clearing the country of Serb marauders and deserters, and raising the national flag of Albania at the palace of Durazzo.

In 1916 the Austrian High Command was seeking a chief for the voluntary Albanian Forces. There was no regular army, as the various tribes fought their own family feuds, and young Ahmed Zogu was the only one to command a trained army. He already had a reputation for his brilliant strategy, courage and nationalism. A born leader of men, he was a natural choice and so at the age of twenty-one he was given the rank of colonel in the Imperial Austrian Army and the command of the newly-formed Albanian Army.

Ahmed Zogu distinguished himself on numerous occasions on the field of battle, having for example, captured a whole company of the enemy. But now his ambitions rose higher. He wished to restore Albanian independence, to create a state, to chase out the Greek troops who occupied the South of Albania. He went to Vienna to show his daring plans to Emperor Franz Joseph.

The Emperor listened to the proposal from the young Albanian officer but told him that he could not take such an initiative to reinforce Zogu with the necessary armament without the consent of his ally the German Emperor, Kaiser Wilhelm II. The Kaiser replied in only one word, "No". His reason for refusal was that Queen Sophia of Greece was his sister. Now the Emperor suggested that Colonel Zogu should be deterred from re-entering Albania and kept in Vienna in a gilded cage with plenty of social life to divert and amuse him.

The next two years in Vienna were the most relaxed period of his life. Ever since childhood he had been in a continual struggle for the independence of his country. Now a handsome young colonel he could, for the first time in his life, savour the charms of Vienna and the empire of the Hapsburgs, now entering the last days of its twilight.

The King went on to tell the young Hungarian countess at his side of his escape from an assassination attempt. He had had an infection in the stomach which turned into a dangerous ulcer. All the surgeons he consulted wished to operate but the specialist was against this. After four days of haemorrhaging the bleeding was finally stopped and for the moment the King was cured. The Queen is of the firm opinion today, backed up by doctors who attended the King in the eleven years he was ill before he died, that had he been operated on at that time he would have been spared the cancer that finally penetrated his whole body.

It was during his convalescence that the King went to the opera accompanied by three ministers of the court. He had been warned by King Alexander I of Yugoslavia, a personal friend, that there was a plot afoot to assassinate him but he chose to ignore it. The only precaution he took was not to leave by the front door of the opera house but by a secondary one. His car was waiting and at the moment he entered it, the chauffeur who was probably an accomplice, turned on the interior light of the car, against the instructions of the King. Several shots rang out, fired by two gunmen who were on the opposite pavement. The King opened the door, bounded out, pulled out a gun concealed in his evening clothes and wounded one of the men. The other ran away. The King's aide-de-camp, Colonel Topalaj was dead and his Minister of the Court, Ekrem Libohova, wounded, but the King was unharmed. It was the first of fifty-five assassination attempts made during King Zog's life.

The Press at that time printed that it was the King's double who had gone to the opera. The Queen confirms that this was false and that the King neither on this, nor on any other occasion would have used a double: it was not in the nature of his character. The plot had been hatched at Valona by certain Albanians, encouraged by foreign agents, who wished to seize power.

All this the King told me in those few hours of our meeting. I

38

was mesmerised. I forgot where I was and listened intently – fascinated. He afterwards told me that the time we spent seemed to him only a few minutes as he loved to watch my face and my various expressions.

The hours had slipped by, and it was five o'clock in the morning when Geraldine joined Baroness Ruling who had been nodding in a chair in the adjoining salon, waiting to take her charge back to the villa.

The next day at ten o'clock, on entering the little dining room to have breakfast with the Baroness, Geraldine was greeted by a heart made of red carnations nearly as large as the table. For the young Countess it was a re-affirmation that the King was pleased with her and that she had not disappointed him.

The whole of the morning of New Year's day the King received members of his Government and the Diplomatic Corps and it was not until four o'clock that Geraldine was summoned for a private visit to the palace. She was accompanied there, as always, by Baroness Ruling and then taken to a salon by a lady-in-waiting of one of the Princesses. From there she entered through bullet-proof glass doors, guarded by two sentries who paced up and down, into a large office scattered with silk carpets that glowed like jewels in the afternoon sunlight streaming through the French windows. The King came forward and greeted her by kissing her hand, which he normally never did, and led her to an alcove where there was a big sofa and easy chairs, and which was shielded from the guards by a screen.

Without any preliminaries he immediately asked Countess Geraldine de Nagy Appony if she would marry him.

"Do you think you could love me for eternity no matter what happens in our lives?"

"Oh, but I already love you," came the reply without hesitation.

On her arrival in Tirana, Colonel Martini had briefed her on court etiquette and how to behave in front of the King. In the ecstasy of the moment she forgot everything he had said and she thought and spoke as her heart and instinct directed her.

They spoke about their religious differences. Geraldine was completely honest when she replied: "I know that I could love you forever but you are a Muslim and I am a Catholic. How are we going to arrange this? Nothing in the world will make me change my religion. Just as we see the moon and we see the sun I have my religion. I can't change it."

The King smiled and said: "I, too, have thought of this and there will be no question of your doing so. We are European Muslims and I have a great respect for your church. It is because of the Roman Catholic church and the monasteries in Albania that we managed to keep our language. You see, under the Ottoman Empire, to speak Albanian was forbidden, only Turkish was permitted to be spoken. But within the monasteries it was different, that is why we owe them a great debt for keeping our language alive. Will you learn to speak Albanian?"

"Give me a teacher tomorrow," Geraldine replied. She already spoke five languages – English, French, German, Hungarian and Italian – and had no qualms about taking on Albanian. The Albanian language is unique. It does not resemble any other tongue and is incredibly difficult to master. Based on ancient Illyrian it has also borrowed words from the time of the Roman and Turkish occupations and the script remains Roman. Within three months Geraldine not only spoke fluent Albanian but was able to give her first radio broadcast speaking her new language.

A characteristic of King Zog was his tolerance of religions other than his own. He had hoped and planned that Albania would become a refuge for those from any nationality subject to political and religious persecution, especially for the Jewish race.

Taking her youth into consideration the King explained that he wanted her to be absolutely sure and said he would wait a further ten days before he required a definitive answer. Meanwhile, they would continue to see each other and have a private talk in his office every day. There was so much about himself and her new country, Albania, that he wanted to explain personally to her so that she would not hear anything second-hand.

When Geraldine left the King's office with two burning spots of excitement on her cheeks everyone ran to escort her to her car plying her with all kinds of questions. What had the King said? Did she love the King? Was she engaged?

She smiled and remained silent.

Not even when she arrived back at her villa did she confide in her beloved Baroness Ruling who was almost a second mother to her. There are moments in life when words spoken between two people must remain theirs forever.

The next three days were filled with getting to know the King's immediate family on a personal basis. On her death bed he had promised his mother that he would take care of his six sisters and dedicated his life to this. They were to become an integral and persistent pattern in Geraldine's domestic life in the years ahead. Apart from the Princesses Adele, Narije, Senije, Misseje, Ruhije and Maxhide there were two nieces. Geraldine was immediately put into a gilded cage and, though foreign diplomats and their wives had expressed a wish to call on her, nobody could approach her without requesting permission from the palace – the King in this case. She had wanted to make some excursions into the mountains and explore the beautiful countryside, but the King was adamant that she should not leave the villa until the engagement had been officially announced.

Each morning she woke to find a magnificent bouquet of flowers awaiting her and a present on her breakfast tray. Every night when she went to bed there were more flowers and another surprise on her pillow. Not even Ivor Novello could have created such a milieu for romance to flourish.

Each day a car called to take Geraldine to the palace for another talk with the King. In Hungary she had only been permitted to speak to men of her own age and the King was twenty years older than she. She found this situation quite natural as she had been devoted to her own father and perhaps at that time saw the King as a father figure. Nor could she resist his charm which dominated everyone around him. Despite whatever ruthlessness he may have displayed towards his enemies and the outside world, to the women in his family he was always tender and never lifted his voice in anger. He was European but had been brought up in the Eastern way.

Historians have criticised the King's luxurious style of living and his extravagance in a country where illiteracy and lack of schools and hospitals were major problems. The fact that he bought his suits in Saville Row, shirts from Sulka in Paris and had his shoes hand-made in Italy were probably his only personal extravagances. In his study he had only the barest necessities of furniture apart from the carpets. In this simple room he spent anything up to eighteen hours a day preferring to receive all his foreign visitors, ministers and diplomats there rather than in any of the grander salons.

According to the Countess Muriel Scherr Thoss, "He was not mysterious but only reserved and had a great deal of self-control and was always polite." This was in a certain contrast with the unmistakable grimness which ruled over his spirit. But this seemed to be a more or less stable characteristic which he carried naturally, unostentatiously – like a well-cut, fashionable suit.

"Although he was a reticent man I could easily see how affectionately he treated his family. In speaking to me about his mother one day he said: 'In the difficult and in the beautiful moments of my life alike I think of my mother. Her memory gives me strength and multiplies my joy.' It was a strange experience to hear him speak about himself."

Until his death the King maintained the role of protector and adviser to his sisters, as would be customary in a Muslim household. He took care of every aspect of their lives and in turn they adored him and were totally dependent upon him.

The King was overjoyed that Geraldine created such a cordial relationship with the princesses. "Family harmony is one of the most important things in human life", was one of his favourite sayings. Love of the family has always been a specifically Albanian characteristic and Zog emphasised it as much as possible. He created in this respect a good example for his whole people.

CHAPTER 6

On 10th January Geraldine gave the King her answer. She had never had any doubts since that first night when they met at the ball and had already written to her relatives in Hungary, "I love him. I have decided: I'm going to marry him. I want to stay here."

The King had written personally to Count Charles Apponyi, Geraldine's guardian, since she was still under age according to Hungarian law, asking his consent and his blessing as she had also done. A letter arrived, by return post, and it was then that the King presented her with a document elevating her to the rank of Princess of Albania.

Now that the engagement was official the King showered his fiancée with jewels bought from the jeweller Osterreicher in Vienna. In giving them all at once it was almost as though the King had foreseen the uncertain future that lay ahead. "I am giving you the jewels I can now," he told her, "for tomorrow we may be without a penny."

One morning when the King and I had finished our talk he called an officer who came in with a large tray of boxes. One by one they were opened. First there was a tiara blazing with diamonds, with a centre piece made in the form of Skanderbeg's helmet.

Among the necklaces was a single string of large graduated solitaire diamonds held together with a diamond baguette clasp. I was still gasping with delight when the King selected a diamond bracelet three inches deep and placed it on my arm. Next he chose diamond drop earrings to match the tiara.

I saw a box that contained a chain of white gold with a cross of diamonds. I could not take my eyes off it. This the King put aside and did not say anything. I also saw him put away three other boxes, one smaller than the others. We spent the next hour choosing gifts for my family — my grandmother, my mother and my aunts.

The King had also chosen jewellery from Bulgari in Rome and Cartier in Paris but I never saw this as the plane that was bringing them crashed and the jewels were lost in the wreckage.

I was not upset about the jewels but that so many people had died in the accident.

It has been suggested over the years that the King used government funds to buy my trousseau and jewellery. This of course was absolutely not true. It was paid for from the King's personal fortune of gold Napoleons which he kept in the safe in his office. These were payment from the sale of thousands of acres of virgin forests that had belonged to the Zogu family to an Italian construction company. Not a single Napoleon came from the State funds.

As a wedding gift the State gave me a large gift of money as I had come to my wedding without a dowry. I had requested that it should be used for the building of a home for poor people who had no families to take care of them and for orphans. The money was still intact in my account waiting for this purpose when I left the country a year later.

In her journal Aunt Antoinette wrote: "The value of the King's gifts was immeasurable: solitaires, diadems, pearls, bracelets, necklaces in such numbers as we have never seen before." The Princess also gave her future sisters-in-law gifts of jewellery, which had been chosen by the King.

The King had decided that Geraldine should move from her present villa. She was shown one which had been previously occupied by one of the princesses and women guests of the King but on seeing its satin opulence and walls covered with mirrors she immediately felt uncomfortable and told the King in her forthright way that she could not live there. She simply did not feel happy there. Instead she was moved to a brand-new villa overlooking the city. Her suite was on the first floor and she spent many thoughtful hours on the balcony looking towards the snow-tipped mountains that surround Tirana.

So many memories so far away and so different from this towering landscape.

I used to nurture my moments alone on my balcony. It was as if this time had been given me to cherish the memories of my childhood and my country. Those wonderful visits to Nagy Appony. I remember them like pieces of gold, the light gold of wheat in summer, the gold of the harvest, the red gold of the forests in autumn and the soft gold of the chandeliers on party nights.

Would I ever again see those joyful feasts for the threshing of the wheat which took place to the sound of gypsy music, or join the peasants dancing the *csardas* drinking the fresh wine or *barack* made from apricots or peaches?

I would never again have the chance to tread grapes with the village girls, or on the days of the great hunting parties leave in the dark to open the shoots for the partridge, pheasants and quails, returning at dawn to a table laden with a real English-style breakfast – which I was never ever to see in England for I went to live there only in wartime.

In this untamed country it all seemed so far away as though I was looking through a kaleidoscope. If I shook it again I could see my grandmother, Countess Apponyi, at the luncheon table saying: "If you don't eat your spinach now you will get it for breakfast." And she meant it. Or those cosy hours she spent instilling her own brand of logic into Virginia and me.

"Never read Freud, Nietzsche or Schopenhauer or any of those philosophers. They are bad for you. If you can get through life believing in the sermon on the mount – "Blessed are the meek" – everything you learn in your catechism will be as clear as the stars in the sky, and the moon and the sun. You will never have the need to seek elsewhere."

Geraldine had hoped to return to Budapest now that she was engaged but the King was adamant that she should remain in Tirana where she would be protected at all times. In his concern for her image he felt that in Budapest she may be subject to an incident that could cause a scandal. He did not trust his enemies not to stage a scene perhaps in a street whereby his fiancée would be embarassed and even photographed for the newspapers. His protectiveness and love for her were absolute. For the moment, at least, she was free to go wherever she liked in Tirana and learn as much as possible about her new country.

She always had her meals with the King and in the evenings they went to his office where he continued his history lessons and talked about his past. In the mornings there were her lessons in Albanian and in the afternoons while the King was occupied with state affairs she made excursions into the countryside with members of her family or new Albanian women friends.

I was received marvellously everywhere, even in the poorest houses, where they did not know who I was. Albanian hospitality is so warm and generous.

Each morning, often at dawn, she went to mass in the little church at Tirana and each time she left the church, people waited to give her small posies of flowers or scattered petals in front of her. As her visits were never planned and irregular clearly they had been waiting for their new princess for some hours.

Through her visits, as well as by listening to the King, she began to learn more about this strange harsh mountain country. In one of the villages she visited the women who were known for the whiteness of their skin as they were supposed to be descendents from the Vikings. To make their cheeks pretty they used juice squeezed from flowers, and noticing this, Princess Geraldine remarked to a woman that they all seemed to look so healthy, the girls with their rosy cheeks and the boys so robust. They are a Mediterranean people and not unlike the Greeks for instance, but in Albania life has always been rough and harsh and, though they crowded round her, neither adults nor children smiled easily. These serious people explained that they had never had time to relax and to take life easily. From childhood it had been one long struggle to survive and thousands of years of foreign occupation were indelibly printed on their faces. Even their poetry was without romance; it spoke of the beauty of the countryside, acts of bravery, love of the homeland and liberty, but seldom of love. Love was a luxury.

On her excursions into the small villages in the mountains the women explained their customs, long cherished throughout the years. When a male child is born he was immediately plunged into cold water. It was considered a good omen as the louder he cried the stronger would be his life. It was also the custom to place a gun of his ancestors under the new-born boy's pillow. When her own son was born and the King did just that, the Queen was horrified but knew that he was only following a tradition stretching far back in time.

A clean house-proud nation, the Albanian women not only kept their houses clean but worked in the fields and, particularly in the mountain villages, they wove cloth to make clothes. Under King Zog's rule the Albanian women had a special status which was not given in any other Muslim country. Polygamy existed in principle, but in reality the Albanian had only one wife and she was recognised and venerated as the woman of the house. A religious respect encapsulated her so that it was virtually unheard of for an Albanian to molest a woman. They circulated freely and even during family feuds and fighting they felt safe to walk peacefully along the roads. Nobody bothered them, for to brigands and honest men alike they were sacred. Now, since the Communist régime has come into being and the country has become atheist, there is no trace of these freedoms.

Physical and emotional fidelity is also another strong trait in the Albanian character. Often the men emigrated to Turkey, to make money to send back to support their families, only returning every few years to leave their wives pregnant and yet another mouth to feed. It was the women who raised the children and often defended them with weapons when necessary. Because of the long years they spent alone Albanian women were more liberated than other women in the Balkans. They were fully privileged to pay calls to any house, for instance, and the Albanian husband was not accustomed to inquire of his wife where she had been and what friends she had visited that day. Before the war, she had enormous power and authority and she was well aware of her status in the family. What matter that she went barefoot or had to walk while her husband rode their mule or even that she did not eat with the guests? She knew that the family all relied on her for her wisdom and counsel. Was not her body building fine sons and daughters for Albania?

It was a hard life, though due to the Rockefeller Institution in America, which came at the King's invitation, the country had now been cleared of malaria. But there was still a great deal of unnecessary illness and mobile clinics and baby care centres were in desperate need. Sitting with the women round the fireplaces and listening to their stories, Princess Geraldine knew that her first commitment when she became Queen was to care for Albanian women. She did not need the King's statistics to tell her — she was seeing it at first hand with her own eyes.

One weekend the King took her to Mati as he wanted to show her his ancestral home. The wild, towering mountains seemed to reach the sky. Much of the family's vast estate was in dense forest lands, miles and miles of them, making the trees of Switzerland seem dwarfed. One old Albanian legend tells how God wished to transport to Montenegro a sack of rocks for some building in that region. He travelled along the Albanian roads and was annoyed to find that half of his load had disappeared into a hole along the way. It is supposed to be the origin of the turmoil of the Albanian mountains and the explanation of their surprising formations.

47

The roads are not only narrow but wind strangely through precipitous gorges and had proved an advantage for the young soldier Ahmed Zogu in the freeing of his country from invading military forces. Lower down in the valleys were miles and miles of gentle forests staining the landscape dark green. The wildlife was rich with bears, wild goats and boars, deer and of course the soaring eagles which were protected by law.

There were also lakes of deep, mysterious and incredible beauty. Lake Ohrida is the largest and deepest in Europe, filled with speckled trout which only breed in one other lake, in Russia. The lakes are fed with sparkling water like ribbons of crystal pouring down the steep mountain sides. It was a paradise, a wild and tumultuous paradise, and with her practical eyes Princess Geraldine already saw the possibilities of turning it into a sportsman's dream, and the possibilities of a vast tourist trade.

In the evenings as they sat talking, the King would smile and say that he had so much to do in modernising his country. Already during his reign, where there had previously been no medical centres or schools, now each village had one, and Tirana itself had one of the best hospitals in the Balkans. Lacking up-to-date equipment, many of the great arterial roads that stretched across the country had been made by hand, a long and arduous task.

One of the first tasks that the King had set himself was to introduce the Napoleonic Civil Code and establish a new form of civil law, to replace the feudalism and superstition that had been the law of the country. The old Albanian law was based on *besa* which is a kind of clan loyalty. It is a word of honour that also embraces family hospitality. The *besa* led to numerous blood feuds and to many invasions. In explaining to Princess Geraldine the real meaning of the word *besa*, fundamental to her understanding of her new country's history, the King told her his favourite story.

"Georges was riding along in his best clothes enjoying the wonderful view and breathing the pure air of spring. The grass on the mountain slopes was velvety green and the fruit trees bowed low with blossom. From afar a church bell rang and Georges noticed a procession which was climbing towards the little stone church perched on a rocky ledge. The colours of the rich local costumes and the steel of the mens' weapons shone in the rising sun. Georges was happy.

"He was returning from seeing one of the most important families in the district and he had received the agreement of the father of Lule that she would be his bride. Georges knew it would not be right to talk to Lule, but he desperately wished to see her returning from church. Lule waş so pretty with her reddish gold hair, milk-white skin and eyes as blue as the wild gentian that grew in the mountains. He waited until he saw Lule coming along a path leaping from stone to stone like a graceful faun.

"Lule too was happy, singing to herself as she wanted to be Georges' bride. As she went along the path she jumped when a figure pounced from behind some trees. It was a young strongly built man with dark black hair, brutal mouth and hard black eyes. 'Lule, your brother refused my offer for you', he growled, 'but I shall not give up. I shall come back with my whole family and take you by force if necessary.'

"'Ridiculous', replied Lule, tossing her head. 'Today I am betrothed to Georges and I shall belong to no one else'. Night fell. A violent storm broke, trees groaned and split asunder, lightning streaked across the sky. On the heavy door of the fortress home of Georges came a heavy knocking. Georges' mother took an oil lamp and went to the door. As she opened it a figure fell on the threshold and muttered *besa*. Georges' white-haired grandfather rose from his place by the fire and said, 'Stay wanderer. Our *besa* and our hospitality are yours. Never has it been said that anyone asked for my *besa* and has been sent away. My daughter, get bread, salt and coffee.'

"Suddenly the light fell full on the trembling form and the mother of Georges cried out, 'Costa my boy. Are you mad? Do you not recognise us? Why did you ask for our *besa*? That really is not necessary in this house which you have known since you were a boy. What has happened to you? You are torn and bleeding'. They handed him coffee and led him to the warmth of the fire. Mountain people do not ask questions.

"'Where can our son Georges be?' the mother asked. 'Why is he not home on such a night?'

"The silence was broken again by thuds on the door. Four men entered carrying a stretcher made from branches on which lay a body covered with a cloth. Taking off their white caps they gently uncovered the head of the corpse. A terrible moan of despair came from the mother and a spasm shook the old man. 'Who did this?' he asked in anguish.

"'Georges was not dead when we found him, only badly wounded. He accused Costa Preshni here,' they explained.

"The old man and weeping woman turned to the form crouched low by the fire. One of the men raised his pistol but the grandfather caught it and cried in a voice raging with thunder, 'Stop nephew! This murderer of my grandson has our *besa*.' The four men turned and left.

"That night while the light of the fire flickered on the dead face of the beloved son three people sat in silence and listened to the storm as it abated in the dawn. At the first ray of light the grandfather turned to the assassin: 'Get up and come with me. I shall accompany you to the boundary of our land but as from midday today guard yourself from our vengeance, as you have brought upon yourself and yours the heavy weight of the law of blood.'"

It was far into the night before the King finished his story.

I had to search the real meaning of *besa* for myself. I said to the King, "Here I am reading Turkish and Albanian history and one sees that the Sultans of Turkey demanded *besa* from the ruling families of Albania. How then has it been possible that there have been so many revolts inside your country during the last five hundred years when they had given their *besa*?"

He smiled and said to me: "Search yourself." One day it came like a flash into my mind. Of course there was no state so that the *besas* were given to the person of the Sultan and not to Turkey itself. Therefore every time a sultan died, and until a new one received their *besas* there was time for the Albanians to rise up and fight for their liberty.

The King also recounted to Princess Geraldine the stories of the old Albanian nobility who, as part of the Ottoman Empire, had once owed allegiance to Turkey. Since the collapse of the Empire in 1913, Albania had achieved independence and this subservience ceased to exist. In the past, historic families like the Vrioni, Delvinas, Bushatis, Frasheri, Koniyzas, Libohovas, Gjonies, Toptanis, Bibdodas and the Dukagjinis had all had their own dramatic sagas. Many of them still had the blood in their veins of the Topias, and of Georges Kastrioti, the legendary Skanderbeg, whose descendant King Zog believed himself to be. This history has a strange, often repeated pattern – oppression, attack, liberation.

50

Though the majority of the country was then Muslim, it had originally been Christian and did not give its soul to Islam until the fifteenth century, when Albania was conquered by Turkey. In the family of the Frasheri they still have the ancient memory of a Christian altar hidden in the cellars of the chateau where Catholic masses were celebrated secretly for centuries despite their apparent change of religion. Today all the mosques and churches have been desecrated. In the climate of fanatic atheism under the régime of Enver Hoxha, two thousand churches and mosques have either been destroyed or turned into cinemas, sports arenas, youth centres, or museums. In the town of Soder there is an atheist museum – a showpiece for foreign visitors.

Geraldine had to learn to adapt to a totally different culture. Hungary, her homeland, was a sophisticated country under the influence of the Hapsburg Empire, whereas Albania was an amalgamation of various tribes each headed by a chief. Fortunately, Geraldine was a good pupil; she learned everything the King explained to her and studied not only the language, but buried herself in the theoretical and practical knowledge of ancient Albanian customs, and the habits of modern Albania. The three months' crash course paid off. She became Queen in every sense of the word. She took charge of a special office, set up at the palace, to deal with the numerous petitions that had accumulated over the past few months. Petitions came from Albanians in the country and abroad, petitions for settlement among neighbours over land, petitions for money and petitions for pardoning wronged prisoners. Her one wish had been to become head of the Red Cross, but as this position was held by one of the Princesses it needed some skilful negotiating on the part of the King before this was possible.

In modern days the parallel again is Princess Grace and her arrival in Monaco. She, too, took over some of the duties which had previously been carried out by Prince Ranier's sister, Princess Antoinette, and found it was a delicate situation. Such royal manipulation has to be done with consummate tact and in this case there were six Princesses all enjoying the cachet of being First Ladies of Albania. The King had made several of them honorary colonels-in-chief of the various regiments, and they appeared on horseback in their various stylish white and gold uniforms with regularity. It was a gesture meant to inspire the Albanian peasant woman with the achievements of modern women and the wonders of the Western World. Each succeeding week the King watched with approval as his young fiancée matured into her new role. That she did it with such alacrity was due not only to her own selfless nature and desire to be a diligent Queen, but to the thorough training that Aunt Fanny, Countess Karolyi had given her in the model village of Zebegny. She instinctively knew how to handle people and situations and with her first-class mind had quickly adapted to what the King called "the art of being a Queen, and the science of ruling."

CHAPTER 7

The days and weeks before the wedding passed in joyful tension until Spring arrived with the blossom-blown month of April. During this period Princess Geraldine had a 'nervous disorder', a possible aftermath of a brain fever she had suffered as a child. The King, immediately concerned, saw that the strain of the betrothal, coupled with perhaps a touch of home-sickness, was becoming too much for his young fiancée and invited her mother and grandmother to come and be with her during the last weeks before the wedding.

Mrs de Strale d'Ekna, her maternal grandmother, came from America and her mother, Madame Girault, arrived from the Riviera. A younger brother, whom she adored, Count Gjula Apponyi, came from Budapest and her sister, Countess Virginia de Baghy de Szechen, from her estate in Hungary. All moved into suites on the ground floor of the Princess's villa.

There was much 'family talk', and every day brought its own special excitement. As Geraldine had not been permitted to return to Hungary, her sister and Aunt Adele did some shopping for her but the bulk of it was bought in Paris by the King, who had impeccable taste and enjoyed selecting clothes for Geraldine. He had ordered a dressmaker to come from France to take Geraldine's measurements and then a form was made of her by the two couture houses, Chanel and Worth, who had been chosen by the King. At no time was she consulted about anything as the King personally selected the three morning dresses, six afternoon ones, three suits, six evening gowns and sports clothes. From Maison de Blanc in Paris he ordered beautiful house gowns and several dozen sets of pure silk lingerie trimmed with exquisite lace. Each outfit had its own shoes, hats, gloves and handbags to match, with packages of silk stockings to tone. It was indeed a trousseau fit for a Queen.

The parcels, huge boxes, always arrived in the morning. In the afternoons the family all used to watch while I unpacked them.

There were screams of joy as I unfolded the tissue paper and held each article up for inspection. I had never seen such beautiful things before because in Hungary we did not have money for such luxuries.

The King had chosen well, because out of the whole trousseau there was only one dress that I did not like. I did not often wear hats in those days, and do not today, but I loved those chic little Parisian models and every one suited me. The milliner had only seen photographs of me.

As the King worked in his office for anything up to eighteen hours a day and seldom left it, except for our meals together, I used to wear something different when I went for our talk every day. He loved to see my excitement.

How could any woman not admire a man who was so thoughtful? Yes I was very much in love. I found the King very handsome with his white skin and golden brown hair and those azure blue eyes, so direct and compelling. And his hands, long slender fingers with manicured nails such a contrast to the fierce life he lead as a soldier when his troops had called him Ahmed the Hawk. And then that wonderful smile. It was his gentleness that had a pull on me.

In those weeks before my wedding I was spoiled as I shall never be again in my life. It was like living in the stories of One Thousand and One Nights.

In February the King had told Princess Geraldine that he had personally sent General Seregi to Italy to invite Count Galeazzo Ciano, the son-in-law of Mussolini, to be a witness at the marriage. It was purely a political gesture for King Zog was walking a tight-rope in his relationship with Italy. At the same time he had sent an emissary discreetly to Victor Emmanuel III, the King of Italy, with an invitation, fully aware that Ciano demanded to be received as royalty and that this request could not be granted to him if genuine royalty was present.

It was a mischievous and dangerous game only thwarted by King Victor Emmanuel tactfully declining, though he did send his cousin, the Duke of Bergamo, instead – much to the annoyance of Ciano. So anxious was Ciano to attend the wedding that certain Franco-Italian talks which were to have been held were delayed by three days to allow him to be present in Tirana.

The world's press were quick to comment on Ciano's presence but in his courting of Albania over the past years, Mussolini had been adroit to advance considerable loans for public works, money that Albania desperately needed to build up the country's resources. A modern port at Durazzo, new roads, bridges, air services, electric power installations had all been provided since 1926 when the Treaty of Tirana was signed under which Albania became, in essence, a dependency on Italy.

Only a week before the wedding a highly significant action had been taken by Italy. The Albanian Government had been refusing to pay the interest on any part of the capital of the loans made by Rome. What could have been an ugly situation was averted when Italy suddenly offered to wipe out arrears amounting in all to some ten million dollars on condition that Albania repaid the principle of the loans inside 15 years. The Albanian-Italian friendship was a thinly-veneered play for time on the part of King Zog, who, for the moment was allowing Albania to become a link between Italy and Yugoslavia instead of a bone of contention as in the past. But the pocket-sized kingdom of Albania had become an important strategic point in the game of *realpolitik*, and among the reverberating effects of the German occupation of Austria in March 1938, not the least significant would be this new importance bestowed on Albania.

An upsetting factor for the bride was the last minute ban on her marriage by the Vatican because she was marrying a Muslim. The King's conscience was clear because, as he explained to his bride-to-be, everything in time would be arranged and that it would be in order for her to take the Holy Sacrament which he knew was to be her strength in her life ahead. Despite the Vatican's prevarication the King ordered all the Roman Catholic ecclesiastics in Albania to be present at the wedding and the Te Deum to be sung in Catholic churches throughout the country. As part of her wedding gift, the King had already promised Princess Geraldine that he would build a small chapel for her own use within the palace. This never happened – there was no time.

The Vatican's displeasure was in fact one of the sensitive areas that was discussed with Count Ciano at the wedding and within a short period of time the Vatican did relent and sent its consent and the Pope his blessing.

For weeks prior to the wedding, gifts had been arriving from all over the world. Admiral Horthy, the Regent of Hungary, sent as a personal present a handsome phaeton drawn by four prancing white Lippizaner horses which was to be used to carry the bride to the palace on her wedding day. Hitler sent a long scarlet supercharged Mercedes, with three large chromium exhaust pipes, a removable roof and lined throughout with white leather. It was a replica of his own and this was the only other one in existence. The Apponyi family gave a magnificent dinner service in heavy bronze, a portrait of the new Queen's grandfather, Count Lajos Apponyi by Lazlo and a collection of the famous Hungarian Herendi porcelain. There were many fine examples of carpets and rugs from friends who knew of the King's personal collection. Mussolini's gift was four handsome copper vases and King Victor Emmanuel's a bronze statue of a mounted Dragoon Guard.

The gifts were not displayed, but were placed unopened in the new guardhouse near the little white marble palace which the King was building for his bride on the heights overlooking Tirana and which was, as yet, unfinished.

Today, when she thinks back Queen Geraldine says that she did not even see many of the presents.

> Now when I see something beautiful I like to look at it, for one of the vital pleasures that God has given us is sight. I tell myself that it is beautiful, pretty, agreeable, but it is good that it does not belong to me. I seem to be fated to lose anything of material value and I accept this as God's will.

On the evening before the wedding there was what was charmingly called 'the bride's soirée', to which all the wedding guests had been invited with everyone wearing the national costume of their country. It was a brilliant occasion with the Hungarian men proud as peacocks in their tunics of gorgeous brocades trimmed with precious furs and buttons of real jewels.

All the reception rooms had been filled with flowers – white roses, lilacs, lilies, carnations, mimosa and lilies of the valley which the King had ordered especially from the Riviera.

Princess Geraldine wore the richly embroidered national gown which had been made for her by women throughout the various regions of Albania. Each had contributed a part of this glorious hand-embroidered dress which was sewn with gold pieces. Though ordinary Albanian brides were expected to provide their own dowry for their wedding, this half-American princess defied tradition. Her gift to the King was herself.

56

The King had declared a three-day celebration throughout the land as his wish was that the wedding would be remembered as the biggest celebration in Albanian history. From the surrounding mountain villages thousands of picturesquely dressed bronzed tribesmen, the Ghegs from the North and Tosks from the South, crowded into Tirana. Before the wedding ceremony at ten thirty in the morning, Muslims and Roman Catholics poured into the churches to pray for their ruler and his bride. Fifty couples who had chosen to be married on the same day in Skanderbeg Square were given a queen's dowry which consisted of a bed, blankets and pillows, the necessities for a honeymoon. The King issued an amnesty freeing hundreds of his political enemies, many of whom had sworn to kill him under the Albanian tradition of blood feud. Since early morning the streets had been crowded as the people danced to traditional folk music. Fifty thousand school children dressed in national costume mingled with the crowds and the King's bodyguard completely surrounded the palace grounds but admitted the crowds inside the walls when in the excitement they pressed close to the palace gates.

For the King it was not only his personal homage to a woman he now loved dearly but the culmination of his career and the desire for world recognition that under his rule his country had, at last, moved from the eighteenth century into the twentieth.

In ten years, by sheer willpower he had brought his country from tribal rule to a constitutional government. Even when he was Prime Minister he had realised that for Albania a monarchy was by far the most suitable form of goverment. Albanians place so much emphasis on the individual personality and since the time of Skanderbeg, have always sought a figurehead to replace him. A man above all others to protect their *Shquiperia* – Eagle Land. As the poet says: "Albanians love to have above their head just a King and a star-studded sky."

Zog had made himself a national hero when, as Prime Minister, during one of the many upheavals in the country, he was shot and wounded three times outside the Parliament building. He calmly walked into Parliament House and despite his bleeding wounds in a calm authoritative voice made not only one of the most brilliant speeches of his career but the longest. As he spoke, all enemy voices were hushed. Throughout all Albania by his moral and physical courage he had become a national hero overnight. Tired of the fomenting unrest, the Assembly proclaimed Ahmed Zogu their King on 1st September 1928, between the hours of nine o'clock and noon and there was not one single voice in dissent. He was a man without fear, a trait that all Albanians respect.

One of his first changes, as well as introducing the Napoleonic Code, was the discarding of the veil. Oddly enough it was the Catholic women who found this the most unnerving since their veils had always been of thicker material than the sheer gauze of the Muslims who were in the majority. This feminist liberation immediately caused a revolution, the quelling of which was one of Zog's first strong acts as King.

On the morning of the wedding Princess Geraldine woke at six o'clock despite the fact that she had not gone to bed until late and been given a sedative to make her sleep. Soon everyone was awake at the villa and emotions ran high as – typically Hungarian – first the grandmother, and then her mother and aunts, began to cry.

Geraldine was astonishingly calm as she put on the pearl and diamanté embroidered wedding dress from Worth that had been selected for her. Again she had not been consulted, but the King's taste was so sensitive that its elegant lines flowed over her willowy figure.

It was Madame Girault's romantic wish that she place the wedding veil on her daughter's head and then from a hidden box she disclosed the white gold chain with diamond cross that Geraldine had admired with the King. It was another touch of finesse that made this man so different. At the time it was reported that the bride was taller than the King, but this was merely the height of her coronet of orange blossom, an insignificant fact that still piques her to this day.

As the wedding was to be a civil one only, it was held in the flower-decked hall of the palace. Followed by her six bridesmaids, all in white, Princess Geraldine entered the room to join the King who looked most impressive in his white uniform, his rows of decorations and his sabre. As Princess Geraldine took his arm the King placed on the fourth finger of her right hand a huge blue fourteen carat solitaire diamond to match the blue white one he had given her as an engagement ring.

The King's witnesses were Count Ciano and Zog's Turkish brother-in-law, Prince Abid, the Albanian Minister to France. Representing the Queen was Count Charles Apponyi, her guardian and uncle, and Baron Frederick Vilany, Hungarian Minister to Italy. Her train was carried by the King's nephew, Tati. Helqmet Delvina, the white-bearded president of the two Houses of Parliament united the couple by reading from the Civil Code.

"The man and wife accept reciprocal obligations to live together in loyalty and mutual assistance. The man is head of the family; the wife follows the civil position of the man, taking his name, and is obliged to follow the head of the family wherever he sees fit to dwell. The man is obliged to protect his wife, to procure her a living according to his means. The wife is obliged to contribute to his nourishment if he is without means."

"I was so nervous that I signed my two signatures with my maiden name Geraldine Apponyi, instead of Geraldine R," the Queen remembers.

The service lasted three minutes. The King then placed her trembling hand on his arm and led his bride to the balcony to greet the thousands milling in Skanderbeg Square. Again and again they returned to wave to the people who were overjoyed to see their monarch so relaxed and fulfilled. It seemed that a whole new era of prosperity was dawning for this nation which had known only turbulence in the past. After this the King led her into the wedding reception, followed by her line of fluttering bridesmaids, the close family and the Court behind. They moved from salon to salon shaking hands and greeting guests. All the Queen remembers today of this part of her wedding was a sea of faces, so many loving faces, and the strange dream-like feeling of receiving reverences from her family.

In a letter to Viscount Halifax, then Foreign Secretary, Sir Alec Ryan, the British Minister in Tirana, wrote: "I am assured that the King nearly forgot to shake the Duke (of Bergamo)'s hand at the end of the wedding celebrations. I understand that the Duke is a distinguished soldier, but he showed few social qualities and seldom smiled. The Count (Ciano) smiled all the time, danced strenuously and flirted outrageously in the intervals between his more serious activities. These had included the laying of the first stone of the new road to be constructed at Italian expense from Tirana to Durazzo."

59

Queen Geraldine cut the three metre wide wedding cake with the King's sabre and her beloved brother Gyula, just fourteen years of age, made a speech. With the permission of the King, the Apponyi family had arranged to bring to Tirana one of the most famous gypsy orchestras from Budapest to play at the reception. They played Geraldine's favourite tunes until, to the horror of the King, his bride began to cry.

They drove to Durazzo for their honeymoon in an enormous open Mercedes. There they came to an enchanting marble pavilion that the King had designed and built especially for Queen Geraldine, overlooking the sapphire-blue Adriatic. Many different coloured marbles had been used so that, perched high on a hilltop, it appeared like a mirage in the golden afternoon sunshine silhouetted against a clear blue sky.

Together the newly-weds drank coffee before the King showed his bride the large reception room furnished in Louis XIV style; the dining room, which was pure Empire since Napoleon was the King's hero; and then upstairs to a Marie Thérèse gilded bedroom where a maid awaited her. The bride chose a white silk nightgown with long bell-shaped lace sleeves and waited terrified in the canopied bed for the King. The only sound was the sea below, lapping against the shore. Quickly and passionately Zog possessed her. Not as a King but as a proud son of the Eagles. His bride was no different from other virgins. No one can explain the deep personal shock and physical discomfort of a woman when she is made love to for the first time, no matter how much she adores the man. She lay softly whimpering into her pillow as the King left her side and retired to a *chaise longue* at the other end of the room.

Time had lost its urgency. When he finally returned to her side and comforted her, with the soft words "*Mein Leibling*", there followed a night of passion until the first shafts of dawn when they fell asleep.

That was to be their last spring of contentment.

CHAPTER 8

On the first day of the honeymoon, while she was dressing as the King was already downstairs, Queen Geraldine found her young maid crying. Why and what was the matter? The frightened girl explained: "I cannot find your beautiful nightgown. Somebody has stolen it." They both looked everywhere as the Queen knew that nobody else had entered the room except the King and his valet. The Queen soothed the maid and said that she would talk it over with the King and the young girl went on unpacking the exquisite trousseau, the likes of which she had never seen before.

That same evening when I found the right moment I said to the King: "Anna is very upset. She cannot find my nightgown." My husband was very fair of skin and I think it is the only time in my life that I saw him blush. He was most embarrassed. He explained to me: "I have told you so much about how we respect women, especially the mother. It was absolutely necessary that you were a virgin and any other foreign girl, who comes here for marriage, has to undergo a medical test. I pride myself on knowing people and it was enough for me to look into your eyes. I did nothing about it because I also knew you would not accept it. At the same time I had to give proof to Parliament so I took your nightgown and sent it to the President."

The afternoon had already been interrupted by a visit from Count Ciano who came to see the King on official business. The Queen resented his intrusion and the King was clearly embarrassed especially when the Italian Minister stayed for four hours.

When the King finally joined her he looked drawn and pale. For the first time during the three months' period she had known him he seemed pessimistic.

"I can see that I shall not be able to do anything with the Italians," he told her. "I tried to make Ciano understand the danger in becoming tied too closely to the Germans. He listened to me but he said, 'To have the Germans as friends is heavy on the shoulders, but to have them as enemies is terrible.'"

Ciano argued with the King that maintaining neutrality, in the event of a European conflict, would be advantageous to Italy. In this way she would have more hope in retaining Yugoslavia and Greece also as neutrals and so keep Albania out of the war.

"I found his attitude in general suspicious. I do not think that he has good intentions towards us but he tried to make me believe it," the King added.

The next day they were not alone either, as all the princesses descended on them. As days passed the Queen slowly realised that she was not only sharing a King with his country but a brother with his six sisters. Each day, too, it was also necessary to give parties for the legations stationed at Durazzo, the Army garrisoned there, and local authorities. It was not until late at night that they were ever alone.

Though she did not fully realise it, these days crowded with family and officials, were to be the pattern of her future life.

I wished so much to be alone with my husband and now we were man and wife it was so much easier to speak about personal matters. I desperately wanted to know the small things that had made him into the man that I now loved so deeply.

He had an extraordinary memory and could tell in detail incidents that had happened to him when he was only three years old. I never tired of hearing how his father had taken him at this age for the first time on his horse on one of the tours of inspection. When he saw how well the child had stood it, he always took Ahmed on his tours which sometimes took several weeks in biting cold, rain and snow.

In this way the child not only got to know the whole countryside and every track and pass through the mountains but he always listened at his father's side when he was dealing with tribal issues in the various villages. There were days when the people came from afar to tell of their problems demanding arbitration on questions of honour, sharing inheritances, disagreements between villages and family blood feuds. Ahmed often went to his father telling him things that he had heard with his child's ears when the people had spoken freely in front of him thinking he did not understand. But he did and never forgot. At five years of age the mountain people already respected his intelligence and sought from this aesthetic looking child his influence. His father was so proud of him. They had a very special father-son relationship.

62

This idyllic boyhood was not to last. When an attempt to get autonomy for Albania from the Ottoman Empire failed in 1901, Turkey asked the Albanian Pasha (governor) for his second son as a hostage. Knowing that the first son was not interested in Albanian affairs the cunning Turks demanded young Ahmed. This came as such a devastating and cruel blow to his parents that Djemal Pasha caught pneumonia and died within a few days.

Concealing her grief from the child and without shedding a tear Sadije watched him ride off with two loyal servants for the long journey to Constantinople, as Istanbul was then called. The trip took weeks with the proud young Ahmed, who wore the red Turkish fez for the first time, staying at various Turkish estates *en route*.

On arrival, and for his presentation to the Sultan, he had been given instructions never to look the ruler in the face but to keep his arms crossed and to prostrate himself at the Sultan's feet. To the consternation of his high-ranking relatives, who had accompanied him for his audience, he merely bowed deeply and in reply to the Sultan's welcoming gesture he stood up and looked him straight in the eyes putting all the sincerity of his young six-year-old heart into the words he had learned to say. This attitude pleased the Sultan and he gave orders that, as in the case for hostages, he was not only to continue his education in the celebrated school of Galata Serail, but he was also to be appointed adjutant to one of the princes.

On hearing this the young Ahmed rebelled. "No," he replied, "I shall never in my whole life be an adjutant to another."

The Sultan's reaction to the boy's honesty was violent: he was forbidden any contact with his family, refused permission to return to his own country and most damaging of all, given no funds. All he had left were his two faithful mountain men.

The Albanians who lived in Istanbul were not rich. They were modest people working as gardeners, café-owners, restaurateurs, cobblers and small-holders, but on hearing the news they met together and placed their savings at the disposal of their young lord. Young though he was, he knew the value of every penny and lived with his retainers in two rooms in one of the old wooden houses in the city.

Even at that age he was already a fastidious dresser and each night placed one of his two pairs of trousers under the mattress of his bed. He studied hard and became thin and delicate on the meagre food and in the penetrating cold of the severe winters. The second winter he caught pneumonia and was only saved from death when a Turkish doctor picked the sick boy up off the street and took him back to his own home. He nursed him back to health and kept him in his house for two years. Ahmed managed to complete two years' study within each successive year and at the age of thirteen made his first political speech in front of a multitude of young Turks. This was the beginning of his political career. His success was so spontaneous that he was carried shoulder high in triumph.

In the summer holidays when he was fourteen years of age, taking four Albanians with him, Ahmed travelled to Macedonia where one of his uncles was managing the large family estates, two of which belonged to Ahmed's family. After having been presented to the whole family, who admired this tall young stripling, he requested a private audience with his uncle.

"I cannot accept your hospitality until you have accounted to me for the years since the death of my father," he challenged the older man. "You have sent no money for my mother and myself. Now you pay me all that you owe and I shall take over the property or I shall cede it to you for a very low sum." The uncle replied that he would pay him nothing until he came of age. Ahmed placed his hand on his revolver and said that he would not leave Macedonia until he had been paid his due.

His uncle looked at him and said, "You would really shoot your uncle?" The reply was crisp and immediate. "Yes."

Ahmed received everything that was due to him and returned to Istanbul rich. He was able to pay those who had helped him and to buy himself a house.

At the age of only sixteen he left Istanbul to return to his country, gathering men *en route* like the Crusaders until he had a thousand 'knights' following him. He arrived at Burgajet triumphant and proud. In re-telling the tale to his wife the King almost cried when he described his feelings on at last being embraced by his mother. Sadije had never doubted that her son was destined to lead men, was not her son born with a caul, which in Albania was a sign of greatness?

King Zog's skill in the art of story telling was unbounded. Contrary to the old Albanian saying, "only crazy men tell stories by day," he was absorbing whenever he spoke. Men and women who knew Zog were always astonished at his almost caressing

64

voice. They found it difficult to equate this aesthetic man, who chain smoked and danced the tango sublimely, with the rugged mountain tribesman of earlier fame. Only Alexander Dumas could have created such a dashing character. This King was real.

The only time that Queen Geraldine had her husband completely to herself was on two trips they made into the mountains. The King wanted to show his impressionable young bride the beauties of his country. On one such four-day trip they travelled by car on narrow stone roads high up in the Northern Mountains. The roads were cut from sheer cliff on one side and dropped into threatening deep ravines on the other. One slip of the driver's attention would have been fatal.

The virgin forests during that spring of 1938 had never been more verdant. First came the groves of feathery mountain ash, pale green beeches, silvery verbascums bursting into bloom like giant yellow candelabra, juniper bushes hugging the roads and, higher up, the mountain sides stained dark green with pines. Always there was the sound of mountain streams gushing down into the rich valleys of wild flowers below.

At dusk the party chose a camp for the night, with the King and Queen and the few guards who accompanied them sitting on the ground round the camp fire as the lamb roasted on the spit. Tales were told in the glowing fire-light as the maize bread, succulent white sheep and goat's cheese, and pots of fresh yoghurt were laid out on the ground. Each district is known for its own *burek*, the paper-thin pastry envelopes filled with cheese or meat or zucchini and nuts. Villagers brought gifts of food to the King and his party.

For the first time since arriving four months ago, Queen Geraldine was able to taste the real flavour of Albanian cooking. Mutton boiled in yoghurt and cheese, meat balls of lamb with yoghurt sauce, cucumbers thinly sliced and mixed with oil, vinegar and herbs.

Dressed in jodhpurs, cotton shirt and sweater she was completely content as they sat under the black velvet sky and breathed the pure mountain air spiced with the scent of pine trees. There was always the haunting song of the nightingale.

The King and Queen shared a sleeping bag lying under the trees within sight of the guards. Long into the early morning they whispered in the dark. Two people sharing their love.

On the last day they spent the morning riding yet further into the mountain crags, exploring hidden villages and greeting the

65

people. Often there would be a small stone house nestling alongside the church dizzily perched on the mountainside. As the King and his bride approached, a venerable old priest would come out and offer to show his chapel. The forms of religion were touchingly simple among these hard-working rugged people.

Lunch was always a picnic seated on the ground on the outskirts of one of the richer villages. By now Queen Geraldine could speak and understand enough Albanian to talk with the villagers and listen to their story-telling.

After one such picnic, when much wine had been drunk – though the King himself never touched alcohol – the driver began to negotiate the mountain road in a frightening way and twice the wheels slipped over the precipice. The Queen was petrified, and members of the entourage begged the King to change drivers.

Despite the Queen's beseeching looks the King replied: "I would not allow myself to change drivers and perhaps be responsible for his death. It is only that he has drunk too much." He then took out his revolver and put it to the neck of the driver and said: "Now drive slowly or I shall kill you." No one ever doubted King Zog and they got back to Durazzo without incident.

Now that she had seen the King surrounded by his mountain people the Queen felt that she knew and understood him better than before. She had seen the freedom of speech between the King and his people and his complete understanding of their forthright yet complicated nature, the result of generations of harsh life. She had also experienced the trust these simple people placed in the King who would always remain in their hearts as Ahmed the Hawk.

Among his own people in the mountain villages the King had been able to forget his grim problems which immediately faced him when they returned to Durazzo.

He confided in Queen Geraldine, and she recorded a conversation they had on 20th May. The King was worried by the attitude of General Pariani, chief of the Italian Military Mission. "It seems very strange", he told her. "He is a capable officer but the activity of the mission is not clear to me, and the armaments we are being supplied with are insufficient in quantity and quality. I distrust our ally more than our enemies. The organisation of the Police by the British Mission is expensive and is not a sufficient counter-balance, but with nothing better it will

66

have to do."

As the result of an earlier request the British Government Office sent Major-General Sir Jocelyn Percy to be in charge of the Royal Albanian Gendarmerie. Serving under him was the late Colonel D.R. Oakley-Hill. Colonel Oakley-Hill was picked as the staff officer because he spoke the language and used to act as interpreter when the general visited the King at the palace. He told me:

"It was in the Spring of 1938 that we British in the Gendarmerie were given letters from the Minister of the Interior telling us that we must leave immediately. Our contracts were negotiated for one year at a time and we had not expected them to be terminated like that. My boss Major General Sir Jocelyn Percy said to me: 'Come on we'll go along and see the King about this.' We went to the palace and I interpreted. The King listened and said that he did not want us to go like that and immediately telephoned the Minister. I listened to the conversation but of course only heard what the King was saying. When it was finished he said: 'Oh yes. That's all right. You can stay until October.' You see he had two sides always to contend with but in the end he always made the decision. I had the greatest admiration for him."

In the month of June all the royal family moved to their chalets on the beach at Durazzo. These beach houses were made of wood and painted inside and out in pastel colours. Queen Geraldine chose a pretty chintz for the new chalet the King had built for them. There was a salon and an immense bedroom with white furniture. From their twin beds they could lie and look out over the blue Adriatic sea. There was also a luxurious bathroom and office. The King's chalet, and those belonging to the princesses and court officials, were guarded night and day.

One of the wedding presents that was now installed at Durazzo was an old, well-travelled parrot. The bird got on the King's nerves so much with its shrieking that, as a joke, he taught it a few well-chosen insults and gave it to his eldest sister. When aroused, the parrot used to shriek at her, "Horrid woman . . . you liar." She had to suffer this because it would have been an insult to give a gift back to the King. The only decent words it knew were "Beautiful Queen".

They were halcyon days despite the ever-present rumblings of discontent in the background. The King's agents reported everything going on in the country and when he heard that Giro, chief of the Fascist workers' organisations and of the Albanian Youth Movement, was agitating a great deal, he told the Queen, "That man is dangerous and has to be watched closely. He uses the worst corruption to gain his ends."

On 25th June General Francesco di Sanlavino Jacomoni, the Italian ambassador offered the King, on behalf of his government, a yacht crewed by Italians. Queen Geraldine was delighted with the thought of leaving the family behind and having the King to herself for a proper honeymoon.

King Zog refused the gift which he interpreted as a bribe. By now he had survived three assassination attempts and there was always the possibility that the food on board might be poisoned. Instead the King said that they would charter it to make a trip to Venice with some of his own servants and if he and the Queen found the yacht agreeable he would buy it.

While embarking, he whispered to the Queen: "I do not like the atmosphere. I do not like the faces of the crew."

The sea was rough so that after only a few hours out the Queen became ill and the King asked the captain to return to the harbour. He refused and it was not until midnight that the King's orders were obeyed. Later the King and Queen heard that had they disembarked in Italy, they would not have been allowed to return to Albania. It was a cunning plot which was only foiled by the King's intuition and the Queen's sea-sickness.

Though acutely sensitive to the advantages of being friendly with the Italians, who now even offered to send their brilliant engineer Trampolini to make a plan to complete the modernisation of the port of Durazzo, he was fully aware of their 'sweet talk'.

"I gave my consent to Trampolini coming here because as well as the port itself there is the draining of 2500 hectares of marshlands near the town. It is vital to have this done and there is no one else but the Italians," he told the Queen.

It was a situation that gave the King many lonely hours in his beach-side study, weighing the consequences far into the night – whether to go ahead with the modernisation of his country using the expertise and money provided by the Italians, or to go it alone with insufficient funds to explore the known wealth that lay waiting to be tapped with modern technology. Though he was surrounded by his own advisers, they were not men experienced in the intrigues of this modern world. The ultimate decision would be his and his alone.

CHAPTER 9

At the beginning of August, Queen Geraldine's sister Virginia and her husband, André de Baghy de Szechen, went to join them at the beach at Durazzo. It was a reunion of immense joy for the sisters, as they had not met since the royal engagement and Virginia had stood behind the new Princess Geraldine on the balcony at Tirana. She was not able to be present at the wedding as she had just given birth to a baby girl which died two weeks later. The doctors had advised that Virginia should have another baby as quickly as possible and she arrived at Durazzo pregnant. By now the Queen was sure that she also was expecting a child so there was much to celebrate.

As Aunt Antoinette wrote archly in her journal: "We noticed today that the Queen was in even better spirits than usual. 'What day is it today?' she asked me before she accepted the mail from her secretary. 'The twenty-ninth of July', I replied.

"There was a soft, happy smile on the Queen's face. She did not say anything nor did we dare to put the question but we guessed that on this day she became sure of the thing which is the greatest event in any woman's life, whether Queen or peasant – she now knew for certain that she was bearing a child under her heart."

Although the world was in the grip of fear of war, King Zog flamboyantly chartered a yacht to sail round the coast line of the southern part of Albania. The weather was beautiful and the sea as calm as a deep blue lake.

It was a family party consisting of the King and Queen, the six princesses, Virginia and her husband and various nieces. On 12th August they dropped anchor at Seranda, a small ancient port filled with fishing boats. During the afternoon the town's authorities came aboard and accompanied the royal party to the quay which was packed with people all dressed in the Albanian costume of that particular region.

The King spoke to them and the Queen was fascinated as this was the first time that she had heard him speak in public. He told them of the plans he had for the nation and emanated such a feeling of pride that the crowds burst into applause.

In the evening the celebrations continued with a dinner for a thousand people in the public gardens of the town, which were planted with fruit trees and brilliantly coloured flowers. Again the news had travelled and people swarmed in from the surrounding countryside and came down from the mountain villages. The magnet was always Queen Geraldine who had added to her own natural vivacity a new assurance with the knowledge that she was carrying the child the country had awaited for so long.

It was not until two o'clock next morning that the royal party was allowed to return to the yacht. The next day they visited Butrino, the place where Helen of Troy found refuge with her people and lived until her death.

> Today I can still see our disembarkation in a little bay shaded by trees and our walk up the valley which was bordered with luxurious trees and a small brook running alongside. In my imagination I could see the young girls and women going to the brook with their water jars on their heads, as they must have done in Helen of Troy's time.
>
> When we arrived at the top of the valley we could see the excavations of a city, a little like the ruins of Pompeii only much smaller, and having a more romantic and intimate atmosphere. Ninety per cent of the relics found went to the museum in Tirana and the rest to the Italians who financed them. As far as it is known the present régime is still continuing with these excavations.

The yacht cruised slowly along the coast until it entered the bay of Valona with the idyllic island of Saseno opposite. Valona is the key to the Adriatic and in the hands of a Free World would act as another Gibraltar. It has the same potential as a natural fortress with its cliffs and rocks honeycombed with deep caverns and tunnels made by the hand of man.

The King already knew that the people of Valona were politically restless compared with the other more pro-monarchy parts of the country and there were already strong Fascist movements afoot. He was determined to speak directly to the people from the balcony of the Town Hall. He spoke for an hour without once raising his voice. When he had finished there were a few moments silence before the people broke into cheering. It had

71

been such a moving experience that old women began to cry and there were tears running down the apple-red cheeks of the old mountain warriors. The King had that rare gift of making a crowd vibrate as a violinist does his instrument.

People are the same the world over with their craving to touch royalty. In Valona they crowded round the open car, pushing and thrusting their hands inside, trying to touch the Queen who was alone in the back seat. Suddenly strong hands lifted the big Mercedes high above the crowds and carried it along triumphantly, to the Town Hall. The Queen recalls today being immensely frightened at the time.

Returning to Durazzo, even though on holiday, the King worked from morning to night on state papers. There was no document or contract that went through Parliament without his scrutiny and signature.

September brought war clouds nearer with the Czech crisis getting worse by the hour. Hitler threatened invasion and Chamberlain, the British Prime Minister, flew to Munich to appease him.

On 22nd September, 1938, the Yugoslavian chargé d'affaires warned his Albanian friends that Italy was preparing to invade the country. On hearing this news King Zog immediately sent for various diplomats to test the reactions of their governments. The winds of change and fear were sweeping across Albania.

Though pregnant, Queen Geraldine resumed her public duties and returned to Tirana to inspect all the milk centres, the Red Cross, hospitals, orphanages, schools, and the shelters especially created for the gypsies who suffered during the cold winters. She wrote copious notes in the pad that she always carried, asking questions, checking the books, prying into affairs which she felt could be improved. Plans were drawn up for new buildings and schemes to be inaugurated after the birth of the baby.

It was a month of great activity as, regardless of the international unrest, King Zog had insisted on celebrating the Feast Day of the Monarchy on 1st September. During the entire month there were civilian and military parades, evening soirées and daily audiences. With the suffocating heat of these last days of summer, and the lack of rest, Queen Geraldine nearly lost the precious child she was carrying.

That afternoon I had taken my usual swim between siesta time and changing for the evening. I used to wear rubber wings and was always followed by a motor boat when I swam far out. The King did not swim but used to enjoy wading out into the water until only his head was visible. It was not only refreshing but one way of escaping from the mosquitoes.

In the evenings before dinner at nine o'clock, we used to spend an hour in the garden listening to the guards' orchestra playing in the pavilion in the grounds. I had as usual taken my embroidery with me and the King was in a relaxed mood as we listened to his favourite jazz and tango tunes. Suddenly I felt completely exhausted, drained of all my energy. I asked to be allowed to retire and went to bed immediately. I fell into a deep sleep and awoke at ten o'clock to find my bed soaking in water.

I was so inexperienced that I became frightened and sent for the King who immediately summoned several doctors and telephoned a leading gynaecologist in Vienna who had examined me at the beginning of my pregnancy.

The doctor told the King that the child would have to be taken away. Thank goodness my maternal grandmother was staying with us at the time. She calmly and firmly ordered the various doctors, who had now gathered round my bed, that under no circumstances were they to remove the child. She then explained that my mother had all her six children safely after losing the water in the third or fourth month.

The doctors conferred and then telephoned Vienna again. The specialist promised that he would come immediately, but for the moment they were to place bags of ice on the lower part of my stomach and that I was not to move in bed. When he arrived four days later he was horrified to find that the local doctors and nurses had followed his instructions exactly and had been replenishing the ice, day and night.

The doctor from Vienna examined Queen Geraldine and found that she had not suffered by this drastic treatment but warned her that it could be a long and slow birth. He also recommended two months of quiet, resting as much as possible. This meant the end of the Queen's personal inspections and her building plans must be put aside.

Within the palace in Tirana there was much to occupy Queen Geraldine. She had persuaded her Aunt Antoinette to take over the financial direction of the household. The personal affairs of the Queen were now managed by Baroness Ruling, who had been elevated to the rank of Dame d'Honneur, and Countess Marie

Rose Wenckheim, a friend of the Queen's from Budapest, had arrived to take over the duties of lady-in-waiting and secretary. It was a promise that the King had given her when she became engaged that she could have someone from Hungary in this confidential position. Only when she appeared at public functions was it necessary to borrow Albanian ladies-in-waiting from the Princesses in order to conform with court etiquette.

On 10th October the King talked to his wife seriously about the Italian problem. He was now deeply committed to co-operating with them and therefore reasoned that at least an appeasement must be made with honour and integrity.

"I shall send General Sereggi (his chief adjutant) to take a personal message to Ciano with instructions to leave a written note confirming the declarations that I have ordered him to make", he told the Queen. "'Albania is today in the hands of Italians, who control each vital sector of the State. The King holds them in esteem and listens to them. The people are grateful to you. What more does Italy want?'"

"Sereggi has the ear of the Italians as he himself is an Italophile, being convinced that under the circumstances there are no politics to exchange against the friendship and alliance with Italy. This is true, on condition that they do not ask anything contrary to the independence and sovereignty of Albania."

A week later Sereggi returned to Albania reporting calm assurances from Ciano. To show their sincerity the Italians accelerated their work at Durazzo and the surrounding countryside, including the drying-out of the marshlands according to the plans submitted by Trampolini that had previously been approved by the King and his ministers.

"God willing, good sense will come to them and they will keep their word," he told the Queen. "We are now left to watch their actions closely and be continually vigilant. In any case I must pretend to believe them."

This period was the most important in my whole life because of the tension that dominated everything we thought and did. It was a period of self-maturing. Apart from the human aspect it developed my insight into the intrigues of the political world and brought me closer to my husband. I was still only twenty-two years of age and his patience was immeasurable as we sat together in the long evenings while I listened to his quiet authoritative voice. Perhaps also my complete joy in carrying our child had given me serenity and understanding which I know helped my husband and also made me love the country and its people for the rest of my life.

By the end of the month, Durazzo was cold and damp and the court returned to Tirana and the normal routine of the palace. The Queen's life fell into an orderly pattern. At eight o'clock she breakfasted with the King and at ten o'clock an elderly minister arrived to continue teaching her Albanian history and language. At noon came a stream of directors of the various organisations that she was associated with and though she was no longer able to travel about herself, she listened and found out what was missing in the Albanian woman's life, especially concerning hygiene in the small villages in the mountains.

The King and Queen always ate alone in their private apartment as this was the only time during the day they could talk. They spoke about the important issues that they were concerned with and made their plans for the future. On one occasion when they were talking about the 'art of government' in relation to human affection the King interrupted excitedly: "That's it. You have found the right word. To govern well one has to know how to love people. Love and affection are the highest necessities of society. Every state employee, the humblest and the greatest, must try to fulfil this necessity." Indeed, the King himself made every effort to implement this ideal.

The afternoon siesta was sacred in the palace and everyone was asked to go to their own quarters. There was complete silence throughout the building, even in the staff quarters. As the King rose early, his siesta fortified him to work late into the night. It was two hours and not a minute less.

Although the public rooms in the palace had been furnished in the French style when Queen Geraldine had first arrived in Tirana in the previous January, in the more personal parts there was a surprising lack of ordinary household necessities. The King had led an almost Spartan life and his food had been sent in from the nearby house of one of the Princesses. Everything was arranged for the great banquets, but there was nothing for ordinary daily life, not even sufficient linen. The bachelor King had simply never been interested in his own personal comfort and his staff were ignorant, coming from simple homes which were run by the women just as they had been for hundreds of years.

When Countess Antoinette Apponyi made her initial inspection as director of the household, she had been horrified to find pieces of a fine, hand-embroidered set of table mats, which the Queen was sent from Hungary, scattered around the palace. Some were in the dining room, other pieces in the bedroom of the first chambermaid and the rest in the office of the royal garage, where they were used as a wall decoration. Each day was filled with surprises: she found that the mattress on her bed was packed with straw instead of the horsehair that she was used to in Hungary; one day she bumped into a valet scurrying along the corridor to the King's office bearing ice in a soup tureen – when the King had telephoned he had taken the first utensil to hand. With her Hungarian background of country estates she was a superb organiser and quickly changed this exotic Oriental court into a well run Western one, which was exactly what the King wanted. Five staff had come from Hungary – the chauffeur and his wife, the cook, personal maid and washing woman.

As Aunt Antoinette wrote in her journal at that time: "The staff is docile, quick-witted and easy to handle. It is a great joy for me to see how the small blunders which had been unnoticed in the past, but disturbed the atmosphere and essence of the whole palace, soon vanished."

In the mornings the golden-haired young Queen and the middle-aged Countess used to sit and pour over catalogues that had been ordered from stores in London and Paris. They spent hours on the inventory that the Countess had prepared and everything which seemed to be missing in the palace was noted and put into two categories. The first was that of the 'necessities' and the second the 'desirables'. Although the King had given the Queen a generous amount to spend on up-dating the palace she preferred to make the purchases gradually. This modesty was exactly in keeping with her character and she rigorously compared prices in the different catalogues so that she could get the best possible bargain.

Just as today the big firms send 'our man' to the palaces of the oil-rich sheiks in the Middle East, so they did then. 'By Appointment to the King of Albania' was a coveted recommendation on their note paper even if back in England they made snide remarks and spoke of 'the toy palace'. Some even tried to bribe the Countess and were quickly sent packing – empty-handed.

76

At last over a period of months, when all the lists were complete the Queen asked King Zog to come to her study. "I would like to show you the plans we have prepared," she told him.

These were not only for the palace but for the reorganisation of this and the various other houses in Tirana and Durazzo, some of which were used by the Queen's personal staff. There was also a villa for her personal guests and members of her family.

When he arrived and was shown the list the King laughed: "You expect me to control what you order?" Quickly, taking a pen he scrawled over the sheets of paper, "First double everything."

Nostalgic for the Christmases of her childhood at Nagy Appony, the Queen discussed with child-like joy what the King, the Princesses, her personal staff and friends at court should receive as Christmas presents. She had wanted to give costume jewellery to her staff but when he heard about this the King was adamant. "They will think they are real jewels," he laughed. Instead she had to ransack her own wardrobe for scarves and lingerie, to wrap up as gifts, as there was no time to get anything else and the shops in Tirana did not cater for Christmas frivolity.

It was the first time in her life that the Queen could have her own Christmas tree in her own home. Two days before Christmas Eve the finest 'royal fir' was selected from the north-eastern forests in Albania and brought to Tirana where it stood in the large drawing room on the ground floor. Although she was six months pregnant the Queen took over the decoration of the tree herself. This immense tree was lit again on Christmas Day for the small children of the two big schools in Tirana who had never seen one before and still remember that afternoon as a fairy dream.

The bells of Nagy Appony had been recorded on a gramophone record and now from a hidden loudspeaker pealed out, loud and clear, the music of the distant Magyar bells ringing in the birth of the child Jesus. "At this moment," wrote Aunt Antoinette, "we thought with pure and great humility in our hearts of the Saviour of Mankind and with deep reverence we glanced at the white-clad figure of the young future mother, the Queen."

Twenty-five members of the close family sat down to a Western-style Christmas dinner with turkey, flaming plum pudding and a table laden with goodies. For one night the King and Queen dismissed all worries and joined their guests playing games but against this background of cosy domesticity, danger lurked in the form of the Italian menace.

CHAPTER 10

On 8th February, 1938 the King dictated notes to Colonel Salmani of the Royal Guards, clearly indicating how concerned he was with the news he had received about the way the situation with Italy was developing. "The news from Belgrade is that Ciano has agreed with Dr Milan Stoyanovich (the Prime Minister of Yugoslavia) to cut Albania in two, keeping the lion's share for himself. The idea was repulsed by responsible Yugoslav circles who consider that the Albanian minority in that country is already too big (nearly two million people) and that it would be madness to want to make it larger. The Italian intention to attack us is now clear, and they can do it alone, without need of active Yugoslavian help. The danger is imminent and I must do everything possible to stop it. However, the disproportion between forces is really too great."

The King had already been trying for some time to interest the Germans in Albanian oil. While keen to exploit the rich fields they clearly did not want to upset Mussolini and told the King openly that Mussolini would be so angry that he might choose to leave the Axis which they could not consider. In his diary Count Ciano wrote concerning the possible German takeover of Albanian oil: "I telephoned Mackensen (Field Marshal H.G. von Mackensen) and informed him that we consider Albania as just like any other Italian province, and that any German intervention would create strong resentment in Italian public opinion. This fact also proves that the Albanian boil will come to a head in a short time. The Serbians have spoken. King Zog is alarmed and very much agitated. Some move might yet be made to oppose our action."

As news of the political unrest began seeping out of Tirana into the mountain communities, King Zog felt it his duty to speak to his people and explain the situation. Today this would be done on television but in those days it was transmitted by issuing a declaration which became the talking point in every village square where men met after their day's work.

The declaration was dated 14th February and said: "As you can see, relations with Italy are worsening each day and Italy is trying in every way to get a foot into the country, fomenting all sorts of trouble. Do not lose courage and hope, I am trying by all diplomatic and political means to guide or even arrest the course of events, but I have firmly decided to accept nothing which could compromise the sovereignty of the Albanian people.

"Truly, even if Italy declared war against us, which is possible as Fascism would profit from the invasion, the great democratic powers are not ready for war and would do nothing to help a country which is not their ally. My aim therefore is to prepare us for any eventuality without giving Italy a hold, which is to say that Albania must do nothing that could give Italy a pretext for declaring war. We must take no action contrary to the Treaty of Alliance with Italy as the whole world would then say that it is our fault and use it as an excuse for their own inertia."

The Council of Ministers decided that a note of official protest should be sent to Italy; and that the Fascist, Giro, and Koci his underling, with other known Albanian conspirators should be publicly exposed and expelled.

It was due to the activities of these conspirators that the King had asked the Queen to change her daily habits and that, instead of taking a drive into the neighbouring countryside after the siesta period they should not go outside the park. One afternoon as they were walking in the park the King said to the Queen, "Look only straight in front of you and without hurrying turn and we will walk back." When they re-entered the palace the Queen demanded an explanation for this extraordinary command but the King only replied, "Later," and disappeared quickly into his office.

That evening the King told her that for a long time he had known that an attempt on his life was being planned. As it was difficult to catch him alone, the Fascist element who were responsible were planning to do away with the King and the succession at the same time. Overlooking the park there was a large building and he had noticed in one of the attic windows a weapon glinting in the sunshine. On returning to his office the King had immediately sent his guards, caught the would-be assassin and had him brought to his office. The man confessed to everything including the sum of money he had been given. Characteristically the King told him to keep the gold but to continue to keep him informed of any other plans afoot.

Two days later Jak Koci, a long-time confidant of the King's, who now turned out to be a two-faced traitor, came to lunch. As they were having desert the Queen spat hers out exclaiming, "Ugh." Koci went green. He trembled as he said, "Do not eat any more!" The Queen did not understand and wanted to explain that it was all a mistake, that instead of making the strudel with apples the cook had used cabbage, a Hungarian dish she detested, but the King reacted immediately, taking Koci by the ear, pulling him out of the room and slamming the door behind him. The Queen saw the King say two words and then, with a kick, push Koci down the staircase. On returning, looking as unflustered as ever, the only words the King said were: "In two hours that one will no longer be on Albanian territory."

Koci had bribed the Albanian cook and the Hungarian woman who worked in the kitchen to add poison to the strudel. Both had come to the King, with the bags of gold with which they had been bribed in their hands to warn him beforehand, but were unable to speak to him.

Within two days the King and Queen had survived a second attempted assassination. Naturally, the Queen was extremely anxious about their safety, but outwardly she remained calm supporting her husband as best she could.

During that week the Queen had received a delegation of the ladies of the various legations who had all brought gifts for the coming baby. The Italian Ambassador's wife, Senora Jacomoni had warned the Queen that one must keep calm and "not move about in one's room." The ladies-in-waiting were most indignant but on hindsight it is now clear to Queen Geraldine that the Italian must have known exactly what was going to happen, and tried to help her in a distaff way.

There was great excitement for the Queen when the luxurious baby trousseau, which she had ordered from Maison de Blanc in Paris, arrived. As she had intended to have several children she had ordered lavishly and once again there were squeals of delight as the exquisite hand-embroidered baby clothes were unfolded from the tissue paper in the large boxes. The young Queen was in remarkably good health despite the two attempts on her life within recent weeks. Her staff had been given special orders by the King that she was not to be upset unduly and he made every effort to keep the desperate gravity of the situation from her.

By now the Italian ambassador, General Jacomoni, had returned from seeing Mussolini and given the King all the appeasements that he could have wished for; and his assurance that Italy had every intention of honouring the Treaty of Italo-Albanian Alliance. Though King Zog pretended to accept this, he knew through his own agents that the Italians were continuing to foment a revolt against him, but by appearing to accept the assurances of the Italians, King Zog was merely playing for time until a war would erupt and occupy their attention elsewhere. He still had hopes of getting help from the great western powers who, in the interests of their own strategy, would maintain the status quo in order to keep the Mediterranean free. Albania was a valuable card in the pack.

If he were to be attacked by Italy the King proposed to draw up three lines of defence: the first on the coast at Valona where the Italians were expected to land, the second and third in the mountains he knew so well. He hoped to conduct a guerrilla war on the second and third lines with the hope that England, France, Yugoslavia and Greece could be persuaded to help unofficially with arms and ammunition.

It was a hopeless situation. Britain and France, throwing blame on Yugoslavia and Greece, did nothing, fearing to push Italy even further into the arms of Germany. Yugoslavia, whose unity was menaced by dissention between the Serbs and Croats and who had Germany on its frontier, could not move. As for Greece, without the support of the maritime powers of the Mediterranean – Italy, France and Great Britain – she was helpless.

Count Ciano had also continued playing his own devilish game. In his diary on 25th March he wrote: "It is not possible to foresee what will be the development of events but it seems probable to me that Zog will yield. I am counting on the birth of his child. Zog loves his wife and in general all his family. I think that he will prefer to ensure a quiet future for his dear ones. And, frankly, I cannot imagine Geraldine running around fighting through the mountains of Unthi or of Mirdizu in her ninth month of pregnancy."

Discussions within the palace went on into the early hours of the morning. Queen Geraldine was not allowed to see any newspapers or to be disturbed by any of the ugly news outside the palace. The King's main concern was that his wife should give birth to a healthy heir, and he did all he could to protect her. When the King and she were alone they used to play games choosing names for the baby just like any other doting parents.

Queen Geraldine chose the name Alexander, which in Albanian is Leka. Even the money is called Lek and the greatest men of the race always bore the name of Leka. There was also Alexander the Great whose father, the King of Macedonia was of pure Illyrian descent and whose mother was an Illyrian princess. In Albanian history there had been Leka Dukagjino and Lek Molosis, both national military heroes.

Just two days before the birth of her baby Queen Geraldine was horrified when she heard the thunderous noise of thousands of people outside surging towards the palace. Rumours were flying about the Italians' plan to invade the country and the Albanians wanted to support their King and needed his assurance on the true state of affairs. They overcame the guards and pushed through the gates into the garden – men, women and children.

> I was trembling. At first it seemed that I heard a great moaning of despair, then the words became more distinct and one could understand that they were calling for arms and ammunition.
>
> The King sent someone out to try and calm them but it was no use. They chanted and shouted until the King himself went out on to the terrace and asked them to go home in peace and in God's name. He told them that since his birth, his work had been to save the honour and independence of Albania and that to the end of his life he would protect the independence and integrity of his country.
>
> The crowds calmed down a little but here and there we could hear sobs. I was standing just inside the palace and the King came and taking me by the hand led me out on to the terrace. The women were amazed and stopped crying and blessed me, as this countered the rumour that I had fled the country. Now they could see me for themselves and quietly they dispersed and went away.

During the previous ten days the gynaecologist Professor Weibel, who had arrived from Vienna, warned the Queen that, just as he had predicted she was going to have a slow birth. This meant that she was not having the usual contractions but was constantly in pain similar to a strong menstrual period. It was so severe that if she had to go downstairs she was carried in a chair.

The Queen's sleep was ruined by horrific nightmares and she constantly begged the King to give his people arms to defend themselves. Patiently he sat with his young suffering wife and explained that he could not do this as he did not want to have a massacre on his hands. It was impossible to put up more than a two- or three-day fight and that if the ordinary people were given arms they would have been butchered by the force of the Italian troops which he knew would be thrown into the attack. It was David against Goliath.

The King had wanted Queen Geraldine to have her baby in the new civilian hospital with its modern equipment at hand should there be any difficulties. The romantic young Queen asked that her child should be born within the old palace where the King had spent the last ten years. Had he not always said that the old building brought him luck? A small labour room was whitewashed and prepared near the Queen's own suite and the baby's trousseau, sufficient for years, was placed in big wooden chests in the new nursery quarters.

On 4th April, 1939, it rained in Tirana – deep, drenching rain covering the city in a grey pall. The King had been in his office from early that morning receiving a steady stream of diplomats, court officials, ministers and his senior Army generals. It had lasted four days now, this unbroken work in an atmosphere of the greatest tension. Faces looked weary. How much longer before the Italians made their move?

The Queen was sitting by the window in her room surrounded by her family: her mother, who had come from the Riviera, her maternal grandmother and Aunt Antoinette. She grew pale and bit her lip. "I think now," she told them. In less than two minutes Professor Weibel was summoned. The Queen underwent a rather lengthy examination in the specially prepared room where the nurses were already waiting and Professor Weibel announced that the birth would probably not be until night but that everything pointed to the fact that they could expect a smooth birth.

All through the day the Queen was in great pain and missed the comforting presence of her husband, who was locked in the conference room. Upstairs a woman was going to give the people a royal child. Downstairs a man was working to save his nation from oblivion.

84

Three more doctors had joined the team, an Albanian anaesthetist and the Queen's uncle 'Nicky' – Count Nicholas Wenkheim, whose daughter Mary Rose was the Queen's lady-in-waiting. Count Wenkheim had come to Tirana from Budapest at the Queen's invitation when she heard that the newly-opened hospital was looking for a head physician. In a short time he was known as one of the leading doctors in Albania. A midwife had also arrived from Vienna as the King wanted every precaution to be taken for the well-being of his wife.

As was the custom, everyone crowded into the room to witness the birth of the baby including the King's eldest sister Princess Adele, and the President of Parliament who was there to see that the birth was constitutionally correct.

The actual birth at three o'clock in the morning had only taken three hours and when it was realised that a son and heir had been born everyone except Professor Weibel lost their heads. They went mad with excitement that it was a boy and a healthy one at that. To facilitate the birth, as it was vital that the child be born in good health, a small slit had to be made. The Albanian doctors were so excited that they forgot to anaesthetise their patient until after the birth.

> I tried to protest without being able to make a sound so I jumped on the bed which caught the attention of Professor Weibel. He promptly told the Albanians off severely so that in the excitement they anaesthetised me too deeply and I woke six hours later.

By ten o'clock next morning, the Queen's room was filled with people. She lay in her big blue canopied bed glowing with happiness. She had recovered after her deep sleep with surprising swiftness. At her side in a white cloud of silk was her new-born son.

The whole family had gathered together. They stood at some distance from the bed as Professor Weibel had demanded this hygienic precaution. The Queen looked at her own family and slowly her hand glided with a careful caress over the head of the baby. She spoke her first words to them in Hungarian: "He is beautiful . . . isn't he?"

They surged forward to surround the bed, disregarding the Professor's warning. The King entered the room carrying a long polished box of rosewood in his hand. He placed it on the table near the bed, opened it and took out a bronze pistol. It was an old Albanian one, a work of art, with the ivory handle intricately carved. The King put the pistol near the baby then took hold of the tiny hand of his son and placed it on the handle of the pistol.

"Be strong and courageous like your ancestors," he pronounced. There was silence – and tears.

CHAPTER 11

The Queen rested all that day blissfully content, with the baby in his cradle at her side. To complete her joy a telegram had arrived from Budapest announcing that her sister Virginia had given birth on the same night to a baby daughter Julia, who became like a twin sister to her cousin Leka.

Outside in the streets at noon there was a military parade, the biggest of its kind that Albania had ever staged. Every regiment was represented as the troops marched with flying colours and bands playing towards the parade ground. The King arrived in his car, at his side his sister Princess Adele representing the Queen and his nephew Tati on behalf of the baby Prince Leka. The march was headed by an elderly soldier in the full war regalia of the old Albanian warriors. In his right hand he held aloft a large bouquet of white lilies of the valley. Behind him rode the formations of the different regiments with every flag decorated with a bunch of lilies of the valley and a long white silken pennant. There was rejoicing all over the country with the rolling of drums, clamour of trumpets, and above all the cheers of the people, "Our life for the King and the Crown Prince . . . For the King and the Crown Prince."

Suddenly out of the clouds a squadron of aeroplanes, flying in close formation, swooped over the city spraying it with white leaflets that fluttered to the ground like huge snowflakes. Lower and lower the planes came so that they were easily recognisable as heavy bombers of the Italian Air Force. Their mission completed they wheeled in formation, creating a display of power, and vanished.

The bewildered people stood dazed as they read in the leaflets a slanderous personal attack on their King. The propaganda had little effect, as the cheering for the King and Crown Prince continued with renewed strength while the people surged through the streets. But the birth of the Prince had forced the Italians to play their hand. Later in the afternoon the news spread throughout palace circles that Italy had presented the King with an ultimatum which would expire next day at noon. All Italians had been recalled from Albania and were crowding to the ports of Valona and Durazzo for embarkation. According to Ciano, "they are now seriously threatened by the bandits to whom Zog has given orders to start a reign of terror." The Italian demands on Albania were strong and punishing. And final.

Economic concessions were demanded which would transform Albania into a minor colony of Italy: military bases were demanded not only on the coast but also inland; all harbours and strategic roads should come under the control of the Italian Army; all appointments in the Civil Service should be revised according to the interests of Italy. In return for all these assurances King Zog was to be allowed to keep his throne and Albania was offered a new loan.

In her journal, Aunt Antoinette related how the Italian Minister had called for an audience with King Zog in the early afternoon. He brought the congratulations of his government on the birth of the Crown Prince, added his own good wishes, and then without any preamble, began to talk about the ultimatum.

"General Jacomoni assured King Zog of the unchanged goodwill of Italy. He tried to persuade the King to his view that he must accept the ultimatum, or rather the 'actual propositions', of the Italian Government. He also spoke about private matters – the Crown Prince.

"'I hope', he said, 'that your Majesty will find the happiest solution,' and added jokingly, 'sometimes one catches the lion through its cub'. Whereupon the King replied without hesitation, 'And sometimes the lion falls together with its cub, defending both himself and his offspring.'"

It was not until nine o'clock that night that the King was able to return to the Queen's bedroom. He looked haggard, worn and desperately sad. He smiled gently as he bent to kiss his wife and the baby who now lay in her arms. From his pocket he took a beautiful string of pearls and a pair of pearl-drop earrings and placed them in Queen Geraldine's hand. He picked up the baby and put him back in his cot and then sat down on the Queen's bed. Unaware of the events of the afternoon she remained silent as she measured the quality of the King's words and the full horror of the appalling situation dawned upon her.

He sat stroking her hand as he explained in a soft, caressing voice that he was thinking of sending her and the baby, with all her family, to the Greek frontier. Up until that moment this possibility had never been discussed, or even suggested.

At first I refused his request. I pleaded that I did not want to go. I could not leave the King in his hour of torment. Not to leave my people. Not to leave my country. I wanted to stay with these people who had accepted me as their Queen.

My husband explained to me patiently and quietly that we were not living in times when we could have found refuge in the mountains. Modern communications and modern warfare made this an impossibility for a woman in my condition and with a day-old baby.

He also told me that the Italians had deliberately chosen this moment, hoping to catch both me and our son and thus have a strong hold over him.

King Zog had the capacity for decision. He was gifted with that combination of wisdom and intuition which makes for swift conclusions. Distinguished memoir writers have criticised the King for leaving his country in its hour of despair. It was not his decision but Parliament's. In the morning, two hours after General Jacomoni had handed Italy's final ultimatum to King Zog, the two houses of Parliament had been in session in the Palace and it was decided then and there that King Zog and his government should leave the country next day after having declared war on the Axis. The decision had been made in the hope that the King could continue to serve his country from the Allied World and keep Albania's integrity inviolate.

While nominally accepting the decision of Parliament the King secretly hoped that the Queen and Prince-heir should be sent to safety, while he retired to the Northern mountains which were his birth place, where the people were one hundred per cent loyal and had not been infiltrated with Fascist propaganda and where he could begin a guerilla war. But this plan of his was completely nullified when he received an ultimatum from Yugoslavia that in the case of any fighting near its borders the Yugoslavs would march into Albania, and that their troops were already massing near the frontier.

When the King left her room, the Queen rallied her strength and sent for her family to explain the situation to them. There was her grandmother, Mrs de Strale d'Ekna, her mother Madame Girault, Aunt Antoinette and Baroness Ruling and of

89

course the six Princesses. Firmly and decisively she gave orders that the larger limousines were to be put at their disposal and arranged a seating plan. Madame Girault was so overcome that she was at fainting point. She not only had her husband Colonel Contran Girault with her but her brother-in-law and the Queen's half-brother and two half-sisters. They were the first to leave for Yugoslavia. Only the Queen's grandmother refused to leave her. No-one, not even the King, could persuade her.

Had she been alone, and not constantly surrounded by confused and weeping women, Queen Geraldine now thinks that she would have directed her personal packing with more sense. As it was, her mind went blank. The two senior women, Aunt Antoinette and Baroness Ruling, who might have helped, had gone to their own houses to do their own packing. Too weak to stand the Queen had to rely on an Albanian maid who went into a complete state of panic. The Queen's temperature began to rise alarmingly and she was near collapse.

Instead of packing the valuable silver gilt service, which had immense re-sale value, or even just a few personal treasures, the only things the maid grabbed were the Queen's fur coats. She did not pack one single suit, cloth coat, dress, pair of shoes or stockings. Not even a set of underwear. The only garment that the Queen had when she left Albania was the nightgown that she was wearing. Nor did the baby fare much better as the weeping nursery-maid selected the most impractical hand-embroidered crêpe-de-chine rompers.

Left in the confusion too were the beautiful Fabergé Easter eggs, and the King's Easter gift of a heart-shaped box which contained the most precious perfumes in the world, all in different crystal bottles.

There was no time to withdraw the Queen's money from the bank and only her presence of mind saved her jewels from being forgotten. At three in the morning, the King received word that a full-scale attack by the Italians had begun at Valona on the coast seventy miles to the south. It was only a question of hours before they would reach Tirana.

The cars were drawn up in the courtyard of the palace and the servants had completed the packing. Everyone went to the car allotted to them and stood waiting. Two valets carried the deathly white Queen, lying on a mattress, down the grand staircase to a Chrysler which had been converted for her use.

Professor Weibel, who was Jewish, had decided not to return to Vienna but to accompany the Queen to Greece. He and a nurse had moved the front seats of the car forward and taken out the back seat completely, leaving a large empty space. This they fitted with a double mattress, pillows and rugs.

The Queen was laid on the mattress and the baby swaddled in shawls behind her, while Professor Weibel sat with the driver. The back door was left open. At the last minute the King arrived, he bent down to kiss his wife first on her forehead and then her hand. It was Aunt Antoinette who recorded in her diary, "At this moment I noticed that Geraldine was not crying – she was smiling. Gathering all her strength she smiled courageously at her husband."

The King bent and kissed the baby on the head. His last words to the Queen were, "Oh God . . . It was so short."

The Queen replied, "God bless you."

The King shut the door and the car's engine roared, moving forward with the rest of the convoy into the darkness beyond. They were heading for the Greek border. It was Good Friday.

Queen Geraldine remembers very little of the next twelve hours as the car travelled over bumpy mountain roads, which were not only narrow but made more dangerous with the last of the winter snow and ice. The King had expressly ordered that all towns were to be avoided because at that stage he did not want his subjects to know that the Queen was leaving the country – nor the Italians for that matter. The route they took skirted Lake Ohrida, by day so beautiful, by night looking like a black sinister sea.

Alone in the back of the car the Queen was overjoyed when she discovered that she could feed the baby herself and had plenty of milk. Though it had been her wish, right from the beginning of her pregnancy, the doctors had thought that this would not be possible. An Albanian wet nurse had been engaged, but during the stress of the last three days her milk had dried up. The only time Queen Geraldine found any peace during those dark hours was when she was feeding the warm baby in her arms. After this she lapsed into a deep apathy and even saying her rosary had lost its comforting meaning. She took no food, drank only a few sips of water and rarely spoke. When she did it was always the same questions. "Is there any news of the King? . . . What do you hear from Tirana? . . . Is there much fighting? . . . There must be some news of the King?"

No-one dared to tell her that the rest of the party were glued to the radio which had announced the occupation of Tirana, the fierce fighting in Santi Qaurante, and the rumour that the King had joined the troops.

In his diaries Count Ciano records: "With the news of Zog's flight to Greece vanish all our fears about resistance in the mountains. In fact the soldiers are already returning to their barracks after having deposited their arms in the garden of the Legation (the Italian Legation in Tirana). The streets of Tirana were deserted and undefended. In the capital the crowd moved through the streets quite calmly. On the roof was a large Italian tricolour and in the courtyard many vehicles."

News similar to this was kept from the Queen who was in no state to receive any more shocks.

Mussolini's son-in-law flew into Tirana at ten o'clock on 10th April, and rushed from the airport to the palace. It is believed that as soon as he arrived at the palace, he made his way to the Queen's suite. As he saw a heap of bed linen, stained by the afterbirth, which was still lying in the 'labour room' Ciano kicked it across the room howling with the anger of a wild animal. "The cub has escaped".

Within about fifteen miles from the Greek border the royal party pulled up in the village of Koritza to rest and to try to make contact with the King. The Queen still hoped that she could persuade her husband to allow her to remain on Albanian soil. When the telephone call finally came through she was so distraught that she was unable to leave her mattress and one of the princesses spoke to the King.

King Zog told about the heavy fighting round Valona and Durazzo. The Albanians were resisting in the only way they knew – with acts of human bravery. In the little town of Chiak, on the road from Durazzo to Tirana, an Italian Army convoy was halted for an hour by a family who established a fortress overlooking a narrow part of the road. They kept up continual harrassment on the column until the house was finally destroyed, with all its occupants, by Italian gunfire. The King's orders to his wife were to proceed as quickly as possible to the frontier. One of the cars was sent to collect Queen Geraldine's younger brother Gyula who was studying at the French Lycée at Koritza, who on arrival was appalled when he saw the beautiful laughing sister he knew

Nagy Appony, Hungary. From a sketch by Countess Margaret Apponyi, 1912.

Tirana as Queen Geraldine first saw it.

Geraldine with her sister, Virginia.

Ahmed Zogu on his presentation to the Sultan of Istanbul, aged 7.

King Zog and Countess Geraldine Apponyi at their official engagement, with four of the King's sisters

Count Ciano acting as witness at the marriage of Zog and Geraldine.

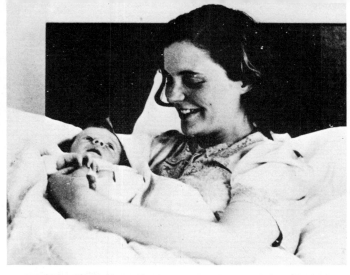

Queen Geraldine
and the day-old
Prince Leka.

Geraldine with the
young Prince Leka.

One of the few remaining official portraits of King Zog (*above*) and two of his favourite photographs of Geraldine (*below*). In Hungarian costume (*left*) and in more conventional attire (*right*).

Prince Leka in 1959.

Queen Geraldine at Leka's wedding, wearing the new crown jewels given her by her son.

King Leka and Queen Geraldine on a goodwill visit to the large Albanian colony in the United States.

now lying in a state of total collapse, both mental and physical.

Just before the convoy left Albania the Queen rallied her strength and ordered the car to stop. Tipping some jewels from one of the sachets she asked that it be filled with soil. It was this soil that was buried in France with King Zog seventeen years later. In all her traipsing around Europe and Egypt the Queen carried that little packet of soil and protected it like gold.

On arriving at the Greek frontier, on one side a group of Albanian soldiers stood to attention as the convoy passed through the barrier. On the other side a Greek sentry, with a fixed bayonet in his rifle, was so overcome by the situation that he lost his hat while running to a telephone. Half an hour later a jeep filled with Greek officers, and an escort of motor cyclists arrived to take the royal party to Florina. This was only a small frontier town and, arriving in the middle of the night there was nowhere to put the Queen. Finally a ramshackle hotel made them welcome and she was carried up the worn wooden stairs to an empty dusty room. Quickly her maid scrubbed the floor before allowing the Queen to be laid on it.

Queen Geraldine was now grey with exhaustion, a wraith in her nightgown and still clutching her baby, whom she would not allow to be taken from her side. Only Professor Weibel and the nurse were allowed access to her room and even then she asked to be left alone in peace.

When I awoke I found near my bed two Greek doctors that King George had sent by special train. They were absolutely horrified at the state in which they found me, not even my linen had been changed. They telephoned to King George telling him that it was necessary to place me in a clinic in Athens. He gave orders that I be taken there immediately with my grandmother, the baby and an officer.

The princesses were distraught when they heard that they were going to be separated from Queen Geraldine. Though they often paraded on horseback with their regiments, of which the King had made them honorary colonels, in reality they had been sheltered all their lives and were incapable of looking after themselves.

When the Queen heard of the plans to break up the party and send her to Athens she refused to be separated from the rest of her suite. The Greek doctors continued to insist until she had a seizure and became so upset that she not only shook all over but large red stains began to appear on her body. At first the doctors were worried that it was puerperal fever brought on by the stress. It was not. This was a violent reaction to the appalling strain of the last few days and her fear that she would never see the King again. It was as if a voice within her warned that the King was in deep danger. Later she was able to prove that her premonition was correct as during those exact hours the King was in grave peril.

Whilst Queen Geraldine fled the country, King Zog was faced with the most important decisions of his life. General John Metaxas, the Greek Prime Minister had informed the King that he could pass the Greek frontier, with his government, but not later than midnight on 9th April and on the condition that he take no military or political action while on Greek territory.

The impossibility of conducting guerilla warfare in the mountains made the King take the definitive decision to leave Albania as soon as possible. Before leaving the palace he had gone to the immense safe in his office and totally alone packed army boxes filled with gold Napoleons, which according to British Foreign Office reports at the time were worth about £50,000. This was the last of his personal fortune made through the sale of family lands over several years. As she was not present, and the King never discussed money matters with her, the Queen has no idea of how many boxes there were. The gold and the Queen's jewellery, were sufficient to keep the King and Queen, the Princesses and a retinue of thirty-six people over the next twenty-six years.

This is not to be confused with the gold bullion, rumoured to be worth £20 million by today's value, locked up in the Bank of England's vaults until such time as Albania pays the £843,947 compensation awarded by the United Nations for the sinking of two British destroyers H.M.S. Saumarez and H.M.S. Voltage in 1946, in what has become known as The Corfu Channel Incident. Albania said at the time that it would not pay and, in any case did not have the money, so the British impounded Albanian gold that had been looted during the war by the Germans and subsequently recovered by the Allies. This gold has remained in the Bank of England, legally say the British; illegally say the Albanians. So bitter still is the quarrel, that the Bank of England will not comment officially on its present day value or whereabouts. This seems to be the main reason why Albania and Britain do not have diplomatic relations and never will until 'the fate of the Albanian gold' is determined.

With a retinue of members of the Government, more than 500 officers of the high command, Mayors and Councillors, constituting a crowd of two thousand, the King crossed over into Greece.

He was never to set foot on Albanian soil again.

CHAPTER 12

When he arrived at Florina the King immediately went to the room in the hotel where the Queen lay, still on the mattress. He knelt down at her side, kissed her and left after two minutes. Looking back later the Queen had the impression that the gaunt and tragic figure before her was near breaking. He was a King who had lost his kingdom but had not yet found a new role. The strain of the last few months was etched into his pale face. There had been days and nights without sleep, but the real and tragic desolation was caused through the treachery and deception that had plagued him during the last months and perhaps even the final realisation of how thoroughly the Fascists had been able to infiltrate the ports of Valona and Durazzo. The Albania of the free man no longer existed.

The King and his following had only been on Greek soil for twenty four hours when Prime Minister Metaxas arrived to ask him to leave Greek territory immediately and proceed to Turkey, explaining that Mussolini had threatened the Greeks if they continued to give him refuge. Even the Greek doctors attending the Queen were stunned. They protested in the name of the Greek King, saying that in the eyes of the world if the Queen should die it would not have been the Fascist invasion that caused it but the attitude of the Greek authorities. Metaxas then put forward another plan: the King should be allowed to accompany Queen Geraldine and his son to Athens with a small personal staff. This King Zog would not accept; he would not be separated from his government and advisers. A compromise was reached whereby the King and his men were allowed to install themselves at Larissa until the doctors decided that the Queen was fit to travel. With these fresh hazards her condition had deteriorated and she was confined to her bed and not allowed to see anyone except the King and her doctors.

In this way I tried to stay calm and recover my strength and I insisted on having my baby in his cradle near me night and day.

I ached to see my husband but knew that he would come to me when he could. Apart from the political situation he now had to deal as much as possible with the future of the Albanians who had gone into exile in Greece with him. The Army had managed to save a small strong box of money which was divided up into enough to give six months pay to all the officers, ministers and officials. Several of them chose to go to Rome where they had money; others to family or friends in Italy who would provide for them; some chose France and the rest elected to go to Turkey. There were a few also who preferred to return to Albania and their families, no matter what fate awaited them.

The King was also occupied and concerned as to which of the Albanian Embassies throughout the world would remain open. The French government closed the one in France. England followed suit, but in the United States, Turkey and Egypt they remained open due to the goodwill of their respective governments and the firmness of the Albanian representatives.

The Greek Government, aware of the Albanian custom of carrying arms, allowed the men to carry their personal weapons with them. Despite this there were several unpleasant incidents such as the time when two army officers went by car to the Albanian Consulate in a Greek port to obtain the necessary papers for them to travel to France. When they entered the Consulate and saw the Italian flag and a large photograph of Mussolini they reacted violently. They threatened the Consul and forced him to take down the flag and then proceeded to stamp on the face of the photo of Mussolini which they had ripped down from the wall. Not content with this, they began to beat up the Consul who immediately called for help from another office. The behaviour of the Albanians was an embarrassment to King Zog and broke the promise he had given to respect Greek hospitality. Fortunately incidents like this were isolated since most of the Greek population were pro-Albania because they too lived in fear of the Fascists in case they should be the next to be invaded.

It was time for the royal caravan to move on. The King decided that his own family party should be split up, with three of his sisters, nieces and nephews, Mrs de Strale d'Ekna and Count Gyula Apponyi going to France accompanied by Albanian officers, and the remaining members of the family to stay with him and the Queen and proceed to Turkey.

The Queen was forced to remain in bed for three weeks during which time she found a Greek dressmaker to make her some clothes suitable for the trip. There were also shoes, stockings and underwear to be bought so that the Queen had a modest enough wardrobe to be seen in public.

The King and Queen and the rest of the party left Larissa by special train on 1st May. The Queen had made a rapid recovery due to the fact that the King was now near her and because of her youthful resilience. King Zog had telegraphed his gratitude to King George and the Greek Government who had allowed them to stay despite continual warnings from Mussolini. At the station there was a guard of honour, a deputation of all the Greek authorities and a large crowd of Albanians, as there was a large Albanian community in that region.

At all stations through which the train passed, and even those where it did not stop, crowds had gathered to catch a glimpse of the King and Queen, shouting "Geraldine, Geraldine" much as they shout "Diana, Diana" today. Some even called out messages of love and hope in Hungarian. The depression of the last weeks lifted as they arrived in Istanbul where there was also a guard of honour and large crowds of cheering Albanians.

It is said that the four most beautiful harbours in the world are Istanbul, Stockholm, San Francisco and Rio. Istanbul is unique for its green islands and fantasy palaces. My only memories of that city were from my readings of Pierre Loti, the French romantic writer, but now I was seeing it all with my own eyes.

There were no longer the gaily painted boats, rowed by men dressed in the family livery and beautiful veiled women, and the dream palaces had now become museums. I do not think I have ever seen such riches piled together in such relatively small museums as in Istanbul. Immense jewels in the turbans of the sultans, precious stones inlaid in the thrones of the sultans, engraved plates and coffee services.

It was touching when we went to the mosques to see old women, still veiled, recognise my husband and come to kiss his hand and ask when the sultan would come back.

My husband knew so many people, with whom he had studied in his youth and who now held important positions of state. As President Inonu was already at his country house we went there by boat. While we women lunched and took a walk, the King and the President locked themselves away for several hours of talk. It was a radiant day on the Bosphorus.

When we entered any of the large hotels, the Turks recognised us and even strangers came up to greet us. I said to the King that even though I could not speak the language and knew nobody, I felt at home. I asked him if we could stay there as I felt that it was as though we were in our own country with our own people. We were understood and made to feel welcome.

Clearly to remain in Istanbul was tempting for King Zog but his thoughts were already ranging far into the future and he felt that Turkey would stay out of the conflict. Therefore when a delegation of highly influential French deputies of Parliament came to Istanbul to invite the King and his entourage to France, he agreed. There he would be near to England in case events took an interesting turn in Albania.

Queen Geraldine was so contented in the beautiful old city that she felt strong enough to accompany the King on all his official visits. The Italian Press reported at the time that she had refused to breast-feed her baby, but this was untrue. The Albanian wet nurse had never regained her milk, since she was now desperately homesick away from her own baby, so the Queen continued to feed Prince Leka herself and always made sure that she was back at the hotel exactly at feeding time.

Just to move the royal party presented difficulties as no shipping company wanted to take the responsibility for carrying them. Instead they were forced to make a long detour across Romania, Poland and the Baltic countries, and from there to France. The party which had been reduced to just the King, the Queen, Prince Leka and nurse, three of the Princesses and twelve Albanian officers finally embarked on the *Bazarabia*, a Romanian boat that was sailing towards Constanza, a Romanian port on the Black Sea. From there they went on by special train to Bucharest where they arrived on 2nd July.

Again it was the same rapturous scene as people crowded the railway stations shouting for the Queen. On arrival at the Athenée Palace Hotel in Bucharest, they were surprised to see Italian guards posted opposite the royal suite, who looked across the corridor with hostility every time the Albanian party went in or out. They were on duty to guard an Envoy Extraordinary who had arrived that same day from Rome seeking an interview with King Carol of Romania on behalf of Mussolini. Presumably this was in the days before hotels had customer relations departments, as the armed Albanian guards spent the day glaring at the Italians who had guns at the ready! After two days and with the departure of the Italian Minister the situation eased.

On the day of their arrival the King and Queen took luncheon with King Carol who received them at the palace steps.

The King, a tall handsome man, embraced my husband and addressed me with a charming smile but that was all. King Zog admonished him saying, "Kiss your cousin". I found him very agreeable, knowing how to charm women although he considered me something of a child. The absence of a woman's hand in the palace was noticeable and I found it rather sad.

After lunch King Carol and my husband were closeted for four hours while the husband of Madame Lupesca, the King's mistress, and some court officials kept me company. From time to time Mr Lupesca got up and went into the offices of the King, each time returning quickly. This restlessness intrigued me but I asked no questions. It was not until we had returned to the hotel that my husband explained the enigma to me. In the neighbouring room was the special envoy from Mussolini, charged to request King Carol not to give us asylum, which in any case we were not going to seek. King Carol had made him wait for four hours and Mr Lupesca's cox and box game was merely to keep a check on him.

In their discussions together, King Zog advised King Carol to come to an arrangement with Stalin, despite the differences of régime, if he wanted to resist Hitler. British support was uncertain and in any case too far away to be efficient.

King Carol replied to him that he was right in political logic but that he could not overcome the deep anti-communist feelings of the Romanian people or his own innate distrust of Russia – Imperial or Communist.

King Carol explained to my husband: "Romanians have fought Communism since its birth at the time of the Russian Revolution, and at the breaking up of the Imperial Army in 1917. They fought it at Bessarabia in 1918, in Hungary in 1919 and chased it out of their own country. They know only too well what Communism means and the propaganda has no hold on them, and then, what confidence can one have in Stalin?"

They had expected to spend only two or three days in Bucharest but were so enchanted with their welcome that Queen Geraldine persuaded the King to stay three more days. This enabled them to visit Sinaia, the royal summer residence in the Carpathians where, for the first time since she left Tirana, the Queen regained her appetite.

Once again the time came for them to move on. It was while *en route* to Warsaw that the King received a telegram to say that the authorities there had been informed that the Italians were preparing to assassinate the King. Such was the naiveté of those pre-war days that a message so important and secret could still be sent by public communication.

On arrival at Warsaw there was the largest crowd that Queen Geraldine ever remembers, all screaming with emotion. In this jostling crowd security precautions were useless so, at a word from the King the royal party closed ranks and shuffled towards the cars without any incident. On reaching the car, Queen Geraldine noticed that the baby was not there. She told the King and then, running as fast as she could, she went back to the train which had already been shunted onto a side line. Desperately she searched from one place to another, asking for the carriage and finally found the wagon with the baby, his German nurse and her personal maid all sitting howling with terror as they did not know where they were. They were quickly taken back to rejoin the party. After this near-catastrophic incident an Albanian officer was detailed to stay with Prince Leka and be responsible for his safety.

The royal party proceeded through the Baltic countries of Lithuania, Latvia and Estonia as the King wished to see these little countries which, like Albania, had only recently gained independence. Everywhere the royal party was greeted with cheering, sympathetic crowds protesting against what the world saw as a monumental injustice of aggression.

A deposed monarch made headline news wherever he travelled in those insouciant days, but the debonair King Zog with his entourage of a beautiful, golden-haired Queen and the raven-haired, sultry-eyed Princesses was irresistible. They had all the mystique and glamour of an Eastern potentate and his harem. The photographers clicked their shutters, purring with delight. In this style the royal party reached the Baltic.

I remember one day that a large German ship arrived carrying strong sun-tanned young men and women who belonged to the Hitler youth. The Latvians shunned them and accompanied us *en masse* to the port when we embarked, carrying gifts of fruit, embroidered blouses, sweetmeats and small posies of flowers.

101

The organised aspect of the Scandinavian countries had always attracted my husband and as we were so near we decided to continue our trip and take in Sweden. With a few other passengers we left on a small boat for Stockholm, waved off by a seething crowd who packed the wharf to see us off. Though we did not know a single face, the warmth of these people touches me even today. There was so much genuine kindness in the world before the horrors of war demolished personal morals and values.

Towards evening the sea became dangerously rough. Baby Leka's cradle was on top of a bunk and had to be held there as the force of the ship rolling could have overturned it at any moment. The Queen was lying on the other bunk desperately seasick. Ten people volunteered to help the nurse hold the cradle, even the elderly court chamberlain, but one by one they were all overcome with seasickness. It was then that the Queen's maternal instinct took over and she rose from her bunk and held the cradle for the rest of the night completely cured of her sickness.

About midnight the captain of the ship warned the King that the gale was becoming so strong that if it lasted another hour he would have to drop anchor at some nearby German islands. For King Zog the news was catastrophic, as having made this lengthy detour he now risked finally falling into Hitler's hands, but without hesitation the King agreed, as he felt that he had no right to endanger the lives of the other passengers. He told the captain to do what he could for the best. Having no sooner said this, the storm disappeared as if a miracle had occurred.

The Queen was up on deck at six o'clock in the morning to see the entry into the harbour of Stockholm which was scattered with little islands covered with carpets of wild flowers. The King was so entranced with Stockholm and the surrounding countryside that he immediately wanted to spend some of the gold Napoleons on buying a small chateau on one of the islands. It was tactfully pointed out to him that the Swedish climate in the winter was distinctly different from the gentleness of the Adriatic.

Once more the Albanian royal family was warmly welcomed. The Swedish Press raved about the rosebud baby with his mass of silky blond hair, claiming that one saw immediately that he was of Swedish descent. The connection was purely hypothetical as his only claim to Swedish ancestry was through Queen Geraldine's step-grandfather, Gustav de Strale d'Ekna, a Swedish nobleman.

The royal party eventually left Sweden, once the baby Prince had recovered from a bout of pneumonia. They arrived in Antwerp at the beginning of August, just three months after leaving Tirana. Three months of constant travelling; three months of the continual stress of organising thirty-six pampered and confused people through the everyday practicalities of living. In this respect, King Zog proved that he was not only capable of running a country but also of soothing the egos of all the different personalities within his own family party, including his wife and sisters.

At Antwerp the cars had arrived overland from Greece and they could continue their journey through Belgium to France where, awaiting them at the Chateau de la May in Versailles, which the King had rented, were the Queen's grandmother, and brother Gyula, and the rest of the entourage who had gone on ahead. The arrival of the Queen's sister Virginia and her husband, who had driven by car from Hungary, reassured her. After the strain of the last months, time rolled back and they were just like the giggly sisters of their childhood, "Gerrie" and "Ginny", talking far into the night.

Virginia told Geraldine how Count Ciano had gone to Budapest on an official visit a few days after the invasion of Albania. There had been a large dinner given in his honour at which several of the Queen's cousins had been present. In his usual conceited way, Ciano was preening himself in front of the ladies when one of the girls burst out: "Have you no shame to pose as a friend of Hungary when only a few days ago you were able to see the bloody linen from the *accouchement* of our cousin Geraldine, whom you forced to flee just twenty-four hours after the birth of her baby?" There was a shocked silence as Hungary was in no position to upset the relationship with Italy at that moment. Fortunately the incident passed over and Ciano merely sulked for the rest of the evening.

The month of September arrived and the granaries of Europe were bursting with a golden harvest, a propitious time throughout history for the start of a war. As in the rest of France no one in the chateau went out but sat listening to the radio. On 1st September, German troops crossed the Polish frontier and everyone realised that it was only a matter of hours before war would be declared. The next day Virginia and her husband,

103

fearing to be cut off from their family, left for Hungary amid tears of anguish.

Whatever thoughts she had of her own family back at Nagy Appony, Queen Geraldine kept them to herself. For the first time, after the excitement of the last weeks, she could be alone with her memories. On 3rd September came those fatal words of Chamberlain from the BBC in London, "This country is at war with Germany." Within hours France had also declared war. The Queen shared the anguish of the millions of women in Europe whose families were now involved in the war.

King Zog had already left for London to rescue £10,000 which had been deposited in the Bank of Italy there some years ago. With accompanying Albanian officers, he arrived at the bank in the City to be greeted by officials with a string of excuses and difficulties. The King was adamant and replied that he would not refrain from using force if necessary to regain his money. Noticing the bulge of pistols and the determined look in their eyes, the bank officials relented and handed over the money.

Once the King returned from London, he moved the household to Brittany, fearing that there would be air-raids on Paris. They stayed in a comfortable hotel and enjoyed for a short while the peace of the surrounding countryside.

> That was the only time in our lives that by common decision, we disregarded the presence of the Princesses and put our problems behind us. We made excursions alone from the early morning until late evening, on foot or by car. We found a small restaurant perched high on the cliffs which only had four tables and belonged to a French fisherman who had spent much of his life in Morocco. He used to cook sole for us which he had caught in the morning and prepared special Oriental dishes for my husband. The restaurant was called Kismet which means 'Lucky Destiny' and we felt that this was true. For me . . . this was my honeymoon.

Returning one night to the hotel the King was called to the apartment of one of his sisters. Princess Ruhije was suffering from severe pains in the stomach and as there were no doctors in the village she had to be taken to Tours. Once again the royal party was uprooted and thirty or so people had to be lodged and fed daily. Queen Geraldine had to arrange all this, no mean feat with so many women to placate, but no sooner had she begun to enjoy the beauty of Tours, when the doctors decided that the Princess required an operation and that this was to take place in Paris. A Swiss nurse, Mademoiselle Elizabeth Aegerter, chosen from seventy candidates, now joined the royal party and was to remain in faithful service with them for seventeen years. While Mlle Aegerter looked after Princess Ruhije, the Queen's hours were filled with moving everyone into the Hotel Trianon Palace in Versailles.

Each day the King left his 'Versailles court' and went to Paris where he met with members of the Government as well as dignitaries both military and civil, such as Marshal Maurice Gamelin, Commander-in-Chief of the French Army, Marshal Maxine Wegand, who was later to replace Gamelin, and General Bethouart who was a personal friend. He spoke to them of the outbreak of war, and of what might be the outcome, even warning of the possible occupation of France. They were all interested in Zog's views but were reserved in their own, as French policy was heavily influenced by the pressure that Monsieur Francois Poncet, French Ambassador in Rome, might exercise. He unceasingly warned them about becoming too involved with King Zog, so as not to irritate Mussolini, and so the King was never offered any responsible post.

> The King often came back from these trips to Paris depressed and told me that the French Army was not sufficiently modernised and that nothing was being done to remedy this state of affairs. He thought the morale of the inactive troops was low and that of the officers, even the highest, not much better. People comforted themselves with the illusion that the Germans, conscious of the impossibility of piercing the Maginot Line, would conclude a peace of compromise. There was nothing to do but wait.
>
> "I am afraid that it will crumble at once. I have even advised them to prepare for a retreat to Algeria in the event of defeat, which would signify the loss of a battle, and perhaps the occupation of Continental France, but not necessarily the loss of the war for France," Zog explained.

The royal party was still staying at the Trianon Palace when at eleven o'clock one night, Queen Geraldine was called to the telephone to take a call from Budapest. It was her sister Virginia who said that she had been approached by the Italian Legation with the news that their government was ready to give the

Queen's family in Hungary all that had belonged to her in Albania, including the immense pile of boxes containing the wedding presents, many of which had never been opened. Without consulting the King, the Queen replied that there was no question of her receiving any favours from Italy. The matter would have to be dealt with at the end of hostilities. Any historical gifts coming from her Hungarian family could surely be claimed in their name, but not in hers. Her suggestion was declined and to this day, despite many requests through international lawyers, the Italian authorities have not relented, nor has she ever obtained the least compensation.

One evening, on entering the room of her fifteen-year-old brother Gyula, Queen Geraldine found him feverish. Taking his temperature she found that it had risen to 104 degrees. An emergency doctor was summoned who diagnosed a dangerous crisis of diabetes. Count Gyula Apponyi asked to be allowed to rejoin his mother who was then living in Aix-en-Provence, so she was summoned to take him back with her. This is why Gyula remained in France during the whole war and explains the tragedy that followed.

Another Christmas had come round and realising how sad the Queen was at living in a hotel all the time, the King now rented a little chateau at Mesnil-sur-Oise and moved the whole retinue yet again. Unfortunately, it was difficult to heat and one after another the whole party caught severe colds until the King in desperation found another property to rent, the Chateau de Segur in the village of Pontoise. Here extra bathrooms and lavatories were added for the thirty-odd people who were by now staying at Mesnil. Finding these large properties was not a luxury for the King but a necessity as their party fluctuated between anything from thirty to forty people, all of whom had no money and had to be taken care of as they were helpless on their own, having little knowledge of the French language.

It was not until April 1940 that they could move into the Chateau de Segur and begin arranging themselves, never an easy task as the Princesses had their own preference as to which rooms they wanted. The Queen now had to try and keep the peace among the entourage of thirty people in their 'court' who were all unhappy at being displaced so many times. As King Zog did not feel it right to do any entertaining in wartime conditions, the Queen's main job was the day-to-day running of her household.

Queen Geraldine is particularly sensitive to atmosphere in a house and felt ill at ease in the chateau. They had only just unpacked when the German invasion of the north of France, Belgium and Holland began.

CHAPTER 13

Now the war, for so long a dark threat on the horizon, was rapidly drawing closer to them. Queen Geraldine was deeply distressed by the sight of the refugees who filled the roads, fleeing from the sudden attacks of the German Panzer troops.

> We watched the pathetic flood of refugees with their bundles on bicycles and barrows walking past the large iron gates to the park. There was very little we could do but we gave them everything that could be useful to them, often tending their wounds and preparing them for the terrible trek ahead. But one could do so little. My heart ached for them.

She could not have known how soon she too must be on the move with them. Meanwhile all the duties of caring for her unhappy household fell on the Queen once more. Just the feeding of them three times a day in a strange country was a nightmare for food was scarce. As few of the household staff spoke French, it was left to the Queen to go with the guards to the markets and buy in supplies to cover the next twenty-four hours. As there were guards and officers to be fed with healthy mountain appetites, apart from the immediate royal family, it was an immense task. Even the Princesses, who preferred a diet of black coffee and cigarettes, were persuaded to take a hand preparing the mountains of vegetables that were consumed each day. As cabbage was one of the more easily obtainable vegetables, every form of Hungarian cabbage dish was served that the Queen could remember from her childhood. When they had first left Paris both the nurse and Queen Geraldine had allowed one of the cases allotted to them to be filled with baby food in preference to their own clothes. They bought up every kind of canned baby food available, and Leka lapped it up like a puppy.

As well as the food shortage they were worried about safety.

> One night the village was bombed and one of the small houses in the park used by the guards was hit. Next morning the

mayor called on the King and begged him to leave the area immediately as his presence was certainly the cause of the bombing which could not be explained otherwise, as all the important centres around there had not been bombed.

The great packing began all over again and the royal circus left for Paris where they spent the night in the apartment in Rue Loti where Princess Ruhije had moved after her stay in hospital. Squashed into the apartment it was impossible for anyone to sleep, so the next day they moved into the Plaza Athenée. The nurse laid the baby Leka on the large bed of the suite which had been reserved for the King, while the Queen inspected and allocated the rest of the rooms and began unpacking their own personal things.

When the Queen returned and wished to remove the baby he screamed and clung to the bed. In his baby language he made it quite clear that he was tired of always being packed up and moved and that he intended to stay right where he was. This he did while the King slept in the baby's room that night.

Even a baby is sensitive to the atmosphere which surrounds him and the eternal moving was infuriating this highly-strung child. I was unhappy too, which did not help, as I hardly ever saw the King who was always occupied with meetings. I simply did not understand why we obstinately remained in Paris.

When at last he had time to take in the situation of an unhappy wife and an unhappy baby the King rented a hotel-pension at Royan near Bordeaux. He hoped that at last he could install the entourage there, where we might be safe until hostilities ceased as by now everyone was suffering 'moving nerves' and tempers were frayed.

We could hear the gunfire from the direction of Pontoise and yet we still remained in Paris. I was sick of it. The King was patient with me and said, "Yes, yes, I understand but we must wait and see what the Government and Diplomatic Corps will do." One evening we were told that the Diplomatic Corps were leaving for Tours that night and that some of the Government ministers were already in Bordeaux.

Early next morning the King said we could begin packing. By now the party had swollen to thirty six people who all had to be squashed into six cars with a lorry for baggage. It was even difficult to find drivers, as among the men only the King's nephews could drive.

I felt so desperately sad when we left Paris as Albanians gathered to ask if they could come with us but this was impossible as already we were far too many people to handle with ease. In the end three of the officers ceded their places to people who were desperate. They subsequently joined the Free French Forces and made happy marriages to French women.

It was eight o'clock in the evening before everyone was ready to leave and it had been an exhausting and sad day. The King and Queen were in the first car driven by one of the King's nephews who could hardly see as he was just convalescing from a severe motor accident which had fractured his skull. In a car behind, bolstered with pillows was Princess Ruhije who was still very ill, and her nurse. No headlights could be switched on and it was a nightmare as the six cars and the lorry edged their way through the pathetic procession of refugees. Such is the madness of war that some women carrying luxurious fur coats, walked in bare feet.

It took the King's cars all night to drive twenty kilometres from Paris, literally crawling along in the dark. At dawn they heard that the Germans had entered Paris and as the cars pulled up to rendezvous in the pale morning light, Queen Geraldine noticed that the one in which the baby, his nurse and bodyguard were travelling had disappeared. For the second time in a few months the heir to the throne of Albania had been lost. As Oscar Wilde's Lady Bracknell might have said "to lose a baby prince once may be regarded as a misfortune, but to lose him twice looks like carelessness."

This was an appalling situation as the car was also trailing a baggage trolley in which were stacked the cases of family jewels and the boxes of gold napoleons. The driver was a faithful Hungarian who, not knowing the French roads, had got lost in the dark and sensibly driven to the nearest police station and stayed there until he was eventually found. Now the party could move forward once more.

We approached Orleans in the afternoon and found ourselves mixed up on the road along with the retreating soldiers, many of whom were wounded and were being dragged along. What heartbreaking scenes. There were few people in France who did not see these miserable queues along the poplar lined roads and your heart was torn when you were in the same position, only better equipped. One felt directly guilty.

Our main problem had been finding petrol to keep the motor cars going, despite the fact that the King had a document from the French Government giving him priority. Sometimes we broke for two hours because we could not find anything with which to fill the tanks.

Just as the royal cavalcade was on the outskirts of Orleans, they heard the sound of planes. There was panic as people in the cars around made for the shelter of the fields and ditches. When they heard the planes, King Zog gave the strict order to his party that they were not to disperse, but stay together. Suddenly the Queen could take no more. Ignoring the King's command, she tore the baby from his nurse and rushed into a nearby railway station which was already packed with mothers with babies in their arms. The children were crying and the white-faced mothers distraught, as they sat there, desperate to know what was happening outside.

They could hear the planes strafing the road. After an hour, when it seemed quiet, the Queen returned to the scene of devastation. Cars had been overturned and people lay wounded on the roadside, but not one person and not one of the royal cars had been hit or hurt and King Zog sat there unperturbed in charge of his party. It was fortunate that the planes were on a return mission and their bomb racks were empty.

The Queen maintained that it was thanks to the will of God that the royal party was not strafed, but the Lord's ways are indeed mysterious and no doubt he finds his own solutions. The fact is that King Zog and Queen Geraldine were travelling in the scarlet Mercedes which had been Hitler's wedding gift to them, an exact replica of his own personal car. The Luftwaffe pilot who would take pot shots at what looked like the Fuhrer's own car was certainly not born then. They had taken no chances, and had bypassed the huge red limousine, concentrating their attack on the many less risky targets.

When they at last entered Orleans, the historic and graceful town was seething with people all seemingly with desperate problems. There was shoving and pushing, screaming and crying. The King wanted to stay the night as he was thinking of Princess Ruhije who by now was desperately in need of a proper rest in a bed. The Queen, who even today panics in a crowd, was determined to continue and escape from the chaos and when they could not find even a single room they pulled out of the city and

111

crossed the bridge.

Not far outside in the forest they saw a shooting lodge and the King negotiated with the owner to allow his party to shelter there overnight. Again it was as if the mantle of providence enveloped the King and his family because towards dawn Orleans was bombed, the bridge was destroyed and more than thirty thousand were left dead or wounded.

> Early in the morning some of the guards went to find something to eat as they did not wish to impose themselves on their host. Food was like gold and we learned to do without. During that time I realised that if one does not eat the stomach can shrink in such a way that one can stay without feeling hungry for a long time. It took my stomach two years to get back to normal when we finally arrived in England.

A baby girl born that night on the estate was named after the Queen. This was to happen on several occasions during their flight south and for some time Queen Geraldine kept in touch with her namesakes. They even wrote to her when grown up but the contacts were lost in later years.

The next few days were spent travelling, sleeping out of doors at night, clinging together and praying. Finally they arrived at Royan and the journey that should have been one day had by now taken a week. Completely exhausted by dirt, lack of food and sleep, they arrived at the small hotel which the King had booked several weeks before, only to find that the military commander of the town had requisitioned the building.

Even the King's persuasive efforts to negotiate failed, as it transpired that the military governor was pro-Italian and therefore anti-Albanian. The governor also had the arrogant idea of asking the men in the party to disarm knowing that to an Albanian this is tantamount to an insult. King Zog refused point blank to this request. By now as the royal party had been recognised, a crowd had amassed outside. From the drivers they heard what was happening and were sympathetic, heckling the authorities. The mayor arrived on the scene and with touching generosity offered King Zog his summer residence some kilometres away for the use of his staff. He also forced the military commander to give a room in the hotel immediately to Queen Geraldine where she, the nurse and baby and Princess Ruhije rested.

112

I shall always remember those two nights in that little hotel as alone and trembling we stayed pressed against each other while the building seemed to be crumbling under the bombardment that Royan was suffering.

Meanwhile, the King sent a cable to President Paul Renaud notifying him of their situation, but before he could get a reply, there was a change of government. Forty-eight hours later he received a reply from the new President, Edouard Daladier advising the King and his party that they should take refuge in a convent which was empty and only a few kilometres away.

The King returned and collecting the Queen and baby, Princess and nurse, moved them to the convent where there was enough room for everyone to have a little white cell to his or her self. These were anguished, waiting days. They listened to the radio with heavy hearts and searched the neighbourhood for food. It was then that the Hungarians in the entourage decided to leave and return to their own country, and the good Baroness Ruling went back to Austria to take care of her old mother. For the Queen, the parting with her own countrymen was yet another sadness but she realised that it was absolutely necessary. She did not want the King to have the responsibility of taking care of Hungarian employees who belonged to her own personal staff.

Each day King Zog set out by car to Bordeaux to try to arrange their future. He returned every evening, often spending hours crouched in the ditches on the way. He was always immaculate and none ever doubted his kingly presence and authority, but in Bordeaux there was general panic and government officials were also reluctant to have a King and Queen on their hands. They tried to persuade the King to continue into Spain as the French situation was worsening and there would be no government in exile in Algeria. Although at that moment he would have preferred to go to Spain, King Zog did not want to add to the worries of General Franco by suddenly having an exiled King on his hands. In desperation, he telegraphed King George VI of England and within hours received a courteous reply welcoming him to Britain and advising him that on a certain date at a certain time, the last boat would leave Bordeaux.

In an atmosphere of elation, the cars were loaded up again and the now smaller party travelled by night to avoid the bombers. Arriving in Bordeaux, they were greeted by a distraught British consul – and not one boat in the harbour.

In letters exchanged between the Foreign Office and the various consuls, which now lie in the Public Records Office at Kew Gardens, it is clear that though wishing to extend a welcome to King Zog, King George VI wanted to be assured that the Albanians would be able to support themselves.

This was clarified for Viscount Halifax by Sir Andrew Ryan, formerly British Minister in Durazzo, who reported that King Zog had taken gold out of the country to the value of £50,000, had an account of $2,000,000 with the Chase Manhattan Bank in America and had £50,000 deposited with Lloyds Bank in London. No mention was made of the £10,000 with the Bank of Italy in London.

Clearly King Zog would not be a liability to anyone and the message was duly passed to King George. The fact that King Zog's entourage numbered thirty people also came under scrutiny as nobody in the Foreign Office could quite understand why he needed to bring so many people to England. Apart from the King and Queen and Prince Leka there was a request for permission including the six Princesses, the Queen's grandmother Mrs de Strale d'Ekna, Colonel Sortir Martini, Professor Xhedadin Nushi, Quzin Kastrati (secretary), four Army officers, a German midwife and nurse, a children's nurse, a lady's maid, four valets and two chauffeurs. The Foreign Office summed it up as 'King Zog's Circus' and questioned whether the Albanian chauffeurs would be any use on the English roads anyhow. And what did even a King want with four valets? On hindsight, this was probably a ruse on the part of King Zog to get permits for two or more officers whom he conveniently labelled as 'valets'.

When they returned to Bordeaux next morning, a ship had miraculously appeared out in the harbour, and the harrassed British consul advised the King that he and his party could depart. Clutching the cable from King George in his hand, the consul escorted the Queen in a motor boat out to the ship. When he saw the cable, the distraught Captain began shouting with excitement; the ship was not only crammed with troops being evacuated from France, but its hospital was overflowing with the wounded. As it was to be the last civilian ship to leave, many Britons who had lived on the coast for some years, were now

114

clamouring to get on board and return to their country. Instead of carrying 800 including the crew, there were now 3000 on board.

In the end the captain gave up his own cabin and found one other spare one for our party, telling me that we would have to embark that night. Back on the quay there were terrible sights that remain with me to this day. I remember a man surrounded by a young woman and three children who wanted a visa for Spain. When the distraught Spanish consul shouted that there would be no more visas issued the man took a gun from his pocket and shot himself through the head.

Night came. The scenes on the quay were no less harrowing as those left behind watched the fortunate ones being rowed out to the waiting ship. Queen Geraldine was standing at the side of the quay with Prince Leka's nurse, holding in her hand her personal jewel case, handbag and a bag of baby food. On the wharf behind them were the cars and all the baggage which two of the Albanian officers had volunteered to try and get to Spain, and ultimately to England. Just as she was about to embark, some drunken sailors snatched the jewel case and bags from the Queen and told her in no uncertain way that she had no right to take anything with her.

The jewellery box was small and contained a few pieces that the Queen cherished for their sentimental value and wore every day: the diamond cross that she had worn on her wedding day; the pearls that the King had given her to celebrate Prince Leka's birth and a few unimportant rings and bracelets. The Queen never took her engagement ring off her hand, and it was to remain there until she sold it to pay for the building of King Zog's tomb twenty-one years later.

There was no time to think of my jewellery when I saw the nurse begin to cry. The sailors were calling for her to throw the baby to them in the motor boat as the sea was choppy and she could not embark easily in the dark with her arms full.

"My good woman don't be afraid. We also have babies and will not let him fall," a sailor called out.

Sizing up the situation and realising how desperate they were for time I took Leka and let him fall into their big, strong, gentle arms. Then I climbed into the launch with the nurse.

These jewels were saved as by a miracle. My Hungarian chauffeur picked them up, when the sailor had ordered me not to take them, and with the rest of our possessions they were packed in the little lorry we had used throughout France and which was parked on the quayside. Leaving Bordeaux he made the long journey back to Budapest and delivered them to my sister Virginia. Such is honour that Virginia, who had lost everything herself, managed to keep them and give them back to me intact many years later when we met again.

On deck, I awaited the arrival of my husband, who by a great favour had a motor boat to himself and two officers who were in charge of our cases of valuables. There were not only the boxes of gold Napoleons which the King had taken from the safe in his office, but also the court jewellery and the considerable amount belonging to the six princesses.

The King had wanted to see that the gold and jewellery were loaded on the ship before he left the motor boat, but the captain was jumping about very angrily as it promised to be a difficult operation to haul such heavy cases aboard in the dark and on a rough sea.

"Please, I am responsible now for the security of the King," he shouted. "Let him come up first. I give you my word the cases will follow."

The King agreed and began to climb up the ropes when to my horror I saw the motor boat leaving without waiting for the chests to be loaded on board. White with rage my husband turned towards the captain and ordered that he should be given the means to follow the motor boat and recoup the cases. The captain replied that he could not allow the King to leave English territory.

There was a shouting match with tempers exploding but in the end my husband left in the ship's motor boat in search of the precious cargo. He came back to the ship two hours later wet through, completely exhausted and without having found anything. He looked shattered but all he said to me was, "You cannot know what it is like to be without a penny and be responsible for thirty-six people, including ten women and a baby."

The King fell into his bunk and slept like a drugged man. Queen Geraldine could not sleep and went on deck to await the first light of dawn when the ship was due to sail. "I never stopped praying." As the first siren blasted, announcing the departure of the ship she saw in the pale morning light a speed boat making towards the ship with a man waving his hands wildly.

He was one of the Hungarian chauffeurs with the two sailors

116

and all the cases in the bottom of the boat. In the early morning light it was comparatively easy to hoist the chests aboard. The King, who was now up on deck, quickly gathered all the French money that the party had, which amounted to hundreds of thousands of old francs, and gave it to the bewildered sailors.

That fact is stranger than fiction has never been disputed. Unable to work in the dark and in the rough sea the previous night, the sailors had returned to the quayside, abandoned their boat and gone to a bistro to drink the hours away until daylight. Satiated with red wine they had staggered back to their boat and lay down to sleep it off. The chauffeur, who had been searching the quay all night, spotted the sailors at dawn and ordered them to take the motor boat out to the ship which was just beginning to move. Though anxious to leave as soon as possible the captain was by now in a more amenable mood and waited for the crates to be loaded on board. Queen Geraldine's prayers had been answered.

CHAPTER 14

On arrival at Liverpool King Zog's party was immediately taken off the ship while the rest had to stay on board under quarantine regulations. Next day the royal party left for London in a special train and were then installed at the Ritz where they were offered special rates as long as they stayed there and did not move to another hotel.

> London seemed at this time to be a paradise of tranquility and I thought of nothing but thanking God for having allowed us to arrive in a safe haven. Many people still did not realise much of what had happened in a world torn apart by war. I remember being invited to tea by a rich old lady who said to me: "My dear Majesty, you do not know what we have lost. My beautiful villa on the Côte d'Azur . . ."
>
> First of all I slept. Deep, safe, precious sleep after those weeks of turmoil. For the first time we were also eating proper food again and the baby quickly settled down to a normal routine. As we had nothing but what we stood up in I went out and bought a few necessities for ourselves, Leka and the nurse. We knew that all our baggage was *en route* to Portugal and it was only a matter of time before we would get it here in London. I had learned not to place too much value on material things but for the second time I was without a completely new trousseau which the King had bought for me in Paris – everything from lingerie to suits from Maggy Rouff and dresses from Chanel – which this time I had been allowed to choose for myself. With his love of oriental rugs there were also the ones that the King had bought in Turkey after we had left Albania. Would we ever see them again? Looking back to those days it is strange how one clung to everyday material possessions. In this repect I think, and hope, that I have changed my viewpoint. In the disasters of today's world even the value of human life has diminished.

King Zog and Queen Geraldine had no sooner settled into their new life in the Ritz when Sir Andrew Ryan, the last British

Minister to Albania, called and, rather embarrassed, asked if the King would like to continue his journey to America as England was now becoming a focal point of the war. He said that a large convoy was being arranged and that the royal party could leave at the end of the week. King Zog listened patiently and replied firmly that he had no intention of moving anywhere as long as he was the guest of King George VI. He reminded Sir Andrew that he considered that his place was to remain in Europe and that he counted on the British Government's political recognition of him as their ally. The King was adamant and insisted: "Now we must stay. We have left everywhere but this time we share the fate of the English, especially those in London." Clearly, the whole subject of their staying on English soil was a sensitive one and there were several meetings before the matter was finally sorted out.

Though several members of exiled European royalty were given refuge in England, the British Government would have preferred that they were removed to safer areas than London. King Zog and his retinue of thirty-odd, living right in the centre of London posed a delicate problem for the Foreign Office. Apart from its own royal family the British authorities were required to give a modicum of security to King Hakon of Norway, Queen Marie of Yugoslavia, King Peter and Queen Alexandra of Yugoslavia, Princess Aspasia of Greece and for a short time Queen Wilhelmina of Holland. Any members of the European royal families who could be persuaded to go to Canada, like Queen Juliana of the Netherlands, were encouraged to leave the active war zones.

The Ritz in Piccadilly was considered a safe enough building as it was built of reinforced concrete which meant that the shocks of any explosions only made the structure shudder without crumbling. It was one of the few hotels in London that did not have its own shelter.

War or no war, bombs or no bombs, every night the grill room in the basement was opened for dinner dancing. In the ladies cloakroom the management put three mattresses on the ground and gave the key to the Queen who arranged that the nurse and the baby would go there at the beginning of the bombing every night, while she would join them later. As they were near the large heating boilers, it was far from safe, but at least the noise of any bombing was muffled and the baby would be able to sleep.

It was on 3rd September, 1940, while they were returning to the Ritz from Mass, that the Queen and her grandmother, Mrs de Strale d'Ekna heard their first air-raid siren. That evening at dusk the blitz began.

> That first night we did not move from our apartments, but even with cotton wool in our ears it was impossible to sleep, as we were very close to Buckingham Palace which naturally was a focal point, and on the other side of Green Park was a large anti-aircraft gun site.
>
> After a week of nightly bombing, my baby woke up in the night with convulsions due to the noise. It was not an uncommon complaint and doctors in the newspapers warned mothers to take their babies as far as possible from London as their ear drums were too delicate and risked being damaged for life.
>
> Tired and distraught, I suggested to the King that we leave London and find somewhere in the country to live, but my husband was adamant that we remain in the capital where he could be in touch with officials.

As the King stayed up most of the night working on various reports he received, the Princesses preferred to be near him, sitting around smoking and drinking black coffee. They caught up on their sleep during the day. Twice, the Albanian family narrowly missed being hit by shrapnel when they were dining in the small sitting room adjoining the King's bedroom. As the Queen got up to close the door, the window was hit and the chair she had been sitting in splintered with shrapnel. Sitting opposite her the King was completely untouched and remained calmly eating his dinner.

On the day the Ritz received a direct hit the whole top storey crumbled and the bedroom of the King and Queen was full of broken glass, fallen plaster and even the bedclothes were splattered and torn with shrapnel. Again as if it was part of a destined plan neither King Zog nor Queen Geraldine was hurt.

For King Zog it was a period of reflection and frustration as much of what he had foreseen could happen in the Balkans was being enacted and he was powerless. It was the moment in history when Mussolini and Ciano were ready to reap the fruit of their invasion of Albania. It was inevitable, the King warned, that the occupation of Albania would lead the Italians towards an attempted invasion of Greece.

120

From his agents in Rome and other sources, King Zog learned in early October that Mussolini was angered at the occupation of Romania by Germany as he said that he had not expected to see the Arbitration of Vienna end in such a result.

During this period my husband had several meetings with Winston Churchill. Unfortunately, they had no common language and the meetings were conducted through an interpreter. I remember him coming back to the hotel laughing as I had not seen him for some time. He told me how he had been kept waiting while Churchill and de Gaulle were in conference. He could hear the shouts of de Gaulle, "La France . . . La France . . . la gloire de France." And then came the rumble of Churchill's voice trying to soothe him.

In his small sitting room, King Zog daily studied the reports that he received and he had talks with several other members of governments already in exile. He found General Sikorski of Poland, and President Edvard Benes of Czechoslovakia sympathetic. Even John Metaxas, the Greek Prime Minister, and other politicians were now making speeches about how it was necessary to assist in the liberation of Albania. According to Queen Geraldine, photographs of King Zog were being distributed among the Greek soldiers. The Greek government explained that it had no intention for the moment of taking the southern, orthodox part of Albania that it had always claimed. They were only giving help to a sister country.

In Albania the guerillas were most active in the mountains, harrassing the Italian forces which were grouped near the Greek frontier. On 29th October, 1940, came the news that Greece had been attacked, just as King Zog had foreseen and by the very same route that Queen Geraldine had taken when she went into exile. This attack failed due to the fact that the Army found itself facing the Greek *Evzones*, who fought bravely in the mountains, and the Albanian guerrillas harrassing them to the rear.

Shortly after this, King Zog and Queen Geraldine were having dinner in their private sitting room one evening when Colonel Sortir Martini, their Court Chamberlain, announced that two high officials from the Balkan Section of the Foreign Office were outside requesting an audience.

During his studies in Turkey the King had learnt classical Arabic, and Persian, and Turkish was needed for his studies at the

Galata Serail and for learning the Koran. He spoke fluent German from his years in Vienna, read and understood Italian perfectly and read and understood French which he later spoke. As for English he simply refused to speak it as he said that only ten per cent of the language followed the grammar. Towards the end of his stay in England he understood a great deal of what was being said around him, but this interview, as always, was conducted through an interpreter.

Although it was late at night, the King left the table and received them. They explained that they had come from the British Government and in the name of General John Metaxas, who by then was in Paris, on a mission to persuade King Zog to go to Athens and from there to the Greek-Albanian frontier where he was to lead Albanian volunteers against the Italians. Imposing only one condition – the guarantee by Great Britain and Greece of the integrity of the Albanian frontiers of 1913 – the King agreed. The officials left late in the night advising King Zog that Winston Churchill had asked to be informed of the King's decision and that a plane would be standing by for a dawn take-off.

> The King called out to me and told me that he would probably go and that I should pack him a small case with changes of linen and uniform. I was absolutely horrified. There we were in the middle of the bombing of London and now he was going off to take part in a mountain war during the winter in Greece.
>
> All my own self-pity vanished when I saw his face. He was a changed man and twenty years had slipped from his shoulders. Absolute confidence radiated from him. He seemed to me even younger than when I had first met him in Tirana. It was only then that I realised the extent of his suffering and frustration during the last year. Hope is the ray of light in a man's life.

The King immediately sent for all the Princesses, who were asleep in their suites, to come to his sitting room, and there he gave instructions to the women and the Albanian officers who were to remain with them. The King was direct, unsentimental and decisive. He spent the rest of the night studying maps with his officers. Sleep was meaningless. By six o'clock in the morning the King was ready and waiting, but had not heard from the Foreign Office. Another hour passed before he sent Colonel Salmani to Whitehall to discover what was happening. He returned at nine o'clock with a British official who apologised that, as the Foreign Office had not received any reply overnight from Greece, he had been unable to come sooner. This delay meant that the King was unable to leave with the rest of the party.

Some time later we heard that the special plane that he was to have taken, with high-ranking British officials on board, had exploded in mid-air and that all were killed. Had he been on board King Zog would have met a similar fate.

After this disappointment, though King Zog occupied himself with the political situation, sending note after note to the various British Government departments with offers of advice, he seemed to withdraw from his surroundings. A King without a crown, a man without a country and now a soldier without a mission in life. Frustration and inactivity are foul breeders of apathy and despair.

Twice in a few weeks fate took a hand in sparing the life of the Zogu family. On the first occasion the nurse had taken Prince Leka into the park for his usual daily outing. Without warning, in the peace of the morning, a bomb exploded in Green Park filling the air with earth and dust. Hearing the noise in the nearby Ritz, Queen Geraldine wanted to run into the park but, when she found that it was sealed off and nobody was allowed in, she spent the next hour trembling with fear and apprehension. The relief was immense as she suddenly saw the nurse returning with the baby in her arms. For once, instead of walking in Green Park the nurse had chosen Hyde Park and so missed the bomb.

On another occasion Queen Geraldine was going to visit a friend but, though normally meticulously punctual, she was half an hour late. When she did arrive she could not get into the street as a bomb had exploded in front of the house which had collapsed, killing one person and wounding three. It had taken place at the precise time that she would have arrived there.

For the Albanian National Holiday on 28th November all the Albanians in London converged on the Ritz to pay homage to their King and Queen. It seemed that just by being together and close to their monarch they gathered strength to carry on without news of their families left behind in Albania.

Just before Christmas the Queen persuaded King Zog to accompany her to Harrods where they could buy their Christmas presents. They were accompanied by two of their Albanian officers, but in the crowded store the King was clearly becoming irritated. In the lift, jostled from all sides, he had his hand in his pocket and turned to admonish one of the Albanians, "I told you to stay close to me." As the royal party got out of the lift the King went on: "My wallet has been stolen." It contained a thousand pounds. Although the Queen was worried at the loss, with his usual *sangfroid* the King insisted on going ahead with the shopping plans and asked for the parcels to be sent to the Ritz.

The King went down again in the lift and this time Queen Geraldine saw him seizing the hand of a little man in glasses who was busy taking something out of the pocket of another man. The moment the doors opened on the next floor both men jumped out, and ran into the crowds. The Queen turned to find the King calmly holding his own wallet and counting the money. It was nearly all there – only five pounds was missing. King Zog had seen the hand of the man with the glasses sliding into the pocket of the man next to him and taking out what he recognised as his own wallet. In this way the first pickpocket had been robbed by the second, but King Zog outwitted them both.

The news from Albania was unsettling and on 6th December King Zog heard that the Italians had lost Pogradec, the Albanian town which had been his last stop before crossing the mountains and entering Greek territory. At first the Albanians had received the advancing Greeks with their typical generosity and hospitality, but their joy was soon to evaporate when they realised that the Greeks were not entering as liberators, but as invaders.

> My husband tried to persuade the British that this was the moment to help him to return to Albania. With the defeat of the Italians by the Greeks there could have been a re-birth of Albanian nationalism under the King, which could have forced the Greeks to leave the Balkans. It seemed to me he had done everything to avoid an undeserved fate for Albania. Alone, with no support in the world, he had tried to defend the independence and honour of his country. He had given his work, his blood, his health for the creation of a modern state in a modern world, but the fight was too unequal.
>
> The King had foreseen the second world war and the defeat of the Axis but he had not realised that during the war, victorious America, as much as Britain, would cede the whole

of the Oriental part of Central Europe, as well as the Balkan Peninsula, except Greece and Turkey, to the Communists. This was not foreseen in 1939 and was even incomprehensible, as it meant replacing Hitler's empire with a Communist one, from Vladivostok to the Adriatic.

In desperation the King exchanged correspondence with President Roosevelt in Washington whom he felt to be a "man of ideals and inspiration". Though certainly not an isolationist, his sickness was already showing definite signs of debilitating him and he eventually sold away the human rights of half of the European World by giving in to Stalin at every request, even under protest from Winston Churchill, who was ready to spend British blood to keep Greece in the orbit of the Free World.

Already, on the very first days of the German attack on Russia my husband had said to Churchill: "Now is the moment to take the strongest guarantees for the Free World's status after the end of the war. Give no help to Soviet Russia before ensuring that they do not take over the territories and advantages that Hitler has won or you will give to the world a régime more terrible than any it has known up until now. Nazism and even Fascism cannot survive but Communism will be much more difficult to uproot. It is poison that crawls through the body like cancer."

Churchill's reply had been ultimate: "No, we are going to give all our unconditional aid to Russia and all our strength to the preparation for the invasion of the Continent. For me the only thing that counts is the total annihilation of Hitler and his Nazis."

At a reception at the Foreign Office, Queen Geraldine told Anthony Eden, "Please be careful of the Communists. They will take over the world." He answered her: "Oh, ma'am international communism does not exist any more." The Queen's Hungarian temperament flashed dangerously as she searched to give him the right answer, but the King touched her shoulder and engaged the Foreign Secretary in irrelevant conversation.

All this caused much suffering for King Zog and on returning home one day Queen Geraldine found him gravely ill in bed, having lost over three pints of blood in a haemorrhage provoked by the old duodenal ulcer from Vienna days. The King was ill for three months before he was able to take up an ordinary life when he immediately resumed his contacts with leading officials, including de Gaulle.

King Zog's admiration for de Gaulle was immeasurable. He felt that the French general's faith, inflexibility and indomitability in maintaining the ideology of the grandeur of France meant that, without a real Government in exile, de Gaulle had been able to do alone much more for his country than all the exiled Governments together.

> How often I listened to my husband's prophecies, most of which were to come true in the future. "Among the many accusations that will be thrown against me is why today I am not fighting in Albania. People cannot know the machinations of politics. We are not living any more in the days of 1914 where individual effort and bravery still counted. Today belongs to the Great Powers of the two sides which manipulate us."

One of the propositions put to King Zog during the next months by Anthony Eden, was to cede the Albanian region of Koritza, which was peopled by orthodox Albanians, to the Greeks, who considered it a Hellenic minority, in exchange for the important region of Kossova Metchija which was attached to Yugoslavia after the Balkan Wars and in which lived more than a million Albanians.

King Zog replied, "Let us take the situation of a father who has two sons. The elder has been taken away from him during his childhood, whereas the younger has been brought up by him. Can one make him the following proposition: 'You will be given back your elder son on condition that you give us the younger one.' That is the suggestion you are putting to me. But I know only too well that in the end I shall have my two sons."

> This is the *raison d'etre* of my son, King Leka, who will never forget that Kossova is an integral part wrenched away from Albania. In addition to his pledge to see a free Albania, he hopes for the reintegration of the provinces. One can understand that he inherited this ideal from the words of his own father, but it has also brought much danger into his life as it earned him the enmity of Tito.

During all this time, Queen Geraldine had wanted to occupy her mind by doing something useful and by taking the official Red Cross first-aid course, but the King did not allow her to; he wished his family to keep as low a profile as possible and not be

126

involved with publicity in the Press. With her lively mind, had she had something useful and fulfilling to do she would have been able to cope with the cramped restrictions of their family life at the Ritz. If they were distressed at all the Princesses did not show it simply because as long as they were close to their brother, the fountain of their lives, and had each other to chatter to, the outside world rarely touched them. They were in every sense women of the harem, but the strain was beginning to tell on the Queen. Always reed slim her face now had a transparent look about it and a white streak had appeared dramatically across the front of her hair. At luncheon one day a guest, who was a physician to Buckingham Palace, took the King aside and said: "This cannot go on: she will have a nervous breakdown. Your wife is a young woman in love with her husband and she needs to be alone with you, as is only natural. Always surrounded by people, she will wilt away. The danger signs are all there."

King Zog was appalled, as he found it perfectly acceptable to be surrounded by family when he was not working, as is the custom in Arab countries even today. It had simply never occurred to him that his young wife, with her liberal upbringing and American blood, would find this claustrophobic family atmosphere a strain. Though he knew that the Queen and the Princesses had little in common, with his Oriental background he had not realised that their proximity at all times would place a strain on his wife. A plan was decided that the household would split up into various units.

King Zog had previously rejected the advice of a life-long friend to make a settlement on Queen Geraldine and a separate one on his son as a precaution for whatever lay ahead in the future. Now he formulated a plan whereby the remaining fortune would be split among the close members of the family and each was free to go their own way. In his mind this seemed a just solution that would be acceptable to everyone, but there was a terrible family row when the Queen was not present, with the Princesses screaming at the King. They absolutely refused the offer and accused the Queen of wanting to break up a devoted family who had never been separated.

When she heard about the Princesses' accusations Queen Geraldine flew into an Hungarian temper herself and refused to accept a penny. She wanted the money to be invested for Leka and not to be redeemable until he reached manhood. This the

King refused to do and it became one of the rare areas of dissension that existed between them. Had King Zog listened to the Queen, King Leka today would have been financially secure and his mother would have been spared years of financial anguish.

King Zog arranged to rent a seven-roomed villa in Sunningdale near Ascot, from 1st June, 1941, but meantime during May the bombing seemed to get worse. One night the whole of the City of London was ablaze. Even King Zog was forced to go down to the grill room in the basement that night.

There for the first time I saw panic which was unbelievable among the British during wartime. They had such a protective attitude to each other and the cockney humour invariably saved the situation. A bomb had exploded nearby and among the wounded was a young woman who had lost a leg and another who appeared to be paralysed. There was ugliness everywhere and people's nerves were in shreds.

That night I retired to my 'ladies room' as usual with Leka and during a moment when the building above us shuddered he took his little golden head from the shelter of my arms and said in English: "Mummy not frightened." The head disappeared again at the next tremor.

At six o'clock in the morning when we went back to our rooms I was distraught. I said to my husband that we only had one child – a two-year-old baby – and that he had not asked to come into this world. I could not expose him to dangers that were not absolutely necessary.

The King had made it clear to me on several occasions that he did not want to have any more children. He felt it unfair to bring any more babies into this turbulent world and our refugee situation. Little Leka was all I had and had become desperately important in my life. Those first hours of his life, when we had shared a mattress together in the back of the motor car, leaving Albania, had forged a link that was not only strong then, but remains so today.

Seeing my desperation the King telephoned the owner of the villa who agreed to allow us to move in immediately. Just as I began packing, my husband said that we would stay a few more days in London. This I could not take. I was totally spent emotionally and physically. I finally left with the baby and his nurse and a few of our own Albanian retinue.

We were hardly out of the suburbs of London when suddenly the world changed and burst into bloom. The country lanes

128

were lined with trees bowing under the weight of blossom and the greeness that England is famed for was all around us. Even the birds were singing. It was like paradise. My heart lifted.

Moving in took some time and it was eight o'clock in the evening before the Queen thought of relaxing in the beautiful garden, which was filled with flowers. Leka was as enchanted as a child entering the Land of Oz and he ran around the garden jumping with excitement and immediately asking if he could have a dog.

It was all so blissfully peaceful. Then suddenly the sky was filled with waves of aircraft swooping over every half-hour. Though the house was sixty miles from London the garden became so theatrically bright that one could have read a newspaper by the glare of what was clearly the burning city. All the telephone lines were down and it was impossible to get through to the Ritz. This first night in the country, so filled with sweet promises and dreams, became a nightmare. Queen Geraldine was condemned to another night of fear, this time for the safety of her husband and not for herself.

The next day at nine o'clock in the morning King Zog arrived with the Princesses and the rest of the staff. They all looked terrible. The King, usually so meticulous, was unshaven and the poor Princesses were yellow with fear and in a dishevelled state. It was some nights later before the blitz ended and the immediate tension abated.

Life at Sunningdale settled into a busy and productive period. Queen Geraldine and Leka used to go for long walks in the nearby woods with the newly-arrived golden cocker spaniel, christened 'Woozy' by the Prince. The household was running smoothly, as apart from two maids, a cook and valet, one of the *Maitres d'Hôtel* from the Ritz had come with them. It was luxury as there were actually two villas making up the royal household.

The only pressing sadness were letters from Hungary which came through Switzerland telling that Virginia's husband, André de Baghy was seriously ill with an infection that no treatment seemed to be able to arrest. Virginia was in her eighth month of pregnancy but managed also to nurse her husband through a series of nine operations. There was no news of Queen Geraldine's mother, or of her brother Count Gyula Apponyi in the south of France, and no news of other relatives who had remained in Hungary. Keeping her own thoughts to herself weighed heavily on the young Queen, who realised only too well the problems that occupied her husband all the time.

After a short time at the Ritz Queen Geraldine had noticed that the nurse was scolding the baby in German, which was her native language as she came from Berne in Switzerland. She asked the nurse to talk to him in French, which she immediately did, even though the accent was rather guttural. The Queen continued to speak to Leka in English until she realised that he did not understand or know any Albanian. The Princesses spoke to him in French and the King spoke in German, as this was the only foreign language that he then spoke fluently. The moment Queen Geraldine began speaking Albanian to the baby, everyone followed. Whenever he could slip away from his nurse, he would find the Albanian officers and sit for hours listening to them. All through his childhood he continued to do this which explains why today he is so at ease with his Albanian people.

Towards autumn, Queen Geraldine saw in a newspaper that Lord Parmoor had died and that his family were going to let Parmoor House. She drove over immediately and arrived just before the RAF authorities who had come to requisition the property. Parmoor House was an immense country house perched on the Chiltern Hills between Henley-on-Thames and the old town of High Wycombe. It was a vast house set in parklands open to the woods, with a home farm adjoining it, and a large vegetable garden. Furnished in the English country house style it was comfortable and eminently suitable for thirty-four people.

> The day we moved in, I took Leka to look around the farm, and arrived just when some fat pigs were being led out of their sties. The farmer yelled out, "Run for shelter . . . one of them is dangerous," and truly, a pig as massive as a wild boar launched itself towards us. Leka, a beautiful child with long golden curls, apple-red cheeks and serious blue eyes rushed in front of me and said very firmly, "Don't move mummy. I will not let it touch you." He was furious when I picked him up in my arms to run away.

Those same Little Lord Fauntleroy curls, the delight of Queen Geraldine's eye, were to be the cause of Leka's first encounter with the tough world outside his own small, privileged one. He came home from a children's party with blue velvet suit and frilly shirt torn, and a black eye. The King immediately ordered that

130

the ringlets were to be cut off and they were, there and then.

At Parmoor House all the servants had been drafted into the Services or factories and Queen Geraldine relied on two women from the village and a man to wash the dishes and tend the boilers. He kept demanding to be paid more than a butler and valet together and one day when there were some important guests from London arriving he went into the dining room and throwing his dirty towel in front of King Zog announced: "I have had enough of washing so many plates! Do it yourself!"

Despite this display of temper Queen Geraldine was obliged to keep the man on as there was no one else to see to the boilers. The Albanian officers and guards had no intention of doing what they considered menial housework or even helping in the garden.

As the Queen's first Christmas present at Parmoor House, she asked King Zog to give her some chickens. A gift of twelve pullets, a fine rooster and a sturdy chicken-coop complete with chicken feed rations arrived.

> At that moment I felt that it was worth far more than any present of jewellery. How I loved my pullets and insisted on feeding them myself and augmenting their rations with waste from the kitchen. And now we had fresh eggs every day.
>
> But I became furious when I found that I was left to clean out the coop every day. In the end I became so cross about this that I only gave out the exact number of eggs for cooking and kept the rest for King Zog, Leka and the nurse.

The household, which at the time numbered thirty people, had arrived to find a vegetable garden ready for harvesting. Every morning Queen Geraldine, little Leka and a guard went to pick the runner beans, and the Queen even grew some potatoes which she gathered when they were no bigger than hazelnuts. One item of food that was not rationed was bread and the Queen became skilled in making bread soup and bread and butter pudding. As Princess Adele, who was in charge of the cooking, did most of it in oil which they bought from Soho, the Queen saved the rations of butter, which she then used to make rum butter sauce. If there was no butter, she served the pudding with a blackberry syrup which she made.

> I got the sugar by carefully storing not only our own family rations but those of the Albanian men who did not care for

sweet food. By now we had a pony and cart just as I had as a child at Nagy Appony and two dogs and Leka was always happy and in good health.

The Queen and Prince Leka adapted splendidly to country life. They made long walks together in the country lanes picking blackberries and taking them back to make jam, jelly and syrup.

Because of the two religions in the 'family' the Muslims gave their ham ration to the Christians who handed over their meat ration to them, and Princess Adele was very clever with her chicken dishes and made delicious yoghurt and cheese from milk they bought from the surrounding farms. As there are many Albanian dishes made with soft cheese and yoghurt, everyone felt very much at home. Pasta was not rationed as it was then not considered proper food by the English, so on her shopping forays to Soho the Queen loaded up with every kind she could find, piling it into the arms of the officers and guards who always accompanied her.

However, it was difficult to go to London often, not because we were far away, but because our petrol coupons did not stretch that far with Hitler's massive red Mercedes. We had to keep the petrol for going to church on Sunday and to see friends. Once a week, whenever there was a suitable film showing at the nearby town of High Wycombe, I took Leka to see it, as I wanted him to feel in touch with everyday life. Here was one small boy surrounded only by grown ups with few chances of playing with children of his own age.

The King had been offered the special rations available to diplomats in both food and petrol but had refused them. As he explained to the Queen, as he was not actively contributing anything to the war, he wanted no special privileges as far as bodily comforts were concerned.

We had no sooner settled in at Parmoor House than we received news that our possessions left at Bordeaux had arrived at Liverpool and been put into store in a warehouse there.

The whole household went out of its mind with excitement as we had purposefully not bought much during the last year, waiting for our clothes to arrive. For me personally I could not wait to wear my Maggy Rouff trousseau and the six fur coats that had been taken out of Albania when we fled and which I

132

had only worn for one year in Paris.

Five people from our suite immediately took the train for Liverpool the morning the news arrived. We did not waste a second. The next morning a catastrophic voice on the telephone told us that everything, except one car, had been completely destroyed by a direct hit from an incendiary bomb. It was purely a material loss but being only human, we women were desolate. In due time the insurance was paid out and the King distributed it among our retinue. The wise ones invested the money and some were even able to settle in England or begin a new life elsewhere.

Disgusted, I looked in the garage one morning, where the infamous scarlet Mercedes was standing, and almost felt a sense of evil. I had wanted to sell the car a long time before, as it simply ate up petrol but again the King would not let me as he felt it would attract the wrong sort of publicity.

Understanding my hatred of the car my American grandmother, Mrs de Strale d'Ekna, next day, sold it and proudly brought me the cheque. The cheque bounced. The car was subsequently tracked down by the police to a garage in Scotland where the proprietor had paid the thief £800 for it. My husband had to reimburse the garage owner and then donated the Mercedes to the Red Cross. His last words to me on the matter were: "Women will never listen."

Years later I was to read that the car was still in existence and had been on display in an exhibition of vintage cars.

At that time the English newspapers were filled with people beating the consumer shortage by advertising things they wanted to sell or exchange. In this way Queen Geraldine was able to obtain a large collection of lead soldiers from all the different regiments, complete with tanks and guns, in exchange for an adult bicycle.

One day I was completely horrified when going into the nursery where Leka had a children's party, to find six boys between the ages of four and six arranging the lead soldiers in an execution firing squad. The nurses were looking on and finding this completely normal.

Despite the cossetting of his babyhood Leka was developing into a fine well adjusted child, strong in body, independent and bright beyond his years. He had learned to ride his pony and thrived on the country air and diet.

One day when I had taken him for a row on the Thames I

decided it was time he learned to swim. Picking him up I threw him overboard. He did not lose his head for a second and immediately began paddling like a tadpole. The psychiatrists can say what they like, but it worked for my child.

The years in the English countryside passed calmly. King Zog remained in touch with other governments in exile and often invited their representatives to meet him in his new home.

Among the statesmen who came regularly to Parmoor House was President Benes of Czechoslovakia. He enjoyed talking to King Zog who found him intellectual and intelligent. One day, just as the Queen entered the drawing room with Madame Benes she found the President upset. He exploded to the King: "I have had enough of the Hungarians – a race I hate. The first thing I shall do on returning is to leave none alive." He knew that he would face continual problems from Hungary, over territory that his own country had seized.

Queen Geraldine turned pale with anger and was just about to open her mouth to tell their esteemed guest exactly what *she* thought when King Zog made a sign to her and in his calm voice said, "Mr President, with such ideas, it is not them who will find death on your return, but yourself. Calm down and let us go and talk in my office."

Only then did Benes notice the Queen's presence and embarrassed, he bowed asking to be excused. Just before the President and Madame Benes left London they went to pay a farewell call on King Zog and Queen Geraldine. When they left, King Zog gave them documents relating to Nagy Appony saying to them: "As I was one of the first victims of Nazi aggression, give us back our property." The President promised. Some weeks later however, the young Massaryk returned to London bringing Queen Geraldine a letter from Madame Benes which said that it was impossible for them to do anything in Slovakia, now a part of Czechoslovakia, as it was already under the communists. Afterwards the Queen tried through lawyers, "but they only considered that I was Hungarian and refused even to negotiate."

News of the siege of Budapest early in 1945 brought fresh sorrow for Queen Geraldine. With many of her family there she could neither eat nor sleep properly for three months. As the Turkish Ambassador was a personal friend of King Zog she was able to get daily reports and saw all the latest despatches which

134

the Ambassador sent by courier to Parmoor House. She learnt that when the Russians had overpowered the city, the troops were allowed to rape and pillage for three days and three nights. For six months no Hungarian could close the door of his house — the few that remained intact, that is.

In Albania the situation was also tragic. All the loyalist and monarchist bands, who since 1939 had fought in the mountains, now found themselves with nothing except their own personal courage. There was no more ammunition, no more food and no more medical supplies. The Albanian loyalists were outspoken, saying that given the command of King Zog, and ammunition, they would continue to fight, though not in the cities, so as not to inflict more ruin and destruction. They insisted that their orders would have to come from London, and they refused to collaborate with emissaries of Tito or from the Greek Communist Party. Orders from the British Government never arrived.

At that time there were three young English soldiers fighting in the mountains in Albania with the Legal Movement, who were monarchists. They were Billy McLean, David Smiley and Julian Amery. Each has written his own book on his part in the Albanian saga and today remain staunch friends of the royal family. They tried in every conceivable way to protect their loyal Albanian bands and especially the leader Abis Kupi, who was to die in New York many years later.

In his book, *Albanian Assignment*, Colonel David Smiley wrote: "When in London we actually asked King Zog to write a letter to Kupi (leader of the Albanian Zogist party) and he had done so, but the Foreign Office refused to let us take it. I did not know the reason but presumed that they did not wish it to be implied that His Majesty's Government recognised King Zog. They were sensitive to being accused of this by the Americans, who were already critical of the support we had given to the King of Greece. It is worth recalling that the Americans had a deep distrust of any form of monarchy, to the extent that when civil war raged in Athens, the American Embassy ran up a white flat and declared themselves neutral in the struggle between the Government and the Communists."

It is today a desiccated, historical fact, lying between the covers of international government reports, that the Allies at that time took a decision to support the Communist penetration in order

135

to create enough power to fight the Germans in the Balkan area. The Partisans received help of arms and ammunition, mines and explosives, clothing and food, communications equipment and even money in the form of sovereigns, as well as military expertise from British liaison officers and NCOs.

As Colonel Smiley wrote: "Without this help, bearing in mind they received none whatever from the Russians, they would not have overcome the Ballists and Zogists in the Civil War. Had British aid gone the other way Albania would be a pro-Western democracy today."

Many years before, during his stay in France, some of his French friends gave King Zog two cases of the finest vintage French champagne that was to be put away and kept to celebrate the Armistice. It was never drunk for this purpose. "You will see that for us there will be no joyful Armistice," King Zog told the Queen. "It is incredible how propaganda acts, even on people like the Anglo-Saxons who do not let themselves be drawn easily. They managed to make a hero out of Stalin, loved by the people. For us will come the relief that the terrible suffering of war has ceased, but we will be without our country which will still be in the throes of relentless suffering."

The Allied advance was now progressing successfully across Europe. In one country after another the bells rang out to proclaim freedom from Nazi rule. At the same time Russia was advancing from the east. The armies met in Berlin and at last "Victory in Europe" was declared. King Zog and Queen Geraldine received more than one thousand telegrams from all parts of the world asking when they would return to Albania.

The King had remained politically active until the end and more than ever he now tried to make the politicians understand how strategically important Albania was to the Free World; how much the English, who wanted a Communist-free Greece, would need a stable neighbour in Albania. But from everywhere there was a negative silence.

I remember the day when we went to a large luncheon party at the Brazilian Embassy. The windows were wide open and we could hear the voice of Churchill announcing the end of hostilities. At the table were only political personalities and I was very sad as all they spoke of was the war to come because of Russia. Everyone at the table realised the grave danger of a world divided by two absolutely contrary ideologies.

136

It was then that the King decided to turn towards his Muslim brothers – to go back and make his base and home in an Islamic country.

CHAPTER 15

Nachat Pasha, the Egyptian ambassador to London during the war, was a very good friend of King Zog, who asked him to contact King Farouk so that the Royal Albanian household could install itself in Egypt. There was the possibility that King Zog could be associated with some kind of business so that he would be relieved of the burden of dipping into his capital to keep his retinue financed. Also behind this move the King had the idea that, with the help of the different Arab countries, he could raise an expedition to Albania with the knowledge that he was leaving his family in the security of a friendly country. Every step he took was to be stalemated.

While these preliminary plans were being made, throughout Europe people were beginning to piece their lives together once more. For Queen Geraldine, with her family so very scattered, this was once again an anxious time as she waited for news of her mother, Madame Girault, and of her brother and sister.

At last she received a desperate telephone call from her mother in Aix-en-Provence who did not know where Gyula, her young brother, was. She had been able to join the King and Queen for a while in London and it had hurt Queen Geraldine to see how much the war had left its marks on her through the privations that she had suffered, all aggravated by her severe diabetes.

Emissaries from the King searched for Gyula for weeks and finally had the news from a hospital that he was returning to his home. He had just come round from a long and serious diabetic coma and was now found to have a lung riddled with tuberculosis. Gyula had fled from home to join the Resistance in Savoy and there, not being able to get his insulin, his diabetes had worsened. Towards the end of the war his group was surrounded and he was bundled into a lorry with the others. When he fell into a coma from lack of insulin he was thrown out of the lorry into the road where some French people had found him and taken him to hospital.

King Zog immediately sent Count Gyula Apponyi to a clinic in

Davos in the hope that the expert nursing and clean Swiss air would cure him. But it did not and he never fully recovered. He died at only twenty-six in 1950 in Merano, Italy, and was buried there.

News now came from Hungary that Virginia too had survived and that she and her two small children were in the Tyrol in Austria. This was disturbing as the French troops now occupying the Tyrol had begun sending back all the refugees. The first train-load to return was machine-gunned at the frontier by the Hungarian communists and everyone was killed. Later Virginia was able to get word through the British Army in Austria that she was in Salzburg and was now working for the Americans. She had left her two children with the family of a forester and had taken a rucksack leaving on foot just as the French troops arrived in Tyrol. Queen Geraldine made every effort to get a passport for her sister to come to London and the Foreign Office promised to give every help. The passport did not arrive.

Although sad to leave England where she had lived for more than four years, and made many friends, Queen Geraldine was ready to move on to a new life. The winds of change were blowing cold. The people had rejected Winston Churchill and in July 1945, elected a Labour Government. After so much physical and moral suffering everybody was now concerned with getting their own lives together. During the whole of the war the Black Market virtually did not exist but with peace came the breaking down of moral codes. Even the Anglo-Saxon patience had begun to rebel at all the restrictions still in force.

The royal party still consisted of thirty people and the Press made merry writing that they were taking "mountains of luggage" out of the country. The Queen claims that this was not true as she herself only had two cases. The trouble was that there were so many people to organise and each had luggage.

Before leaving London, Queen Geraldine took Prince Leka to a chemist to have him weighed and was asked, "What vitamins have you given this eight year old?" He was just over five years old but looked three or four years older. Like all the English children he had thrived on the vitamins, cod liver oil and orange juice which they had been given throughout the war.

After having lived for so long under the perpetual grey skies of England, those devastating pea soup fogs and the bone-biting

139

cold of an English country house I was longing to see the blue sky, shining sun and lyrical moods of the desert. The days at sea in·a converted British troopship were long and as usual I felt desperately seasick the whole trip.

We were met on arrival with great courtesy by the Governor of Cairo, a representative from the palace and a line of officials. We had been accepted in Egypt not only by King Farouk but on a vote of parliament we were treated as extra-territorials which also carried all diplomatic privileges.

Nothing was examined at our entry which was to cause great difficulties eight years later as there were no official record of our possessions. I liked Port Said with its clean wide avenues, graceful people, fine buildings, and sweeping long deserted beaches. Here Leka really went wild as we ran with him letting the salty wind whip our faces and bodies, revitalising us so that we went back to the hotel with ferocious appetites. I felt like a young girl again.

Queen Geraldine had only been in Port Said for two days when she was called to the telephone. As she did not know anyone in Egypt she was most intrigued to hear a voice so similar to her own. It could only be one person – Virginia.

With her two children and three suitcases the intrepid Virginia had hitch-hiked a lift on an American military aircraft from Vienna to Cairo. Knowing nobody on arrival she had gone to the Albanian Legation who put her in touch with her sister. When Virginia arrived at the hotel she immediately began to unpack and pressed into Queen Geraldine's hands pots of cream and then took from her blouse a large diamond brooch. Hidden in the cream were all the jewels that the Queen had left behind on the quay at Bordeaux in 1940.

The two sisters talked all night. Virginia spoke of the death of her handsome young husband; he was only twenty-eight and she twenty-four. Though she was to marry twice more he was, and remains, the great love of her life.

During the siege of Budapest, Virginia had fled with her babies and gone to earth in a small place on Lake Balaton. Their cousin, Baron Peter Inkey, found her there without any money and took her to his chateau of Iharosbereny, not far from the Austrian border. Before the Russian advance he had decided to place himself on the list of those who had disappeared and made Virginia his heir. He advised her to become the representative of the Red Cross for the province and the chateau became a

140

hospital. In this way she was able to work, look after her own children and even manage to hide other children in the towers so that with the help of Hungarian underground workers they could escape being recruited by the German army. She also risked her life with the Underground who helped the Swedish nobleman Count Wallenberg, in rescuing Jews.

One night while she was lying on a mattress on the floor of one of the large salons, she woke to find a bayonet on her chest. She had been denounced and it was the Gestapo who had come to arrest her along with Countess Kendeffy, Baroness Inkey and their children.

The Sergeant prodded the women and said, "There is one among you who has been a Queen." He ordered them to follow him. Virginia protested that this was not true and insisted that at least she should be able to collect her belongings. Once in the corridor she ran towards the room of a general who was a German relative.

The general emerged in his pyjamas protesting furiously and explaining that if the Countess Apponyi was arrested the farmers and peasants would not bring any more food for the German troops. Virginia was left under the guard of the Wehrmacht in the chateau but her two friends were taken away. Now she had six children to care for, all under the age of four years. It was the kindly general who arranged that she was sent under guard to the Tyrol from where she managed to escape.

Some days after Virginia's arrival in Egypt, by special train the whole party moved to apartments in the Mena Hotel facing the pyramids. The station at Cairo was decorated with the flags of the two countries and Queen Farida had sent her ladies-in-waiting to pay their respects to Queen Geraldine.

Two days after their arrival, while King Zog left for the palace to speak with King Farouk, Queen Geraldine and Countess Virginia de Baghy went to call on the beautiful young Queen Farida. They drove through two iron gates in the park before stopping at the iron grilles in front of her palace. As no man was permitted beyond these gates, Queen Geraldine and Countess de Baghy walked the last few steps. There awaiting them stood the Queen, a slim, elegant figure with a finely boned, extremely pretty face. Everything about her was delicate and feminine.

From the few words that I had alone with the Queen I could see that she was not happy now, although I knew that it had been

141

a marriage of love. During tea the three adorable little princesses came in and then we left promising to see each other often. As soon as there was a divorce both my husband and King Farouk avoided my requests to see her. I only saw her once more in Egypt but happily since living in Spain I have been in touch with her often, especially when I go to Paris. She has an expressive talent for painting although in the beginning it was tortured. Now it is much more serene with lyrical landscapes of the Nile. She still has her arresting looks but there is an air of infinite loneliness about her. She and two of the princesses, who have grown up into pretty young women, were at Leka's wedding.

King Farouk later visited us one afternoon in our apartment at the hotel in a jovial mood and he was especially respectful and attentive to my husband as he was young enough to be his son. Both Kings sat in their fezes absorbed with each other. With me he also seemed at ease because we could speak English together.

At that time King Farouk had charm, intelligence, a certain kind of bravery and a headful of dreams. Even then there were the signs of the decadence and gross flesh that was to bring about his downfall and death. King Zog was concerned for the young King Farouk because he saw that, within the flamboyant frame, was a sensitive and essentially kind man. He continually advised King Farouk to bring in Egyptian courtiers instead of the foreign riff-raff with whom he surrounded himself. Farouk's guards were the only men he really trusted and these were plain men from the Albanian mountains, one of whom had been with him since birth and stayed close to the King until his death. The two Kings would talk for hours but soon it was clear to Queen Geraldine that King Farouk was becoming bored with so many political discussions. Probably on the advice of his ministers, who feared the influence that King Zog was having on their young King, he began to space out his visits. The authorities may well have become apprehensive of King Zog's desire to involve Egypt in the creation of a united Arab world, composed of all the people of Islam with Albania as the only independent Muslim power in Europe, which in itself could be a strategic and creative force. President Nasser was to bring this dream to fruition during his period of office when he formed the United Arab Republic.

The political situation was very frustrating, and meanwhile the Queen still had to deal with all the everyday problems of her difficult household. Somehow she had transformed the apartment she occupied with the King and Leka into a real home. It is a magical gift that she still has today. But the constant worry was causing stress. Mental stress has always taken a physical toll on Queen Geraldine's health and now she went down with dysentery. As she had nearly died of it when she was a child she immediately went to bed but the rest had only lasted three hours when an agitated nurse came to tell her that Leka had the same illness.

From this moment I no longer thought of my own illness and neglected myself which was bad, as it took years of suffering from amoebic dysentery before the doctors managed finally to cure me. I was distraught as I watched my healthy Leka become a skeleton. He was badly treated by an English doctor who in reality turned out to be a vet, after which we had the best paediatrician in the Middle East but not even his treatment did any good. Every night Leka had a fever of over a hundred and his strength was literally being burnt up.

Finally, we went to the Anglo-American hospital where he stayed for several weeks and was treated for everything – yellow fever, malaria, tuberculosis and so on. We thought he was cured but no sooner had we been back in Mena House for three days the fever returned. He was completely dehydrated and seemed to be without life. We called the paediatrician in the middle of the night who lifted the boy's eye lids up and said, "We must give him an injection." To which Leka, who had appeared as if dead, jumped up and shouted, "No."

The next day Virginia came to me and said, "You do not see it because you are with him every second but Leka cannot live long like this. Take him to Paris, London or America but you must save him."

An Egyptian doctor who was living in the hotel heard of the Prince's illness and offered to look at him. Queen Geraldine trusted him completely when he said he had trained under the famous professor who had nursed King Zog in Vienna. He examined Leka, looked at the reports of the other doctors and summed up: "This could have been the boy's death but today with penicillin we will get him out of this within a week. He has streptococcus in the tonsils which has spread to the glands."

There was no penicillin in Egypt at that time, but through King Farouk's kind influence, and the efficiency of the British

Embassy, they were supplied within twenty-four hours, even if it did cost £14 for each ampoule of 100 grammes. Leka was cured in ten days.

The King and Queen went by car to Alexandria, crossing the desert, where they were able to see for themselves the mystery of a mirage.

> The desert always gave me the impression of anguish although I made many romantic illusions for myself about everything to do with it. To many people it gives the impression of liberty, of flowing, of eternity, but for myself I get a kind of claustrophobia. I have a heavy head, as when I am smothered by mountains.

For the first few weeks while they were looking for accommodation the royal party stayed at an hotel. In an Islamic world, which they understood, and preferred to the dullness of wartime London, it was thought that the Princesses would have been more content. But this was not the case: they were only happy when they returned to Paris for periods of a few months in the summer heat. Their world centred on the Place Vendôme and the Rue Fauborg St Honoré, where shopping was their delight. Only the King's eldest sister, Princess Senije refused to be separated from the King and Queen and insisted on spending every waking hour in their company.

In a letter to Baroness Ruling, Queen Geraldine drew a picture of the monotony of their family life: "One of the King's secretaries is a wonderful bridge player and saves my evenings for me. Every evening I play an excellent *partie de bridge*. The rest of the family go into another salon and play rummy or poker. I cannot do so because the poor Princesses are so embittered with life on the whole that I just cannot swallow the atmosphere. Only I must say that everyone looks old. Also this climate forms wrinkles you know, and if one forgets what a smile means, well then nothing is left."

King Farouk sometimes visited King Zog and Queen Geraldine without announcement. He would shut himself up with the King for political discussion, then have dinner with the family and stay on for a game of poker which finished in the small hours of the morning. In the beginning the Queen used to join them and was

144

always a winner. The stakes were never more than £5 but she was able to hide away her winnings until she had saved up enough to buy a set of emerald cuff links for the King which her son Leka now wears.

Prince Leka had been enrolled at the Victoria College and although only ten years of age, he looked more like a fourteen-year-old especially when seen against the finely-boned slim Egyptian children. With the classical features he had inherited from his father and his mother's wide blue eyes he towered like Gulliver over the Lilliputian Egyptian children. The Queen wrote of him to her former governess:

Well Leka is going to school. I hope that it will be the making of him. Of course at first it was a tragedy, sobs and tummy ache every morning for a week. The teachers insisted on putting him in a class much too high, because of his height and so on, but we intend now to engage a tutor for him to take care of him until he is twelve.

He is terribly quickly influenced by kids a bit older than himself, especially the children of one of the royal princes, and they give him ideas especially from the religious point of view, which makes me unhappy.

Leka has been allowed to grow up in a way too much as a child of nature. He needs a good moral influence next to him, whom he will respect and look up to, so that he will believe in him when he says what is right and wrong. We must give our only son the chance to grow up to be a man of character, fearing none but God. Despite what I write Leka has grown into an independent clever boy in spite of all the spoiling, surrounded by adoring adults, and now also plays an amusing game of tennis and rides quite well. He is completely without fear and has the head of all Albanians and is often just as stubborn. But I feel that with firmness and patience anything can be done with him.

In the first reports on Prince Leka his teachers said that his oral work was excellent but that he was hopelessly impeded by his written work. He spoke Albanian, English and a little German but if he was to progress, the King and Queen felt that the only solution was to have a private tutor.

In Egypt, life was at last flowing smoothly for the Albanian family. The strawberry haired Virginia became one of the belles of the social scene. This delighted Queen Geraldine who hoped that

145

the right man would come along at the right time and marry her vivacious sister and take care of her and her two small children. As King Zog did not like to mix with the social scene and rarely went out, one feels a pang of sympathy for the young Queen who was not permitted to dance, or even accompany her sister Virginia, who was enjoying every minute of Cairo life. The only time that the Queen had for sightseeing, window shopping or visiting her new women friends was from the hours of four o'clock in the afternoon until eight o'clock in the evening.

Though she seldom went sightseeing, Queen Geraldine treasured her visits to a small wooded place near one of the bridges spanning the Nile from where one could see the *felluca* with their colourful sails and eat pigeons grilled in the open over a spit. Another part of the town, where she enjoyed walking, looked from the outside like a jumble of delapidated old houses, but inside was an Aladdin's cave of exquisite marbles and mosaics. In the Spring she played tennis at a club on the island of Xamalek enjoying the luxury of Egypt with all the other ex-patriots.

King Farouk and his court moved every summer to the magnificent palace of Montaza at Alexandria, overlooking the sea and surrounded by a large garden blazing with exotic flowers. There were tennis tournaments, concerts, bridge tournaments almost every night in private houses and of course, sumptuous dinner parties and dancing under the star studded black velvet sky. It pleased King Farouk that along the coast he had his own Royal Mile with exiled European royalty seeking favour and refuge. At his invitation, Queen Giovanna of Bulgaria, after the coming of the communist régime there, arrived in Egypt with her little son, King Simeon, and her daughter, Princess Marie Louise, and was followed by her parents, King Victor Emmanuel III and Queen Helen and a few months later by their son, King Umberto of Italy.

One day when King Zog and Queen Geraldine were having lunch, an aide-de-camp announced that an adjutant of King Umberto had arrived to say that the Italian King would like to visit King Zog as soon as possible. The interview was arranged without delay. It was to be an historic and touching reconciliation between the two nations.

The King asked me to change my dress – so I put on my prettiest gown – but to remain in my room upstairs. He told me that it might not be a comfortable interview with an interpreter between them, though he felt that King Umberto was coming with an open heart. My husband felt that despite the fact that King Umberto had accepted the crown of Albania, he had been forced to do it and that he had always been against the invasion of our country. He was deeply against Mussolini's aims but was up against an indomitable dictator.

From my window I watched the car arrive and I saw the handsome King get out accompanied by two aides. About ten minutes later our Court Minister, Colonel Martini came up to fetch me. I went down feeling very nervous and emotional. When I went into my husband's office I found the two kings both looking embarrassed. My husband said to me: "King Umberto is trying to express the remorse that he feels as well as that of King Victor Emmanuel. Will you please embrace him."

I kissed the tall king on both cheeks and he kissed my hand and we all sat down. Speaking in English King Umberto asked me to try and explain to my husband that he was not personally consulted in any way. It was Mussolini the dictator who forced the crown of Albania on his father. As he explained:

"As soon as I was King of Italy I refused this crown and it will never be thought of again by my family. I want also to express my own personal feelings and respect and admiration that I have for the person of your husband."

Although I knew that my husband had understood most of the conversation I translated it into my kind of words. King Umberto had asked me to do it from my heart and whilst I was talking to my husband I noticed that the Italian King had tears in his eyes. Seeing this, and being so very touched, my husband got up and took King Umberto in his arms.

King Zog then made the generous gesture of saying to King Umberto that he would like to visit his father, King Victor Emmanuel the next day. King Umberto was clearly delighted and said that he had one request to make as his sister Queen Giovanna was living nearby alone. "I know that she wants to see you but because of what has happened she has not liked to approach you", he said. King Zog's reply was: "From your father we go immediately to your sister."

And so began a life-long friendship that continues today between Queen Giovanna who now lives in Portugal and Queen Geraldine in Madrid. They correspond and telephone and there is never a year that they do not see each other.

I not only feel a great admiration for Queen Giovanna but an affection that has only deepened with the years. Her example and advice have been extremely useful to me in my relationship with the other royal families. She has also consecrated her life to doing good works to which she has given all her great gifts of intelligence, sense of values and tenacity of will.

Egypt at that time was a hot-bed of intrigues and gossip and soon the news of the reconciliation was all over Alexandria. King Farouk called on King Zog soon after and asked excitedly: "Now tell me is it true?" Not wishing to be left out of such an historic event, which after all had taken place in his country, King Farouk gave a glittering dinner reception in the Montaza Palace to which he invited King Zog and Queen Geraldine, the two Kings of Italy, King Victor Emmanuel and King Umberto, and representatives of all the other Royal Houses – the Romanoffs and Hesses, the Ottoman family, Queen Giovanna and her sister the Countess Calvi de Bergolo, who was the eldest daughter of King Victor Emmanuel.

This was a time of peace for the family after the turmoil of war. A time of peace and of reconciliation.

CHAPTER 16

The summer ended. King Zog, Queen Geraldine and their entourage returned to Cairo where Princess Ruhije again became seriously ill with cancer. As Queen Geraldine wrote to Baroness Ruling: "No one could bear to watch the agony that she went through. Her suffering in France was nothing compared with this. The martyrdom she is going through you would not believe. The doctors say that they have never seen such heroism and she still wants to live. When she was in the last agony of death her moans were so terrible that I went down to the chapel of the French hospital and prayed to God that she would have peace. Whilst I was there she was delivered, but it was awful as it was the first time that I saw death so close and it shocked and scared me.

"The poor family showed no resignation at all and were in an awful state of grief. The only one who kept them all normal, with his great kindness and patience, of course was my husband, but they are still sitting about all day in black veils. Yet their poor sister is surely happier in heaven. King Farouk gave orders for an official funeral so Princess Ruhije is buried in the citadel of Cairo.

"My darling is the same as ever. I do not think that the years have made a difference in him, at least people say that he doesn't look older than forty. But of course the poor dear is everlastingly worried. Since Leka has had no recurrence of the bad illness he had in the beginning, I have come to love Egypt with its blue sky, the sea in Alexandria where King Farouk has built us a chalet on his own private beach, and the Nile in Cairo which in several places reminds me of dear old Budapest. The only thing one misses are the forests, hills and plenty of green. One has everything one wants, although things are expensive and now because of restrictions certain luxury items may disappear from the market. But I still get a thrill to go into the shops."

By late Spring 1947 there was a feeling of unrest in Egypt and a growing hostility among the ordinary people against foreigners. One day when Queen Geraldine was out walking with the wife of one of the Albanian ministers, she saw a large crowd coming from a mosque carrying placards covered with Arabic slogans and in their hands bundles of propaganda pamphlets. Individuals in the crowd were distributing little bags filled with gold pieces. On the pamphlet was written a verse from the Koran, a quotation from Karl Marx and finally a text combining the two ideologies illustrating the compatibility between them. It was dangerous and inflammatory material. When Queen Geraldine told King Farouk what she had seen, and asked him why he had re-opened diplomatic relations with Soviet Russia, his reply was: "The British have forced me to do it." She was sharply reprimanded by King Zog for asking such a question, for he did not want the Queen to make political comments.

At that time King Zog was in contact with the Kings of Saudi Arabia, who had shown great interest in his plans for the creation in one of these countries of a military force, which could invade Albania at the right moment and free the country of the Hoxha communist régime. Albanian delegations were received and letters were exchanged with gifts of gold. The Government of the United States was also favourable to such a plan, particularly the military services, who wished to build a training camp for Albanians in Libya. The whole project was a failure from the outset.

Apart from his political activities, the King also wanted to find a way to invest the last of his capital which was fast diminishing. He was offered a large farm property not far from Alexandria but on investigation he found out that he was being asked twice the price given to other people. In the end the Queen had accumulated several files of the businesses they had been offered, but with the King's great mistrust of everything and his native shrewdness it nearly always turned out that his instincts were right.

I have an impression that Providence wished us to do nothing, as immediately afterwards there were large agrarian reforms and we would have lost everything anyway.

For Christmas the King took the whole of his household to Upper Egypt, although the Queen who was very tired, would have preferred to go alone with her husband. Every day they were accompanied by the whole household. They travelled from Luxor to Aswan and then the length of the Nile to Wadi Halfa. Staying one week in Luxor, they made daily excursions to the Valley of the Dead.

> I recovered under the marvellous sky at Aswan where quietness enters one's spirit and even death does not seem filled with fear. There is no more marvellous sight than the pure temples of Karnak in the moonlight. I would like to think that I shall see all this again before my old age.

Though Queen Geraldine had enjoyed travelling with King Zog, who was knowledgeable in the history of the Middle East, it was no substitute for the unrest that she felt in her spirit.

In the month of May 1949, approaches had been made to King Zog when he received two American delegates, Mr Robert Low and Mr Robert Minor, and from England Julian Amery and Colonel Neil (Billy) McLean. Although the King did not like Geraldine to be involved with his political activities she was now present at all important meetings acting as his interpreter, simply because he did not trust anyone else. The Albanian monarchist leader, Gaqi Gog, a former decathlon champion, kept the record of this particular encounter. The meeting went well and a report was sent to Jefferson Caffery, the United States Ambassador in Cairo.

The most likely reason for this new initiative was that the Anglo-Americans, through their intelligence services, had been able to collate sufficient information on the people in Albania to realise that in spite of any reservations that they might have had (particularly the Americans who were not pro-monarchists) the only leader who still maintained credibility among the people of Albania was King Zog. Strangely, because of the clan structure of Albanian society, and because of King Leka's activities today, this mantle of credible leadership has been passed on to him. This characteristic of the Albanian people is little known and little recognised by Western governments today.

The motive that forced the British and the Americans to consult with King Zog was that by far the largest majority of the Albanian refugees recruited as fighters would not have volunteered without his tacit approval.

Two months later, in Rome, it was agreed in principle that a small force should be landed in Albania with the purpose of raising Loyalist supporters to overthrow Hoxha. A decision was reached concerning the composition of a united front for this

151

purpose. On 7th July immediately after the agreement was settled, Colonel McLean flew fom Rome to Cairo and a few days later travelled to Alexandria for a second meeting with the King. He was joined by Julian Amery and Robert Low, who in reality was an intelligence officer.

The meeting opened disastrously. "We rather blundered in, proud of having pulled off the Rome agreement and we imagined that the King would accept what we put to him," McLean recalled to Lord Bethell. They explained to the King that the United States and Great Britain wanted to form a united front composed of all anti-Communist Albanians living in the West under the leadership of Midhat Frasheri, leader of the Balli-Kombetar — the National Front. Such a group would include Republicans and other anti-monarchists supported by the U.S. This meant that the question of the future role of Albania would be left in suspense until the day that the Albanians could freely, by plebiscite, express their preference, but meanwhile the royal prerogatives would be considered suspended.

The King rose angrily from his chair. The Queen had never seen him in such a cold rage before. He ordered through her that the American and British delegates leave the room, saying:

"It was I who made Albania. I left the country with the National Assembly's authority and it is my duty to defend Albania. I refuse such a condition and find that it is incomprehensible that you could think of formulating such a proposal, as a King cannot suspend his prerogatives, because it is illegal. I cannot pass this duty on to anyone except my heir.

"Before I left Albania the National Assembly charged me to defend abroad the independence and integrity of the country, and this is part of the Royal Rights."

Only Julian Amery stayed behind to apologise and try to placate King Zog. He asked if the King would allow the talks to be resumed the following day when a new plan would be presented to him under another aspect. King Zog agreed.

The next day the officials returned in a different frame of mind. They accepted the point of view of King Zog and asked that he would re-examine their proposal which was as follows: that it was the hope of the Government of the United States that the King support with all his heart their proposal, the sole objective of which was to establish a united front of the Albanians living abroad.

152

The King agreed to their proposal adding "a united front grouping all exiled Albanians who were *anti-Communist*."

On 14th June 1949, the King signed the following declaration: "I welcome with great satisfaction the formation of the Albanian United Front, as the way to achieve unity among the Albanians who are abroad, and also to bring moral comfort to the Albanians in their own country, which is now under the domination of a Communist Government of foreign obedience.

"I will give, with all my strength, my support to the Albanian United Front and its committee. I shall persuade all Albanians so that they give their loyalty to this movement whose aim is the recovery of Albanian independence in all its integrity.

"I consider this method as entirely compatible with democratic principles.

"I declare that I exercise none of my royal prerogatives against the Albanian United Front – against its activities or its committee, presided over by Midhat Frasheri, under the condition that they do not go against the aspirations of the Albanian Nation and that their only aim is the recovery of Albanian independence and the integrity of its territory.

"This declaration concerning the general lines will be published the day that the different parties mentioned in our first meeting proceed to the formation of a committee of the Albanian United Front."

He also came to an agreement with the American representatives on the following points saying:

"After the declaration that I signed on 14th June 1949, I am going to add to it an addition which is an integral part of my declaration and which can be summarised in three points.

1. Given that I represent the legality, I demand that all questions of primary interest be brought to my attention, for discussion by the directing committee of the Albanian United Front, in full collaboration, and if shown to be necessary, by the good offices of the competent American authorities.

2. In accordance with the principles of legality mentioned above and being constitutionally invested, I will form a government in Albania totally neutral during the training period which will follow the liberation of Albania.

3. I sanction the choice of Midhat Frasheri as President of the committee and director of the Albanian United Front, by reason of the entire confidence that I have in his patriotism, but in the

case where Midhat Frasheri resigns, or for other unforeseen reasons, I must be consulted on the directing of committee members. These three points detail and condition my declaration which should not be published until after the realisation of the agreement of the different national Albanian parties."

In the autumn, *en route* from New York to Cairo, Midhat Frasheri died of a heart attack. While the members of the committee were searching to select another personality as strong as Frasheri, American interest waned. The great impetus was over as all their projects for the countries behind the Iron Curtain were placed under the administration of the Free Europe Organisation. Once more Albania had been diplomatically pushed into the background.

In 1951 King Zog was asked if certain of his officers, who knew the country well, given the possibility of being able to enter Albania under cover, would collect vital information that was required. Personal contact with loyal Albanians from the outside world had been impossible due to the rigid attitude of the Serbs who either imprisoned the messengers if they were caught or murdered them. Most of the men from the north or the centre of Albania did not know enough to try the dangerous crossing to the south where they could enter Greece, whereas those from the south could not go north. What still functioned were bases outside the Yugoslav frontier which relied on letters arriving via Turkey.

The King replied that while he was willing to give all the help that he could to such a mission, his men must not be given any orders that could provoke an uprising as it was not yet time. The King called his men to him and explained the situation, adding that he would give his consent for those who volunteered. There was silence and they all had tears in their eyes because, as some of them admitted to the Queen later, it seemed that at long last they could do something for their country and that all hope was not dead.

During the following days the volunteers came to the villa requesting private audiences with their King. I could see how moved the King was by these talks. In the end five in all – half of them – decided to go.

At the moment of departure, after we had said an emotional goodbye to them their chosen leader, Captain Zenel, came to find me and gave me a few pieces of personal jewellery that belonged to him, asking me to keep them until he returned. Nobody, except the King, knew of his request nor of my conversation with the captain. Some weeks later we were told that they had entered the country where a base had been arranged for them for their stay which the King had insisted should not be longer than five weeks.

Time passed and we had no news. One day in the spring of 1952 an American official came to tell us that they were worried as the radio no longer seemed to be in their hands and they feared that the whole group had fallen into a Communist trap. They had asked all the questions in code and received the correct answers but the sending of the morse messages had been different. This they were told was because the operator had been wounded in the right hand and was therefore transmitting with his left.

The King instinctively felt that something was wrong and asked that no more men be sent in after them as this would be an even greater loss. The Americans insisted that they wished to save them and asked King Zog what question could be asked to which only the leader of the group would know the answer. It was then that Queen Geraldine, who had been present acting as the interpreter, suggested, "Why do you not simply ask the Captain where he left his jewellery," and she related the moving scene with the young Albanian soldier. Only he would know the answer to this question and would supposedly reply something like, "with the mistress of the house," or "with my second mother."

The news of the party's arrest was finally announced years later on Tirana Radio on 1st January 1954, and their trial took place on 6th April. The transmission was so strong that the King and Queen were able to pick it up in Alexandria. During the trial the captain's last words were, "Do not ask anything more. You can see that I have told you all that you forced me to say. Long live the King." They were all executed on 15th April.

Later the Queen was to hear that when the American official asked the operator about the jewels he seemed to have been annoyed and replied, "We have had enough of your stupid questions. All personal objects are in the luggage left in Greece." Immediately the Queen knew that it was all too tragically clear that the Albanian soldiers had been betrayed. That there was a traitor in the high administration in either the United States or

Britain. That traitor we now know was Kim Philby.

Not only had that group been caught but a second one, despite the King's advice, had been sent in to rescue them and they were also caught. Brave men had been senselessly sacrificed.

One of the amusing anecdotes that seeped through from Albania in the early fifties, illustrating the mood of the country, concerned the fact that the new Communist régime was discouraged by the lack of co-operation among the mountaineers. A delegation of officials was sent to the Mirdites Mountains and called all the chiefs together. One after the other the officials mounted the dais, speaking of all the benefits that Communism had brought the country. They demanded an answer so the oldest man of the community got up and spoke slowly for all to hear.

"We only know one thing, that our country has for centuries been under the yoke of the invader. We asked God that the Romans should leave and that the Devil should come, but that we be left a free homeland. We asked that the Slavs should go and that the Devil come, that the Turks should go and that the Devil come. Finally, after a lapse of time, when we had known the good feeling of being free, then the Italians came and we started again to pray that in their place the Devil should come. And now the Devil has come and we can no longer find anything to pray for."

King Zog and Queen Geraldine had moved into their white villa in Alexandria. The Queen's joy was unbounded as she arranged the villa exactly as she wanted and walked around admiring her new possessions. The Durazzo honeymoon villa, with its beautiful marble, was a *fait accompli* from the King, but this new villa she had watched rising out of the soil and helped choose the marbles for the grand staircase herself. It was her very own home in every sense of the word.

Her joy was short-lived when the King announced, "I do not think that we will be able to live here for long, as I neither like the situation in this country, nor in the world. It seems to me we are facing another war."

He was also aware through his own intelligence agents, though he had not been officially informed by the British Government, that British officers were already being trained by the republican Balli Kombetar for infiltration into Albania. On the same day that the military experts had met the King, an advance guard consisting of the first two recruits were already boarding a British

156

military aircraft near Rome for Malta where a training camp had been established.

Through land agents in London, Queen Geraldine spent all that summer looking through prospectuses to find a suitable property in Rhodesia which would allow her and Leka to live in a peaceful land with a good climate. For Queen Geraldine it was thought that a change of scene might ease the deep sadness. She was still suffering from grief at the death of her mother Madame Girault, in 1948, and of her brother Gyula who, with all his vibrant charm fought gallantly until the end against two infected lungs and his diabetes. Now her American grandmother, who had shared so much of her wartime experiences, had died in New York as the aftermath of a broken femur.

In the autumn, Prince Leka caught pneumonia and bronchitis and despite penicillin was desperately ill. It was a tragic time for Queen Geraldine as the whole family blamed her for allowing her brother to play with Leka. The Princesses were convinced that he had caught tuberculosis from Gyula. It was streptomicine that saved Leka, but it was now absolutely necessary to take him to the mountains to recuperate.

While the King and some of his officers were away in America, Queen Geraldine and Prince Leka went to the Lebanon where in the then peaceful and beautiful countryside, he soon grew strong and healthy. By now he had grown into an extraordinarily handsome youth and was accepted as intellectually bright beyond his years.

> We were received in Lebanon as though we were still on the throne and I was able to visit the whole country. Albanian refugees came in bus loads to see me and talk to me. We took food together and spoke of loved ones and the country that they all yearned to return to one day. To an Albanian, nothing in the world replaces the beauty of the Land of the Eagles.

The Queen had made a vow to cross into Syria and see more refugees but when the news of the assassination of King Abdullah of Jordan broke on 20th July 1951, the frontiers were closed.

In America, apart from meeting all kinds of leading personages whom he hoped to interest in the Albanian cause, the King bought a magnificent mansion on Long Island, which because the house was so big and therefore considered a 'white elephant' cost only $100,000. Set in beautiful parklands, it could easily shelter

157

the forty people to which the household had now swollen.

For the Queen her return from the Lebanon to Egypt brought only stress and sadness. The new villa had been sold to a Saudi Arabian Prince and Queen Giovanna, who had become her closest friend, had left Egypt to settle in Spain. One day when she was sitting in the garden of the Hotel Mediterranean, a small boy pressed into her hand a letter addressed to her. There was no signature but in bad French it said: "Egypt is becoming a dangerous place for the King, for all of you, but especially for you. So leave immediately. You are too much loved for anything to happen to you here."

On showing the letter to the King he laughed and said, "Anonymous letters should never be taken seriously," but the Queen had deep misgivings. She was frightened.

There was unrest in the winds blowing from the desert. The atmosphere in Cairo was tense, everyone was nervous and there was trouble in the streets. Within weeks, the famous Shepherd's Hotel, filled with guests, had been burned to the ground. The pro-Nasser mob attacked property indiscriminately: a hotel, then the hospitals. Even Alexandria was not spared from the burning and pillaging. The political situation became very tense for a while, but fortunately the rioting died down and an uneasy calm prevailed. For Queen Geraldine however this calm was not to last. Her husband's health deteriorated suddenly.

I was sitting in the hairdresser's and my hair was still wet when a car drew up blaring its horn and in rushed one of our officers saying, "Come quickly. The King is very ill." He did not know any details. I threw off the towels and rushed into the car and instead of the usual time of twenty minutes it took to drive to our villa, with full blaring horn we did it in ten minutes, scattering the traffic right and left.

I rushed to the King's room. I was absolutely horrified. There was blood everywhere. In the bed, dripping on the floor, staining the bathroom. The King was lying on his bed, fully dressed but in a deep coma. The first thing I did was to telephone for a doctor who arrived soon afterwards. By then my husband had lost five pints of blood. Under the doctor's care he regained consciousness. The haemorrhage had been a severe one but was now contained.

For three days King Zog was drip fed, after which the Queen prepared all his food, beginning with a milk diet, to help him

158

regain his strength. Although it was to be a three months' convalescence the King refused to have a nurse and the Queen took complete care of him night and day. In a city where cholera and such infections broke out frequently she was taking no chances in having the Egyptian male servants look after the King. Though reasonably clean and well trained they did things, "that made my hair stand on end."

By spring 1952 the tension had become unbearable in the country, and pro-Nasser feeling was running high, demanding the abdication of King Farouk. The King arrived early in Alexandria with his family and, weak as he himself was, King Zog tried to get word to King Farouk that he wanted to see him, as he felt he might be able to help with advice and possibly save the monarchy. One evening Queen Geraldine watched as the four roads that converged on the villa were closed off by trucks filled with soldiers. She was told that a "high personage" would be coming to see the King that night. King Zog wore a silk dressing gown for the occasion and sat in a chair throughout the night waiting until six o'clock in the morning. King Farouk never came and soon the trucks disappeared. Three days later King Farouk was surrounded in the Montaza Palace by his own police.

> One afternoon soon afterwards, towards three o'clock, I saw from our garden a disturbance around the royal yacht in the harbour. Through binoculars we could recognise the unmistakable figure of King Farouk embarking. The town was silent. I turned to my husband and said:
> Everything has happened without blood flowing, but there is going to be a reaction. It is not tactful to stay in a country whose monarch has been forced to abdicate. Now we must go.

They had known six settled years in Egypt, but now with the King becoming increasingly ill they had to set out on their travels once more.

CHAPTER 17

Those next years were a nightmare for Queen Geraldine, a nightmare she can still hardly bear to recall. After 1950 her husband's health worsened steadily. There would be times of hope as he seemed to make a recovery, but these were to be cruelly dashed by the continual recurrences of his illness. Throughout those eleven years the Queen was never far from his side, watching over him with distress as despite everything that could be done he grew weaker.

They lived quietly in Cannes for a while, and the Queen nursed her husband constantly. She was sure that all his illness stemmed from that ulcer which was not treated properly in Vienna. Now nothing could be done.

On 3rd January 1961, King Zog's household moved to Paris. The journey was made possible because of the King's own will power and the services of their devoted French physician, Dr Bourgois Cavardin, who agreed to travel with the King, who was now in constant pain. The doctors had warned the Queen that the least jerk of the train could be fatal and throughout the journey she was so worried that she arrived in Paris with nervous cramp in her stomach. When they arrived at the villa at Ablon there was so much mud that it was impossible to drive the car into the grounds. The King became impatient and though he had scarcely walked in years, he found the strength to climb the hilly path on foot.

On arrival the Princesses took to their rooms and lay down leaving Queen Geraldine to cope with a sick husband, a house badly in need of cleaning and no servant to help her. For three weeks she struggled on alone until she, too, became ill. She had simply reached the end of her strength and was no longer able to cope with the washing and lifting and all the care that a terminally sick man required. The doctors decided that as King Zog was now so ill he should be placed in the hospital of Foch at Suresnes, which had the best research laboratory in Paris.

Then began for me a calvary from which to this day I do not know how I was given the strength to survive. Because it was a Sunday afternoon, the director of the hospital was not there and the whole of this large building seemed to be understaffed. I had been promised that I could have an adjoining room to my husband's so when they wheeled the King into a little room cramped with a bed, chair and bedside table, I immediately looked for my room and the bathroom. I was shown a curtained-off cabinet with lavatory, hand basin and shower and that was all.

When I asked about my room the nurse replied tartly: "No one of the family is allowed to stay in hospital with the patient." I insisted that it had been arranged with the director and demanded a communicating room. "That is absolutely impossible," she replied. "We will put a mattress on the floor near the bed. This is only for one night and tomorrow we can sort it out with the administrator."

King Zog was furious and wanted to leave immediately but he was far too ill to take another move so I made light of the situation. I told him, "It isn't the first time in my life that I have slept on the floor."

The next day I contacted the Minister of Health, and a cousin of mine talked to him. As for the hospital doctor neither my husband nor I wanted to talk to him and for that first week he seemed to be all the time in the laboratories. Nobody cared for my husband and I had to continue to nurse him. When I saw that for the first ime in his life he was getting bed sores I took myself into the lavatory and cried my heart out.

Each day I watched the King becoming weaker and weaker and I could not understand why. It was as though his personality, his soul, his whole being was going little by little. I fought to have outside opinion and the best professor in Paris came to see the King, which was as well, as the resident doctor came to tell me that his mother was dying and that he would not be able to attend my husband.

When he saw that he had become yellow with jaundice the King whispered to Queen Geraldine: "I do not need to use the revolver as I see now why I am so weak." During his illness he had kept his gold revolver, that had saved his life so many times, on the bed beside him, but the time had come when he was too weak even to pick it up so he asked for the Queen's small revolver inlaid with gold that had been given to her in Albania.

The Queen had surreptitiously asked Prince Leka to take out

161

the bullets but when it was placed on the table near the King he ordered, "Open it." When he saw that there were no bullets in it he made his son put them back. The reason for the revolver was not because the King could not stand the suffering, but because he had said if he knew for certain that he had cancer he would put a bullet through his head. His dread of the disease which had killed Princess Ruhije was bitter.

The revolver episode had so horrified the Queen that she begged every doctor who passed the King's room to go in and say some encouraging words. This was difficult, as in the Foch Hospital the King was already a man condemned to die: here he was only the patient in the room at the end of the corridor.

On the day that it was apparent that King Zog had developed jaundice, one of the first signs in terminal general cancer, the director of the hospital called Queen Geraldine and Prince Leka, who was not twenty years of age, into his office and told them bluntly that the King was dying. Prince Leka went white but as soon as he left the room he telephoned the most famous American cancer centres pleading with them to accept the King as a patient. One by one they checked with the director of the Foch Hospital, only to be told the sad truth. The King could not be moved. Queen Geraldine remembers this day as one of the worst of her life. Not only was the man she loved going to die, but she was to be left with the enormous responsibility of taking care of the Princesses and the whole royal entourage.

> On the day that we knew for certain that my husband had cancer I cabled Mr Ostier, in New York where I had left the last of my important jewellery, and asked him to send in Leka's name $10,000. I knew that whatever money we had left in the French bank would be frozen should my husband die. There was a contract in New York that the jeweller could not sell under a certain sum but alas he did not sell much over it. Today my jewels would be worth a fortune.

Amidst her own personal grief the Queen demonstrated her realistic attitude to life, which is, even today, very much at the heart of the woman.

One of the last people to speak with the King was his sister-in-law, Virginia. She sat on his bed and he held her hand. "Liebling, don't leave your sister alone," the King said in a voice now so weak that she could hardly hear. "I know that she is perfect for

162

all she has to do in her job of being a Queen. She has the strength and the political knowledge but I would ask you to help her with our son. To guide him to make the right steps in his life." Virginia kissed this man she had grown to love and admire and whispered, "I promise."

Three days went by until the King finally fell into a coma. Three days of agony, stress and infinite sadness as Queen Geraldine watched the man to whom she had devoted her life slipping away. On the third day the King became conscious for a short while, long enough to see Prince Leka sitting by his bedside. It was then that he told him of his dream. How he had seen Queen Geraldine, now beautifully aged, standing on the prow of a ship that was sailing into Durazzo harbour. Words that King Leka was to repeat to me twenty-four years later in a drawing room in Belgravia.

Now that she realised that King Zog was dying, Queen Geraldine asked the hospital that he should be given morphia as, even when he was unconscious he thrashed from side to side in his bed clearly in distress. The Princesses, who waited at the clinic every day, heard of the Queen's request and ordered that no morphia should be given because of their religious beliefs. Instead two Albanian guards were placed either side of the King's bed in case in his agony he should fall out of bed and injure himself. He was to be denied even the dignity of a peaceful death.

On the Sunday afternoon of 9th April 1961, Prince Leka, who had been constantly at his father's bedside over the last few days, had gone to the cemetery at Thiais, near Orly, to make arrangements for the King's funeral which everyone had realised would take place within the next few days. Queen Geraldine was resting in a nearby room, which had been empty awaiting a patient, when one of the Albanians woke her and said: "Come quickly." When she entered the bedroom King Zog opened his eyes, gave a deep sigh and died. As she recalls that moment today, "God gave me the courage to close his beautiful eyes before I knelt at his bedside to pray."

The room was suddenly filled with the family wailing in grief. Death had deprived the Princesses of their whole reason for living and now they were unable to contain themselves. *Moret i Squiptarvet*, Bird of the First, King of all the Sons of the Eagle, who had survived fifty-five assassination attempts, was no more. Their cries of lament could be heard throughout the hospital.

One of the King's old friends, who was also present, immediately went to call the head Imam of the Paris Islamic community. Shortly afterwards four Imam with flowing robes arrived at the hospital and threw up their hands in horror. They immediately turned the King's bed towards Mecca just as nurses came to take the body away to the mortuary chapel. This was an unacceptable idea for a King and a Muslim.

Leka had returned from the cemetery and seeing our distress, threw out all the hospital officials and nurses and placed two Albanian guards, with poised revolvers, outside the door of the room. No one dared to intrude.

That moment my son had become a man. He led me gently to the hospital chapel and left me there to pray while he arranged with the administration for the body of the King to be placed in a nearby small hall. Candles burned at the foot of the bed as my son, with the officers of our suite, watched over their dead King.

It was there that Queen Geraldine took her farewell of this man she had loved with all her heart from that first evening in Tirana.

With the anguish of the Princesses, and her own desolate grief Queen Geraldine collapsed. Her sister Virginia, who had arrived at the hospital, took her to rest at a nearby hotel where a doctor was called to give her sedatives. It was the beginning of another long illness.

During the whole of that night and the following days, Albanians from all over Paris and the near surroundings came to pay their last homage to their King. The news had been flashed on television and cinema screens, over the radio and on the front page in the evening newspapers round the world. Albanians arrived on the Franco-Belgian border by carloads as there was a large colony in Belgium. There had been no time to collect visas and the French gendarmerie, sympathising with their tear-stained faces, allowed them to enter France for a few days. Even in Sweden when they had heard that their King was dying the Albanians had managed to find the money to fly to Paris and share those last moments.

From the hospital they streamed through the deserted streets to the hotel to pay their respects to the Queen. Her beauty was unrecognisable in her suffering and some did not even realise who the slender figure in black was. Others greeted her in the traditional Albanian way, *Rroft Mhbreti* – Long Live the King!

This acclamation was taken up so that it echoed through the still town, drenched in moonlight.

As I listened to their greetings and saw their proud faces I felt that the veils of time and sadness had disappeared. My spirit turned to former times in Tirana, in another Europe, in another world. I also felt a sense of pride that I had given them the tall handsome young man standing by my side who would be their future King.

From the hotel the Queen was transferred to a hospital. It was a sanctuary for tortured souls with small bungalows for each patient and set in a beautiful garden. On arrival she was put into a wheel-chair and taken to a bungalow where a pretty maid – in reality a nurse – immediately put her to bed. She was given sedatives. Every three hours a tray of delicate food arrived in the Queen's room but she had become so weak through not eating that she was unable even to lift a glass of water.

Prince Leka went to visit his mother every day but after a week of intensive treatment the director of the hospital telephoned him and said, "Your mother is dying." The twenty-year-old Prince was horrified and demanded to know why. "She has no real illness," the doctor explained: physically and mentally Queen Geraldine was "burned out". The Prince immediately went to the hospital and facing the director in his office placed his revolver on the table saying: "My father died because of a French hospital and I will not let my mother die too. You *have* to do something."

The French doctor thought before replying, "We have the idea that she has lost the will to live. Would you allow our chief psychiatrist to try to get out of her subconscious the reason why?"

Twice a day a sympathetic doctor spent about an hour talking to the Queen. They spoke about everything including life itself. After a few days he told Prince Leka that he thought he had found out what was wrong with Queen Geraldine. "She does not want to live because she has lost her husband."

One of the problems that was subconsciously giving the Queen added distress was what she was now going to do with the Princesses. She had promised King Zog that she would take care of his sisters. Queen Geraldine does not break promises easily but she now felt that she could not take on the responsibility.

165

Prince Leka listened to his mother and said brusquely: "I will remedy this immediately. You are not going to stay here long and I suppose as I am your only child that we will live together. I will take care of the aunts. They do not want either you or me. We will go our way and we will help them to go their way."

It was not until the doctors decided that it would be a good idea to give Queen Geraldine male hormones that she began to improve and get her strength back. The first morning when she got out of bed she saw there were bars on the window. She called the maid who immediately fetched the doctor. He explained gently to the Queen why she had been placed in a mental hospital. She had gone down to 41 kilos and with her height of 1.77 metres she was a living skeleton. The doctors had previously feared for her nervous stability, but now she had recovered sufficiently she would be allowed to go out in the garden.

Six weeks after entering hospital Queen Geraldine was strong enough to leave. After spending a few days in Paris in her sister Virginia's apartment Prince Leka drove his mother to Madrid where her friend Queen Giovanna was waiting in her villa to take care of her.

Towards the end of the Albanian Queen's stay, Queen Giovanna arranged that she was again officially invited by the Vatican as this was the only way that she was permitted to enter Italy. Queen Geraldine was required to give her word to the Italian Government that she would give no Press conference. During her audience with Pope John XXIII she again asked for his support in putting forward her claim for war damages. As a result, Queen Geraldine had an interview with a senior minister who promised, "Si . . . Si . . . Si . . .," but once again her plea was in vain.

The Italian Press made the most absurd allegations about Queen Geraldine, writing that she had changed her religion to become a Muslim and even that Prince Leka now wanted to become a Catholic! The Queen was so angry that she persuaded an old Albanian minister to telephone to the Government saying that if these allegations were not immediately refuted in the Press, on the front pages next day, she would hold her own Press conference.

This was done, as clearly the Italians did not want me to talk; to tell how my personal money, left in the bank in Tirana, had

166

been confiscated and all the wedding gifts pillaged. I could have told how a friend bought pieces of our silver-gilt dinner services which were on sale on the Riviera and a great deal more.

Back in Paris I had one of the most painful experiences of my life. I decided to pawn my fourteen carat blue diamond engagement ring as I now needed money to arrange for a tomb on the King's grave. There had only been three hundred francs left in the bank account and I wanted to erect a monument over the King's grave of which all Albanians could be proud.

I took my ring, which my husband had bought from Cartier, off my finger, and pushed aside any memories as I sat in the offices of the *Mont de Pieté*. This was no time for tears. With infinite gentleness in her face the woman advised me to sell the ring outright which I did and even got a good price. My son was able to keep track of it for some years as he hoped one day to be able to buy it back for me. For whoever is wearing it now it is merely an extremely beautiful diamond ring but for me it encircles a lifetime of memories.

The rent and food in the house at Avlon, where the Princesses and four officers were living, still had to be paid. Taken care of all their lives by their brother, the Princesses simply had no idea about money and it never occurred to them to sell some of their jewellery to help Queen Geraldine with the finances. They had been brought up in a completely different world and had never learned to adjust to paying their own bills.

Realising that there was only one way to handle this delicate situation, Queen Geraldine decided to call on them with Prince Leka so that they could all discuss the future. She had not seen her sisters-in-law since the King's death as they had not visited her in hospital when she had been so ill. When she arrived at the villa at Avlon there were about a dozen other Albanian women present who, on seeing the Queen, fell to their knees and kissed her hand begging her to take them to live with her. "As Allah wishes", the Queen replied and went in to greet the Princesses, who were draped from head to foot in black and grouped like the chorus in a Greek tragedy.

Everyone sat down as Turkish coffee was served by one of the women just as it would have been before any formal discussion in Albania. While the Princesses sat in front all the rest of the women stood at the back near the door. Prince Leka and Colonel Martini were the only men present. In a calm voice Queen

Geraldine began talking: "You realise by the first of next month you will have to leave this house. As you know the King could not leave us anything so Leka and I were wondering if you would accept to live with us in an apartment in Paris."

Prince Leka, who had no idea of what his mother was going to say, blanched white as celery. Princess Senije, who had always been the spokeswoman and was the closest to King Zog, began pacing up and down the salon. Suddenly with a face filled with fury she screamed, "Under no condition will we live with you." The Queen looked at Prince Leka and he looked at her. They understood each other.

Prince Leka then began speaking, asking the Princesses if they really understood the financial situation. Their faces remained impassive as he explained that the Queen had found a pretty apartment and there was room for a living-in servant, a luxury which the Queen herself did not have at that time. Princess Senije answered that they did not need a servant as Princess Adele would do the housekeeping. It was then explained to them that Princess Adele, who was not present, was going to be taken care of by her own children as two of her daughters were married to rich husbands.

The Queen realised from their stony faces that the Princesses did not intend to come to any decision immediately, and rose to leave. As she reached the outside hall all the Albanian men and women who had been standing outside the door listening said to Queen Geraldine: "We have heard every word. We can be witnesses and we thank you for having made the right decision." In the car Prince Leka was cold and quiet, and when Colonel Salmani, who was sitting next to the driver, began to talk nervously, he ordered, "Be silent."

Now that the problem of the Princesses seemed to have been set aside, Queen Geraldine still had to face what to do with the entourage of officers and guards. Though he would be present Prince Leka felt that it was correct if his mother broke the painful news to them, as by now they had become like members of the family. Two of the officers went back to England and took up work, three were accepted in France as political refugees and were given a pension, and three went to America where the Queen found places for them. The only two that she could not accommodate were Colonel Salmani, who had been Court Chamberlain all those years and who, in any case, simply refused

168

to leave her, and one of the guards. The Princesses were at last found their own apartment in Cannes, with a servant to take care of them, and the Queen, Prince Leka and the two remaining Albanian men moved into an ugly little apartment in Paris.

The person who saved my sanity in that tumultous time was the Hungarian Countess Gisele Alvensleben de Schonborn, known to her friends as 'Gigi'. She collected me in her car every Friday afternoon and I stayed the weekend with her at her pretty villa near the golf course at St Nom la Bretche. The Countess died early in 1986 but I shall always remember how the warmth of our friendship increased with the years, like wine maturing.

For the first time since she had been married and to the fury of Colonel Salmani, Queen Geraldine now went out alone in the streets of Paris. It was like a bird being free from its cage after twenty years of captivity. A mixture of heady excitement and fear.

CHAPTER 18

As his mother lay struggling with her loneliness and despair in hospital Prince Leka had taken over all the family affairs: life has no mercy on the weak. Too ill to be told, Queen Geraldine was totally unaware that on 5th April more than seventy representatives of Albanian groups and colonies scattered around the world had gathered in Paris. Under the presidency of Admadis Bey Frasheri, a former diplomat, they had formed a commission of ten. They had come together to honour Prince Leka in his consecration as King of the Albanians – in contrast to King Zog who had been King of Albania.

There was no pomp, no ceremony. In a room in the Bristol Hotel in Paris, kissing the flag of his country, the twenty-one-year-old Prince, now an imposing six-feet-eight, became King Leka I, until that day when in a free country his people would declare their definitive will. Towering over the men around him he stood tall and proud. In a moving but strong voice he said: "I, Leka, King of Albania, at the moment at which I climb the Throne of the Kingdom of Albania and take into my hands the royal powers, swear before Almighty God to safeguard the unity, the independence of the State and territorial integrity of my country.

"I will safeguard the Constitution and I will act exactly in accordance with it and according to the Laws in force, while always having the good of the people in sight. May God help me.

"In this present moment when I take upon myself this heavy task, I appeal to all Albanian people for help to fulfil my mission as King of Albania with honour."

Royalist Albanians abroad are not rich, except for one or two families in America. They are simple, hardworking folk who have made great sacrifices to keep the spirit of the Monarchy alive. That their king had spent only three days of his life on Albanian soil had no bearing on their devotion to him. In his voice and demeanour they detected the willpower and unyielding strength of King Zog, who had brought pride and honour to a country

170

which previously had been only a wild mountainous land of feuding tribes.

One of the subjects now uppermost in the minds of Queen Geraldine and her son was King Leka's future.

I made him understand that no one would respect him if he did not work, as we had little money of our own and still had responsibilities to be met. I got in touch with the Krupps family in Hamburg and they offered to take him on as a trainee on a small salary on the condition that he stayed in Hamburg and learned to be an arms dealer. This had to be refused as I certainly could not live in Hamburg under these conditions. We still had six people dependent on us and this was not the right solution.

During the next few months in Paris, King Leka, who had liberty for the first time in his life, was never at home. Often, the Queen was worried for his safety, but a private detective was out of the question. She knew it was only a natural reaction against the anxiety of his father's illness, which had lasted eleven years. One night at eleven o'clock the doorbell of the Queen's apartment in Neuilly rang and she could hear Salmani speaking in his fractured French. He came to her room to tell her that there were two French officers outside who wanted to speak to her. She quickly put on a housegown and asked them into the salon. Colonel Salmani wanted to stay but Queen Geraldine told him in strong Albanian that he was to stay outside.

It seems that when necessary I can freeze people. It is not in my character but I sometimes get an injection of ice cold strength as if it comes from some higher power. They had come from the French Intelligence and Security Service and told me "We come like this as we don't want you to be molested. It is necessary to inform you that the young King cannot go about and come home at all hours of the night. There are four men, from the Albanian Embassy, at either end of the street day and night watching every move you and your son make. That the Albanian Embassy is causing you so much trouble worries us but we are not capable of guarding your son."

Without hesitation I replied, "He is over twenty-one. He is armed. He is never alone but always with friends and I cannot keep him caged in this small apartment." They got up and with great courtesy saluted and said, "We have done our duty and we can only leave him in the hands of God."

Naturally, next day when I had composed myself I told Leka of my midnight visit. His reply was typical and I said, "Now you talk to Colonel Salmani, as I said to him last night that I would not speak about the visit until I had told you."

Though the two Albanian officers in the household were furious that the young King should be given such liberty, after all they were responsible for his safety, Queen Geraldine was delighted when, after this incident Leka, his cousin Julia and two young friends decided to leave Paris and go by car to Spain and Morocco. While they were away the Queen, who had found a Hungarian servant to come for half a day to clean the flat and prepare the food, was still in deep mourning. The days were never long enough and the nights were everlasting. Her whole body ached with loneliness. Life without King Zog was void of purpose. Theirs had been a marriage of dedication and intensity and they had been rarely parted.

On his return, King Leka spoke enthusiastically to his mother about Spain. He had seen General Franco twice, had become friends with Prince Juan Carlos and stayed with his old friend King Simeon of Bulgaria with whom he grew up in Egypt and whom Queen Geraldine considers to be her second son. While there he had talks with an import and export firm who discussed the possibility of employing him and this was to be the deciding factor in the Queen's determination to move to Spain. She was also pleased with the friendly interest that General Franco had taken in her son. Leka had told her that after each of their meetings he had come away with the feeling that he had been in the presence of a great man whose opinion he valued. Up until General Franco's death, he and King Leka met about once a year. Queen Geraldine says that one of the most important things that the General did for her son was to teach him that as a leader of his nation he had to stand on his own feet and answer to no one except God, his people and his conscience.

The friendly ambience of Spain had so impressed King Leka that after long talks together he persuaded his mother that both for political and practical reasons it would be better for the family to move there and take up residence. He received a surprisingly warm reply when he wrote to General Franco, not only including an invitation for the King to take up residence in Spain but also

172

assuring him of all possible help in his battle to free Albania.

Upon the royal family's arrival in Spain, after a second meeting with General Franco, King Leka was granted "political asylum and extra-territorial rights" which enabled him to fly his own flag. The invitation naturally included Queen Geraldine and members of the King's household.

Hardly had the Queen settled in Spain in a small furnished villa that Queen Margarita of Bulgaria had found, than she was telephoned from the Prado Palace that General Franco's wife wished to call. Queen Geraldine returned her visit and met General Franco for the first and only time. He took the Queen and King Leka into his private library and talked to them for an hour. "I had the impression of a serious, severe and ascetic man and I could well believe that he worked eighteen hours a day for the good of his country," the Queen recalls.

Queen Geraldine was now living in the fashionable Puerta de Hierro area near the Royal Golf Course in a villa complete with a swimming pool and a garden. King Leka took over the task of employing five servants, all for the price they had paid for the Hungarian one in Paris who only worked half a day!

King Leka's ambitious plans for the export and import business crashed as the Spanish firm now insisted on his investing some capital which had not been mentioned in the earlier discussions. As there seemed no other possibilities for him in Spain mother and son decided that he turn to his father's friends, the Arab kings, where he knew that he would be welcomed. He made contact with Prince Faisal of Saudi Arabia where King Leka was treated like a son and introduced to leading Saudi Arabian businessmen before he returned to Spain with a handsome gift of money and the suggestion that he should return to Saudi Arabia very soon and that this time he should bring Queen Geraldine.

Life never runs serenely for long in the world of emotional Albanians. No sooner had Queen Geraldine begun to enjoy life surrounded by young people – the friends of Julia and Leka, and her god-daughter Melissa who had arrived from England to stay with her as her lady-in-waiting – than the two Albanian male members of the staff with not enough to occupy their time, fell out.

One day the Queen returned home to find that the guard was locked up in King Leka's office, where he kept his collection of arms, and that Colonel Salmani was stamping around, brandishing a revolver and vowing to kill him. It was purely a question of jealousy, boredom and hot Albanian blood.

> When I saw the situation I determined that I was not going to stay in the house. They had to sort it out for themselves. I told my son that Colonel Salmani must get a room for himself outside the villa, and while the air cleared I went to stay a week in Madrid with my Spanish friend Fina de Calderon.
>
> I was terribly annoyed that the Colonel would not allow me to pay any visits or go shopping anywhere unless I was always accompanied by a lady-in-waiting or preferably himself. It was a claustrophobic situation that I could not accept in this modern age.

The day King Leka returned from Saudi Arabia, filled with his own plans and excitement, Queen Geraldine told her son that she could not tolerate the situation any longer. King Leka told Colonel Salmani "Your disrespectful, outrageous attitude has to stop and I wish you to find a room elsewhere." The Colonel refused. The King then added, "All right, but you must apologise to the Queen and you will never interfere from this day on in her activities." Eventually, the situation returned to normal.

Accepting the invitation of Prince Faisal, Queen Geraldine accompanied King Leka shortly afterwards to Saudi Arabia, taking with her one of the last Napoleons which she had made into a bracelet for Princess Effat, Faisal's Turkish-born wife. In an antiquarian bookshop King Leka found a beautifully illuminated Koran which he presented as a gift to their host. On arrival the Albanian party, which because it was an official visit included Colonel Salmani and Madame Sula who acted as the lady-in-waiting, were met by the Minister of Protocol who asked the Queen whether she would not prefer to stay at the palace of Princess Effat? Queen Geraldine replied that she wanted to be near her son, and they were installed in a luxurious suite in the best hotel. It was lavishly furnished in satin and huge moquette upholstered furniture, but like many Arab houses everything had a forlorn look, and was in need of repair as there was not a single woman on the entire staff of this huge hotel. Around the suites were spacious balconies but the blinds were always kept drawn, not because of the sun, but as a precaution against outside eyes catching a glimpse of the Queen.

The day after our arrival I went with Leka to visit Prince Faisal in his simple villa. The Prince embraced Leka and took my hand. I thought him the most amazing personality, so wise, with such strong penetrating eyes that seemed to pierce through to one's soul.

Behind him stood deaf mutes with crossed swords and at his feet, squatting on the floor, was his interpreter. For Leka and I, armchairs were brought near the Prince so that we could talk without strain. The conversation was conducted in English, which the Prince understood and spoke well. I saw with pleasure that he loved Leka and I believe that it was the open honesty of a young man that made him say to me, "You have a very handsome, intelligent and good person as a son."

There is a timeless ageless quality about the Bedouin race. Despite their modern cities that have risen from the sands, certain moral attitudes have never changed. Their women are protected and their courtesy is from another age.

Prince Faisal had insisted that Queen Geraldine should stay a week in Saudi Arabia so that she could visit the various hospitals and schools that Princess Effat had founded. This also enabled the Queen to have time to receive members of the Albanian colony there, made up of Albanians who had left Egypt at the same time as she and the King, and had settled in Jeddah. When she set out one day to see an elderly bed-ridden couple the Queen was appalled when the official car in which they were travelling, and which was not curtained, was almost crashed into and abuse was hurled at her every time she stepped out of the car. She was bewildered until her lady-in-waiting, who spoke fourteen languages, explained: "They are angry because you are not veiled. You are a foreigner and your face is unveiled." It was during one of the critical times with the first influx of American and British women, whose husbands were employed there, and who were walking the *suqs* and streets in short dresses, bare arms and even shorts.

Within minutes a convoy of police converged on the Queen's car and her chauffeur and aide were severely admonished as she was escorted back to the hotel. In future she was never allowed to drive without an escort. When the Saudi officials heard who the Queen had intended to visit the old couple were immediately brought to her on stretchers. It was a meeting they would never forget.

As a Muslim, Prince Leka wanted to make the holy pilgrimage to Mecca. This caused a great deal of confusion in the hotel as there was not a suitable robe in white cotton in his size and no time for a tailor to make one. Prince Leka suddenly said, "Bring me a double bed sheet," which they managed to drape around him in the prescribed style. Accompanied by Colonel Salmani, and several Saudi Arabian friends, he made the *hadj*. He returned in the evening completely exhausted by his spiritual marathon. The Prince was to make two more such pilgrimages and today knows the Koran completely by heart. Just as Queen Geraldine never travels without her rosary, so her son takes a copy of the Koran.

This visit to Saudi Arabia was the beginning of a long-standing friendship between the Albanian King and Crown Prince Faisal. They spoke as brother to brother, and Prince Faisal invited the young King to talk freely about his problems.

Nevertheless it was with pleasure that mother and son returned home to Spain where, surrounded by beautiful young people Queen Geraldine began to live again, and through them laugh again. All her married life she had been surrounded by older people, and in latter years especially, shrouded with ill-health. It was as if she was reborn and as her new young friends preferred to speak Spanish even this gave her a fresh outlook on life. Apart from her son Leka and his friends she now had Melissa Bligh to talk to. The villa was filled with the sound of young laughter.

The youngsters took the Queen with them to see Flamenco dancing and singing in the old traditional restaurants. They explained Spanish history and culture to her. They discussed the Spanish Civil War, and spent long nights telling her of their own dreams.

I thought that going to a cocktail party at an embassy was like going to a ball in my youth. Just to put on party dresses again and make inconsequential light talk. It was like stepping into another world.

The embassy social round in Madrid was becoming more and more interesting and I went a great deal to the French Embassy and those of the Arab countries, especially Iran. So many beautiful women in glittering dresses. I took up bridge again and managed to become a good player which is one of my joys today.

As Leka was so often away, I took over his duties and dealt

with the vast amount of correspondence we received each week from all over the world. In these ways the emptiness was filled.

During that time Queen Geraldine met again the Marques Perico Pratt de Nantouiller and his wife Lily. With these good friends she dipped into the high society life at Marbella where they had a house and entertained on a grand scale. This Spanish resort on the Riviera had not yet gained its jet-set image of today and elegance still prevailed. There were private balls with two orchestras, five or six hundred guests, and dancing until dawn. As Gibraltar was still open it meant champagne and caviar at every party. It was the first time since 1938 that Queen Geraldine had danced, and she saw each ball through the eyes of an eighteen-year-old debutante. King Leka was now doing successful business and so for the first time she was able to spend money on couture clothes.

> You cannot believe what a thrill it was for me, because I had never spent much money on clothes. Though several times in my life I had couture clothes they had mostly been chosen by the King. When we left England to go to Egypt my husband wanted me to look my best and went and chose my dresses from a young English couturier, Norman Hartnell. Though essentially a masculine man, my husband was completely at ease in the world of women's fashion and always admired his sisters' lavish wardrobes.

Some months later King Leka, who had been travelling a great deal in the Middle East, told his mother that he must make another trip to Saudi Arabia on business. It was the time of the Yemen war and for weeks he was unable to write or communicate with his mother.

Eventually Queen Geraldine had a telephone message that the Saudi Ambassador would like to call on her. He arrived and said, "I have a message from the King for you. He says that you are not to worry as your son will not be permitted to go to the Yemen war. He has been seen training for it, running round the hotel in full kit at four o'clock in the morning. In any case he is far too tall for guerilla war and there is no way we could take care of your giant son."

> Whenever he was away I was never idle. I interested myself in the administration of the building of homes and orphanages. I

had this longing that if ever I went back to Albania, at least I would be fully trained in the modern administration of social health services.

In April 1968 Queen Geraldine had been in Switzerland to see a specialist and heard that Queen Victoria Eugene of Spain was dying in a clinic in Lausanne. When she arrived at Lisbon, where she was going to stay with Queen Giovanna of Bulgaria, she found her waiting at the airport dressed in deep mourning. Queen Giovanna greeted Queen Geraldine with the news that the Queen of Spain had indeed just died.

As royalty the world over always travel with black clothes, in case of suddenly being plunged into mourning, Queen Geraldine went up to her bedroom and slipped into a black silk dress before going downstairs to speak with Queen Giovanna about the situation. As soon as they sat down, Queen Giovanna said "You should leave tomorrow and return to Lausanne where the Queen is to be buried."

> We had not decided what to do, as we drank a cup of hot soup, when suddenly the telephone rang and it was Leka. "Where are you ringing from", I asked him as I never knew where he was in the world. "Cannes", came the reply, "not one but two of the Princesses, Senije and Myzejen, have died this evening of heart attacks." I screamed and Queen Giovanna took over the telephone. Leka explained to her that the third Princess Maxhide was ill with circulation troubles.

During the last years in Cannes the Princesses had become wraith-thin, their deep-sunk eyes framed with hair as black as a raven's wing. Though King Zog had sent them to finishing schools in France and given them an educational trip to America, they always remained indifferent to the outlook of the Western woman, except in the luxurious clothes they wore. The days, weeks, months and years had slipped by drinking black coffee and smoking cigarettes in the seclusion of their apartment. Only occasional visits to the Casino in Monte Carlo broke the monotony of their rigid lives. When King Zog had died they had been robbed of their reason for living and never recovered from the shock. Perhaps of the whole family, Mussolini's invasion had brought the most suffering to the six Princesses in this tragic Albanian saga.

178

Princess Maxhide was never to know of the death of her sisters. In those last weeks, when she lay in a clinic in Nice which King Leka had arranged, it was as if a grey veil had descended over her eyes and mind. She was to die just three weeks later.

Queen Geraldine told her son that she would go to Cannes immediately but Queen Giovanna took the telephone and explained that Queen Geraldine was unwell and could hardly stand. The King immediately replied: "Mother please . . . don't come."

The Princesses were taken by hearse from Cannes all the way to Paris. Behind them was a car brimming over with flowers tied with scarlet and black ribbons, the national colours of Albania. King Leka, who had to leave immediately for South Africa on business, had made all the funeral arrangements. In death the Princesses would be beside King Zog, the man they worshipped. Countess Virginia Apponyi travelled from Munich to represent Queen Geraldine and Colonel Salmani the King.

It was an emotional scene in the cemetery at Thiais as buses came from Brussels, Sweden, Germany, Belgium and all over France, filled with ordinary Albanians. It was not as if they had personally known the Princesses, who had always led lonely, insulated lives, but to their countrymen they were a link with the past. The Princesses represented an era when Albania had been brought out of the past by the remarkable achievements of King Zog. They were part of Albania's first, and last, Royal Family and that was all that mattered.

Thinking that Countess Apponyi was their Queen they fell on their knees at her feet, amid the wailing of grief. The only sound in the heavy cemetery air was their calling the names of Queen Geraldine and King Leka, over and over again.

Queen Geraldine and her sisters-in-law had never been close, they could not be. Their worlds were centuries apart and the Princesses' jealousy of the beautiful young Hungarian who had captured the love of their brother was of paranoic dimensions. The Queen could never understand the circumscribed, old-fashioned lives they led. She was always a modern woman, interested in the world around her, determined to play her part in any endeavour which might one day be of use to the country she had lost.

She became active in the work of the International Red Cross and sometimes travelled on their behalf.

One of the countries which interested me most was Switzerland. Everything is so fresh but the only thing I miss there is a soul. In 1971 I was asked by a firm in Madrid, who were working in conjunction with the Red Cross, to represent them on a business visit to Iran.

I was to be paid for my services in smoothing the way for Swiss business contracts and was delighted to have the chance to earn money in an honourable way. In Iran I was in direct contact with the Empress and her mother, Madame Diba, a delightful lady whose life was filled with the joy of her grandchildren and helping her daughter in the work of modernising Iran. They were both daughters of their country.

The Empress and her mother needed equipment for the hospitals they were planning, both big and small. In Iran they had the oil money to do everything that I had dreamed of for Albania so many years before.

Born plain Farah Diba, the Empress came from a traditional Persian family and had been brought up to realise, in the modern way, that she would have to earn her own living and take her place in the world of men. She went to the French Lycée in Teheran, and then to Paris to study art and architecture. It was in the second year of her studies that she was to meet the Shah who had spent ten years in trying to find the right wife to replace the lovely Empress Soraya who could not bear him any heirs. It was a love story with many similarities to that of King Zog and Queen Geraldine. It is said, that only years later did Empress Farah pluck up courage to ask the Shah why he had chosen her from all the hundreds of eligible women. "I am touched by your simplicity," he told her. It is a reply that King Zog may well have given, describing his Geraldine.

Much has been written and spoken about the Empress Farah. The first time I saw her she was still young, filled with vitality and goodness which radiated from her. She had just completed transforming an old army barracks into an orphanage. The touching detail was that she made the whole concept look welcoming. Half of the building was for the baby boys with everything in blue and the other half for girls, all in pink.

During a family dinner I had with them, the Shah, who had a great sense of humour, teased his wife in French and asked her what were her great aspirations. Full of enthusiasm her face was buttercup bright as she replied "I want to take over

180

everything that is to do with health but, oh dear I love our country's art. Don't forget what I did at Ispahan."

The Shah smiled sadly and answered "Don't forget that the first thing we must think of is bread for the people."

When Queen Geraldine had arrived in Teheran, Kadar, the head of the Communist government in Hungary was on a surprise visit and as it was a diplomatic embarrassment for the Queen to meet him, she and her sister Virginia who accompanied her, and King Leka were flown to Ispahan where they were given rooms in this dream palace. The Empress had been the inspiration for collecting all the great artists of modern Iran to create this architectural wonder of the modern world.

Queen Geraldine had her business meetings and much was planned. However, the whole operation was to take place over a period of three years and because of the downfall of the Shah and the Pahlavi dynasty these plans never came to fruition.

While he was in Iran, King Leka was to be involved with a business set up by the Shah, who wanted to help his young 'cousin'. The deal included supplying mobile cranes for the Ports and Shipping Authority of Iran and as these contracts were very large, King Leka was able to make a reasonable profit.

As a result of this successful deal King Leka gave his mother a set of court jewellery to replace those which she had had to sell over the years. It was a handsome set of a tiara of sapphires and diamonds, a brooch and matching ring with the head of a lioness as Leo is the Queen's birthsign. Apart from an eternity ring set with diamonds this is the ring that she never takes off her finger. An interesting heavy ring, it is one of the first things you notice on meeting Queen Geraldine.

CHAPTER 19

On 10th October 1975, King Leka was married to the Australian Susan Cullen-Ward, whom he had met seventeen years before at a dinner party in Sydney. Their courtship was a long one, set against the landscape of three countries – Australia, England, where they renewed their friendship, and Spain where Susan Cullen-Ward had gone to study art after a course in interior and industrial design in Sydney. Her parents, Mr and Mrs Alan Cullen-Ward had a property near Parkes, New South Wales, but now lived in Drummoyne.

> Susan was among the young crowd that Leka went round with in Sydney. I liked her immediately when he brought her to meet me in Madrid. She had a natural charm and an honesty and directness about her that was very attractive to me. Her face is classic, fine-boned, with long blonde streaked hair. Her presence is serious and dignified and I thought she had all the qualifications to by my son's wife.
>
> I immediately noticed a devotion and admiration for whatever Leka discussed. She became like one of the family. She took a studio, was in and out of the house, and very soon I began to love her. I kept silent about her to Leka because I knew that if I suggested that Susan was the perfect mate for him he would have rebelled. I kept my thoughts to myself until one day Leka came back from Teheran with a diamond engagement ring in an oval form. Tears came into my eyes when I thought of the immense blue-white diamond one that I had received. He had hardly arrived and shown it to me before disappearing out of the door. An hour later the happiest telephone call came. Their voices were vibrant with joy. "Oh ma'am", Susan said, "I am so happy and though it is late we are coming over immediately to hug you."

The official announcement of the engagement had to wait as there were many problems to be solved. Although there was no official parliament in exile, King Leka still needed to obtain the goodwill and consent of the old leaders scattered around the

182

world, especially in America. All this took time and a great deal of correspondence. When at last Queen Geraldine was able to announce it officially the engagement was celebrated with a grand luncheon party for fourteen in the Royal Golf Club at Puerta de Hierro which included Prince Juan Carlos and Princess Sophia.

My main concern over the next weeks was how I was going to provide a wedding suitable not only for my son and future daughter-in-law but for all the Albanians who had remained so faithful to us over all those years in exile.

Knowing that such arrangements would take a long time I immediately began writing to all my relatives round the world. At that time there was a wave of hatred against Spain from all over Europe so that many of my vast family, survivors of the last war, wrote: "We dare not come." They were living as refugees in the Argentine, Vienna or in Germany. Delighted as they were to hear our news they also explained that they could not come unless their passages were paid. Those nearer at hand like France, Italy, Belgium and Switzerland were not such a problem. Leka looked over the whole of the Albanian invitations, assisted by his men. He arranged to invite two religious heads from America, Imam Isa Hoxha of New York, and Imam Vehbi Ismail of Detroit.

Queen Geraldine and King Leka quickly came to the point when they realised that the money available would not be sufficient. Though the King had saved some from his business deals, and Susan Cullen-Ward had a little money of her own, it was still necessary to find a great deal more. In Spain, to take a mortgage on a house usually takes anything up to six months to arrange but, with the help of a sympathetic government official, Queen Geraldine got one in twenty-four hours. It was a small sum which she knew that she could pay off fairly easily over the next three years.

The King had decided to have the civil wedding in Biarritz so that he could be married under French law, the nearest to the Albanian one which King Zog had adapted from the Napoleonic Code and because of this there could be no question of the legality of the marriage in the future. This was to be followed by a Muslim ceremony and a reception for 2,000 in Spain. Apart from Prince Juan Carlos and Princess Sophia (General Franco was then still alive) the Marquess Carlos Navarro had told the Queen that all the Government with their wives would be present at the wedding reception which was to take place in a beautiful old walled Moorish Palace near Toledo belonging to Queen Geraldine's friend, Fino de Calderon, the Spanish painter and writer.

Three days before the wedding, the royal party set out by car from Madrid for Biarritz. It was composed of Queen Geraldine, King Leka, his fiancée Susan, her parents, Mr and Mrs Cullen-Ward and her brother and sister, three Albanian officers and some Spanish friends. They were extremely worried about how they were going to cross the frontier, as this was the time when there were protest marches up and down the Champs Elysée demonstrating against Franco and Spain, but all went well.

Once in Biarritz they were installed in the Palace Hotel, that stylish wedding cake perched over the sea, the favourite holiday ground of the Duke and Duchess of Windsor. On the day of the wedding, Queen Geraldine met an old friend, the American-born Peggy, Duchess of Nemours in the street and invited her to attend. The mayor of Biarritz, Monsieur Guy Petit, had agreed to conduct the marriage but had requested that it should be strictly private and that the Press were not to know until after the ceremony. He was frightened that the Albanian Embassy would make a protest which would have been upsetting for everyone, and especially the bride and Queen Geraldine. The mayor arranged his office with flowers, the bride wore a cream dress and jacket and the service was simple and dignified.

In his address to the bridal couple the mayor spoke of the link between Albania and France and of the fact that King Zog had been invested with the Order of the Legion d'Honneur. Monsieur Petit hoped that King Leka and his bride would have many children and be able to return to their country. The civil ceremony was followed by an intimate Muslim one in King Leka's suite where Queen Suzani (the Albanian translation of Susan) was the only woman present. Queen Geraldine was by then fully occupied in finalising details for the reception in Toledo. The wedding luncheon which followed lasted until six o'clock in the evening and some time afterwards Queen Geraldine was called to the telephone to hear a frantic Fino de Calderon speaking from Toledo. She said that she had received anonymous letters that bombs were going to be placed on her estate if she went ahead with the wedding reception because of

184

the royal guests and high-ranking Spaniards who were going to be present.

It was midnight before Queen Geraldine could track down the restaurateur José Valentine who had been engaged to take care of the catering. On her arrival back in Madrid eighteen hours later, a proud and beaming Senor Valentine took Queen Geraldine to see his own charming garden restaurant near the village of Illescas. It was not a Moorish Palace, nor the Royal Golf Club, but the restaurant had an Arcadian charm of its own and had space enough for the 2,000 guests. Instead of tables laid with silver-gilt and Sèvres they were dotted with dozens of posies of multi-coloured flowers, and the restaurant was transformed into a bower of flowers . . . young and joyful.

In the last-minute switching of plans two thousand guests had to be advised, as well as a complete re-organisation of the buses and cars that were to take the guests to the new venue, a mammoth task. Through television, radio, newspapers and telephoning Queen Geraldine personally took over the task of making sure that everyone knew. At midnight on the night before the celebrations the head of the Spanish Government telephoned Queen Geraldine to explain that General Franco was very ill, and that due to the political unrest the whole of the government could not appear at the celebration: there would not be sufficient time to arrange security. A quarter of an hour later Prince Juan Carlos telephoned her and said: "Auntie I am sure that you have been expecting this call from me: we have been deliberating all night and as the government ministers are not coming they have asked me not to appear at any celebration at the moment."

It was a feeling of disappointment but at the same time a sense of relief. I was terrified of anything happening to Prince Juan Carlos. I had enough to worry about in the person of my own son.

I nearly went out of my mind, so many people became hurt. The Iranian ambassador in Madrid was very angry because he had telephoned that he was delivering the wedding gift of the Shah and Empress. The person who had answered the telephone did not speak any language except Albanian. "A representative of the Emperor cannot be treated in such a way", he claimed. It was arranged that next morning I would receive him at ten o'clock at my villa and he brought a beautiful gift of turquoise earrings and a brooch from the Shah and Empress Farah.

185

In a pretty gesture to her new country Queen Susan had decided herself that she would like to wear a traditional Albanian wedding dress for the reception. Her parents had brought with them from Australia the family dressmaker, who was shown a photograph of an Albanian wedding dress and a scrap of authentic embroidery. Her clever fingers were able to create the white silk under-dress over which was worn a gold embroidered black coat incorporating the double eagle emblem of Albania. Round her neck, hanging on a golden chain, she wore a miniature of Sadije Zogu, mother of King Zog. King Leka had chosen to wear the uniform of colonel of the Royal Albanian Guards with the Order of Skanderbeg, which had been initiated by King Zog as the country's official decoration. Queen Geraldine looked stunningly beautiful in an azure blue silk dress that had been created and given to her by the Spanish couturier, Marble Junior. For the last time she wore all the new court jewels which King Leka had had made in Teheran. On her first visit to the *finca* where the newly-weds were making their home Queen Geraldine gave all the jewellery to Queen Susan except the tiger-headed ring.

International royal families were represented by Grand Duke Vladimir and the Grand Duchesses Leonida and Maria; Queen Farida and her two daughters; King Simeon and Queen Margarita of Bulgaria; Prince Michael of Orleans and Princess Beatrice of the Netherlands. The Duke and Duchess of Seville, and the Duchess of Cadiz were among the top Spanish society also present. Albanians had come from all over the world and included two shepherds from New Zealand who had spent their life savings to see their King wed. From Calabria and Sicily they came, wearing their traditional Albanian costumes. There are whole villages in these regions which still speak an old Albanian patois which even Queen Geraldine finds hard to understand.

It had become something very special – a folk wedding, so different from my own. Instead of the ornate Hungarian and Austrian court uniforms many of these guests were dressed in colourful national costume. Apart from myself there were two other Queens in exile, Farida of Egypt and Giovanna of Bulgaria. Cables from all over the world were read out including one from Queen Elizabeth of Great Britain. The wedding cake was cut by my new daughter-in-law with Leka's sword and then to my horror I saw that the young people had

186

begun to dance. We had been especially asked by the government not to dance, but how can you stop the exuberance of joyful young people. Leka allowed them to dance for about twenty minutes before the orchestra played the national anthem of Spain and the Royal Albanian one.

King Leka and Queen Susan left for their honeymoon in the South of France and on their return the newly-weds went to their *finca* outside Madrid on which they had paid a deposit guaranteed for them by the Bank of Oman. A carpenter had been called to the *finca* to build shelves for a collection of small exquisite objects that they had both collected over the years. Queen Susan had just arranged them when the whole thing collapsed, and most of these precious antiquities were broken. "I have a feeling that Sue felt this to be an ill-omen about the house, though she never spoke of it," Queen Geraldine recalls.

Within months there were two upheavals that were to change the history of Spain. Queen Geraldine and her son and daughter-in-law were sitting in the garden of her villa when they heard a terrible explosion. They immediately turned on the radio to hear the news that a bomb had been thrown into the car in which General Carrero Blanco was travelling. He was the President who had been entrusted to continue with General Franco's government, which Prince Juan Carlos was to inherit. Queen Geraldine believes that this horrifying bloodshed certainly hastened General Franco's dying agony.

For exiles like Queen Geraldine it meant a breakdown of the law and order that Franco had instigated and a change in the whole moral structure of Spain. All three in her family not only attended the funeral service of the General, but were present at the crowning ceremony of the King Juan Carlos in the Cathedral in Madrid.

The young King looked magnificent, with his family surrounding him and it gave a warm feeling to all of Spain and Spain's friends that such a handsome, virile and steady young man took over without any bloodshed after three years of the worst civil war known in Europe and forty-eight years of different kinds of dictatorship.

All these activities tired Sue emotionally. This girl from Australia had suddenly become part of the solemn pageantry and the maelstrom of Europe. She had her first miscarriage and it took her a long time to recover.

CHAPTER 20

In March 1977, King Leka had two important business deals to be completed in Thailand and, in honour of a promise that he had made, suggested that Queen Susan should accompany him. When his business was completed in Bangkok he planned to take her into the interior where the real Thai people live and where they could see this gentle race of beautiful people in their own surroundings. Queen Susan was on her way to Australia and this was to be a welcome break in her journey.

Before leaving London, King Leka had bought a collection of guns to give to his hosts, such as the King of Thailand and various ministers and heads of departments and also for Saudi Arabian friends, as he planned to go there straight from Thailand, while Queen Susan visited her parents. The guns were bought legally in London and were to be taken to Thailand to be engraved in gold as presentation pieces to the various recipients. It was merely an old Albanian custom that King Leka was honouring.

After spending two weeks in Bangkok on business the King planned to make a trip to Northern Thailand, the Chiang Mai and Chiang Rai areas. It was to be part tourist and part professional interest as several highly skilled military units were operating in these areas, and the King wanted to see for himself how such units are trained and if they differed from European training methods.

During the time he was there he visited several interesting border areas and the border patrol camps where he was given some surplus operational and communications equipment which was desperately needed by the Free Albanian units.

After several more days visiting the various patrol units, under an official military escort, King Leka returned to Bangkok with a Highway Police Patrol escort so as to prevent any possible trouble on the Chiang Mai-Bangkok road. It was normal practice that the Highway Patrol should escort a diplomatic guest.

On arrival in Bangkok the King and Queen went to stay with their close friends, Colonel Willis H. Bird and his wife who belongs to a prominent Thai family. Colonel Bird has lived in Bangkok since the end of World War II and is a highly respected member of the local community. Two days later Mrs Bird received a telephone call from a member of the police, whom she had every reason to trust, who said: "The wrong elements have a full list of the equipment King Leka received in Chiang Mai. They insist on taking it back and to avoid the embarrassing situation of having to raid your house it should be dumped in some place where it can be found."

Not wishing to cause any trouble to his hosts King Leka did this, with the exception of the weapons that he had bought in England as gifts. The equipment was duly picked up by the police but despite all the assurances made in the telephone call they did not honour their promise and raided Colonel Bird's house. King Leka, His Highness the Shan Prince and Captain Khemwong Mengrai, who was acting in the capacity of aide de camp were arrested.

That the whole operation had been stage managed very carefully was evident as every newspaper in Thailand not only sent a reporter to the police station where the King was taken but also to observe and write about the raid on the house.

At six o'clock in the morning on 1st April, Queen Geraldine was telephoned from Bangkok by William Bird Jnr. to tell her that her son had been arrested on an arms charge. He told her that the authorities had refused to recognise the King's diplomatic immunity, despite his being in possession of a valid diplomatic visa from the Thai Government. He asked that she should immediately contact the necessary authorities in Madrid to clarify the situation.

In moments of actual crisis Queen Geraldine has a remarkably clear head. She does not panic or over-react. She just gets on with what is to be done in the immediate future. By half past eight, after several abortive attempts, she got through to the Zarzuela Palace but was told that she could not speak to either King Juan Carlos or Queen Sophia. Every Friday in Madrid there is always a meeting of Government ministers, presided over by the King and he is always incommunicado on that day.

At noon Queen Geraldine called on the Thai Ambassador, who was unaware of what kind of visa King Leka was using, although the Embassy must have got clearance from Bangkok, and appeared not to know anything about the situation. Queen

Geraldine insisted that he send a cable to his government to find out what was happening to her son.

All that day Queen Geraldine sat telephoning her friends throughout the world. She called Teheran to try to speak to the Shah only to be told that he and his family were in Kisch. However, the Iranian ambassador in London was able to make contact with the Ministry of Foreign Affairs in Iran and to get a message through to the Shah.

English family friends, Colonel Charles Inigo Jones in London and Julian Amery, who was returning from a holiday in Zermatt, were both contacted by the Queen. Colonel Inigo Jones immediately went to see Julian Amery and discussed the possibility of alerting those American senators who had proved so often to be friends of Free Albania and Julian Amery promised the Queen that he would speak to the Secretary of Foreign Affairs in London to ask him to make inquiries and the Thai Ambassador who was a personal friend.

When Queen Geraldine telephoned the Jordanian Embassy she was told that there were only two Arab countries who had embassies in Thailand and these were Egypt and Saudi Arabia, therefore the Jordanians could not help. By the afternoon Queen Geraldine had spoken four times to Colonel Bird to check whether any of her actions were having any effect in Bangkok. By evening she was beginning to get desperate.

All that was known was that King Leka and His Highness Captain Khemwong Mengrai had been moved from the police station to Bangsui Police Station where they were being held. The open cage in which the King was held was generally used for overnight arrests, and the only food was either bought from hawkers in the street, or supplied by Colonel Bird and his family. Other people were held in the cage: a variety of transients ranging from children to hardened criminals of both sexes. The only special privilege granted to King Leka was access to the station telephone.

In desperation Queen Geraldine again telephoned the Royal Palace in Madrid and through the kindness of the young girl on the switchboard was put through to King Juan Carlos and Queen Sophia who assured her that they were doing all they could to secure King Leka's release. They told her that they had sent orders to the Spanish Ambassador in Thailand but as Queen Geraldine was quick to point out, "This is not enough." If the

190

Shah could personally involve himself then it would be natural if King Juan Carlos did the same. This was purely the reaction of a desperate mother fighting to rescue her son.

The following morning at nine o'clock Queen Sophia telephoned Queen Geraldine to say that King Juan Carlos had given an order to the Minister of Foreign Affairs, Senor Marcelino Creja, to cable the Minister of Foreign Affairs in Thailand to find out the exact situation.

Monday was a bad day. Colonel Bird had telephoned Queen Geraldine to say that the situation was getting worse. She could no longer get in touch with King Juan Carlos as he and the Queen had left Madrid. By now the world press were on to the story with headlines such as "King Kept in a Cage" and such like. Even Colonel and Mrs Bird found that official doors were being closed in their faces. Highly placed people in the Military Government, who had at first been helpful in trying to clear up the situation, now began to back out of any involvement.

As King Leka was to say later: "There seemed to be a powerful force blocking any attempts to free us. This force became more and more apparent as the days went by."

The situation had become so complex that all efforts were now being made to pevent any direct contact between King Leka and Colonel Bird although Queen Susan had been permitted to speak on the telephone to the King on two occasions. She had obtained the telephone number of the prison via members of the Albanian community and was also given reassuring information of the King's health from members of the Australian Press.

With time passing Queen Geraldine then decided to call on the help of King Leka's proven friends, the Saudi Arabians. The Saudi ambassador in Madrid saw her immediately and promised to notify Crown Prince Fahd, as well as the Saudi Arabian Embassy in Bangkok, giving instructions that if bail was granted, the Saudis would pay it.

Mrs Bird answered Queen Geraldine's call to Bangkok with this latest news, but assured her that no bail would be required and there was now a gleam of hope that the prisoners would be released. Through sheer perseverance by Colonel Bird's son, Lieutenant Pinyo Vajaradesa was reached and he immediately called the Police Commissioner to enquire why such an action had been taken against the King and a Siamese Prince. Unable to get a straight answer from either the Police or Foreign Office,

General Pinyo took the matter to General Krainsak Chamanan, deputy Commander-in-Chief of the Thai Armed Forces, who immediately ordered the Foreign Minister to his house. General Krainsak had been away from Bangkok on a golfing holiday hosted by one of the Western Powers and, strangely enough, at a club where the facilities did not include a telephone.

As King Leka and Prince Khemwong Mengrai were no longer at the Bangsui Police Station, but had been transferred to the civilian Lahu Special Penitentiary, the order for their release had to go through a Supreme Court Judge. It was at midnight on 5th April, King Leka's birthday, that he was finally released and the Shan Prince two days later.

Like gigantic shock waves Albanian communities around the world had been aroused by the indignity of what had happened to their King. Thai embassies and consulates were forced to shut down because of the demonstrations and militant threats by the Albanian communities. The situation became particularly acute in Australia, Belgium and Paris. Queen Susan had been telephoned by the Australian Commonwealth Police and asked to try to control the Albanian Community. She replied that she was unable to do anything due to the intense emotional feelings engendered by the incident, but she promised to speak to the King's representatives.

Following his ordeal, King Leka continued his stay in Thailand as the guest of General Krainsak, where an intensive post mortem was carried out on the whole bizarre affair. It became clear to everyone that some powerful forces had been at work to compromise King Leka and try to paralyse the activity of his military organisation of Free Albanians. There had been rumours, which were never disproved, that there was to have been an attempt to assassinate King Leka by poisoning while he was being held captive. To this day it remains a mystery as to who was behind this incredible blunder on the part of the Thai Government.

About a week before King Leka arrived in Thailand there had been an attempted government coup, and on 20th April General Hiranyasiri was executed for his part in this affair. It is possible that King Leka's arrest was a final gesture to discredit the existing Thai Government. The leaders of the coup must have known that the Thai royal family were on holiday at their palace in Chang Mai, the Army commander was out of Bangkok and it appeared that part of the police force was under the influence of the anti-Government element. By alerting the Press to King Leka's impending arrest they might have hoped to discredit the Government even more.

As no one claimed responsibility for King Leka's arrest those members of the Government who were in Bangkok at the time did not seem anxious to be associated with any action to effect his release. In the late 70's the Governments fell with great regularity whenever disagreement arose over defence, financial expenditure or the Far East policy. These coups have never been against the Monarchy and they, in their turn, were extremely careful never to become involved.

It was known that at the time Thailand was under tremendous pressure from Communist guerillas and had the country made more enemies it would have made the situation more precarious still.

As the ambassador of one foreign country in Bangkok was to say at the time: "If this can happen to King Leka, who holds a diplomatic visa, how reliable are our credentials as embassy officials in Thailand now?"

As soon as King Leka was released, the Thai Government did everything possible to amend the blunder and the King, who had been officially accepted to visit the country on this and at least ten other visits, was flown out of the country by Royal Jordanian Airlines with a friendly send-off by the Thai military authorities who had continued to assure his safety until such time as he left Thailand.

For Queen Geraldine the whole experience had been traumatic. It was to take some months before the horror of it all could be erased from her mind and she regained her nerves. From that day on, every time King Leka is travelling to a foreign country, she is never at ease and sits by the telephone awaiting his call: "Mum . . . its Leka."

193

CHAPTER 21

Although she has spent all her life in Europe, Queen Geraldine has never forgotten her American roots. And in recent years it has become like a second home to her as it contains the largest colony of Albanians outside their own country. A colony of devoted loyalists invited King Leka to visit them and suggested that he bring Queen Geraldine and Queen Susan with him. They arrived in New York on 30th May 1976, but after a few days went straight on to Toronto and to Petersborough which has the largest Albanian community in Canada.

In one day it was scheduled that Queen Geraldine should visit two old peoples' homes, an orphanage and a hospital. She was accompanied by Queen Susan, the wife of the mayor of Toronto, and by leading Albanian women. It was tea-time when the Queen arrived at the old peoples' home and sitting on the lawn in their Sunday best were all the old ladies. Their delight was almost overwhelming as they saw the Queen coming towards them with outstretched hands and that very special smile, and greeting them warmly. Though the years have been everlastingly turbulent there is no sign of this stress marking the Queen's face and in addition to the mystique that surrounds all royalty, Queen Geraldine has a special charisma.

> Seeing the old Canadian women did not upset me as they looked alive and interested in life around them but when I saw the vacant, hopeless expression on the men's faces I felt desperately sad. They had given up all hope, all reason for living. They were impassive as though carved in wood. In a clear voice so that everyone could hear, I said, "I hope never to hear that an Albanian family cannot take care of its own old people."

Towards the end of her stay Queen Geraldine made a suprise visit to Washington that no one, not even her son, knew about. She wanted to meet for herself some of the official and private friends that her son had made over the many years he had been visiting

America. At her request the American press left her to enjoy her visit in private and to this day she is profoundly grateful to them. Despite this, the Queen had hardly arrived in her room when Baron Blomberg, who had been acting in the capacity of a public relations officer for Free Albania for several years, arrived with lists of people who wanted to meet the Queen. It was more than she could have physically managed in a month and certainly not in four days.

On the first morning the Queen was received at the Capitol by three senators and on the second morning three ministers, and every midday the party went to the Army and Navy Club. The Queen remembers these gentlemen as being "charming, cultivated men but they did not know one thing about Albania." The exception was Senator Jesse Helms, who has never wavered over the years in his determination that it is the duty of the Free World to rid Albania of communism.

When Queen Geraldine arrived back in New York, Albanians came all day and every day to pay their respects to her, each clutching a small envelope of money which was all recorded by Colonel Salmani and went to the Free Albanian cause. The Queen did not see or handle a cent of it except a gift of five hundred dollars from an old Albanian lady who insisted that the Queen should use it for herself to buy something personal.

Of all the cities that Queen Geraldine visited in America, outside of Washington, she liked Houston the best. "The people are welcoming, genial and well-mannered and I felt at home."

On a later trip to New York in 1979 visiting the Albanian communities Queen Geraldine got up at six o'clock one morning to go to one of the poorest, sleaziest areas in the Bronx where Mother Teresa of Calcutta had opened a "meditative house". Everyone wanted to be part of the Queen's visit so in the end there were five cars full of men – Muslim and Christians. When the party arrived Mother Teresa and a young nun were standing in the small door to greet the Queen.

> I found Mother Teresa so tiny. I wanted to kiss her hand and she wanted to kiss mine so we were both rather embarrassed. This frail wisp of a woman who only seemed to come up to my waist was dressed in a simple grey cotton habit and wore a silver cross. Her worn calloused feet were encased in slip-on sandals of brown leather.

It was Mother Teresa's face that I remember best. Her sallow skin was not wrinkled but etched in deep grooves like leather. A face that showed all the suffering of the world. Her eyes were bird bright and intelligent, with the light of God in them.

Born Agnes Gonxha Bojaxhin in 1910 in the city of Skopje near Kossova which was then Albanian territory before being ceded to the Yugoslavs after the last war, Mother Teresa was the daughter of a grocer. She joined the Sisters of Loretta and worked in Ireland before going to India, and it was while she was principal of St. Mary's High School there that Mother Teresa found her true calling in life. It was to the under-privileged in India that she decided to dedicate her body and mind. She created fifty schools, orphanages and houses for the poor there, and in 1952 founded the Pure Heart for Dying Destitutes. In 1979 she was awarded the Nobel Prize for her services to mankind and used the money to further her work among the destitute of India. She is now a world famous daughter of Albania.

The home that she opened in New York was different from all others. Ever the realist, she explained to Queen Geraldine: "New York does not need physical help. It is no use my going with my little basket like I do in Calcutta. Christ gave me this inspiration to open a house of prayer for all these millions of souls who have desolate moments."

The basis of the work in New York was a seven-line phone-in service where desperate people could ask for help. They were either talked to on the telephone or one of Mother Teresa's experienced helpers would set out and find them wherever they were, bringing words of comfort and practical help.

In England this kind of work is done by the Samaritans, for whom the Duchess of Kent mans the telephones from time to time, and in Monaco Princess Caroline instigated a similar service for the young girls and boys on the Cote d'Azur called "J'Ecoute" where if they were at odds with life and susceptible to drug temptations, they could phone in to an understanding, anonymous ear, often the Princess herself.

With customary Albanian hospitality Mother Teresa found places for all our party and gave us fresh bread, fetta cheese and coffee. She told the men to look around as she wanted to talk to me alone. We sat down in the corner of the room and she explained to me many things about her life's work and then looking directly into my face said, "I pray every day for you and your son."

At that moment I felt a kind of comfort, a deep peace and an enlightenment, for it is Mother Teresa's prayers that protect Leka from his would-be assassins. No one could ever be in the presence of Mother Teresa and not feel her strength and stillness. Emotionally inspired, I said: "I would like to come to India and help you in your work."

"You can help in many ways but not in India. God gives his holy strength in many ways to many different souls," was her direct reply.

With her all-seeing eyes Mother Teresa did not have to be told Queen Geraldine's history of illness. She only saw before her a body of such delicate proportions that it could not stand the degradation of the poor districts of Calcutta. Mother's need is for young, strong, virile volunteers who can lift the rotten flesh of the dying, and face the foul air, without vomiting. In Mother Teresa's infinite wisdom she also knew there is another role in life for Queen Geraldine – to inspire hope in her countrymen deprived of their homeland and keep the spirit of Free Albania burning bright.

Mother Teresa and Queen Geraldine joined the rest of the party who had been waiting in the distance. Everyone felt the strength and peace that radiated from her as she spoke in Albanian and told how for years she had tried to get a permit for her mother and sister to join her in America. Pressurised by authorities in the different countries the Hoxha régime had always promised that permits would be possible. They never came. Finally both her mother and sister died of infleunza. There was silence as everyone present realised in their hearts the little Mother's own personal suffering that she had lived with all these years.

When Queen Geraldine told Mother Teresa, "I can't understand that such a thing could happen to you," the old nun replied: "Perhaps I also have to be part of a martyred country."

Just before leaving at six o'clock, Mother Teresa led the Queen into the chapel where they knelt and prayed side by side. Albania was not far from their thoughts. As they parted at the door both women spontaneously embraced and kissed each other on each cheek. "Outside my hour with the Holy Father Pope Pius XII this will remain the most enriching human encounter I have experienced," Queen Geraldine said.

King Leka's involvement with the United States goes back many years. He first met President Reagan as Governor of California when he was returning from his visit to the Vietnam war zone. The King routed his trip back to Europe via Hong Kong, Taiwan, Honolulu and California. They had several meetings and established a rapport that has remained. On returning to Spain and hearing that Ronald Reagan was standing as a candidate for the Republican Party, King Leka had the idea to send him an elephant, the emblem of the Republican Party. As the King tells the story:

"My mother was already in Marbella so I thought I would take my boat and go down and see her. My former secretary Maureen Cropper had come from London and was once again acting as my unofficial secretary assisting me to write letters to the various people who had helped me on my recent trip. We were a party of fourteen all told.

"In California I had noticed on President Reagan's desk several elephants and promised him that I would add to his collection from one of my travels. We decided to sail on to Gibraltar and I asked my mother if she would look for one in the shops there. She searched in vain.

"It was then that Maureen said: 'You know Harrods can get anything from a camel to a corgi,' and I said, 'Great. Why don't you get on the ship's phone and call Harrods?' And this she did. Now what I had been talking about was an ivory elephant or a carved wooden one and she thought I meant a live elephant! Several calls later, by the time she had made all the arrangements with the gentleman in Harrods who didn't blink an eyelash, it suddenly clicked that she had ordered a live one. By that time I was so amused, and Harrods anyway thought it would be great publicity, that it was agreed that I pay the £1200 for a baby elephant and they would take care of the air freight. I was in for a penny and in for a pound. The London store used the elephant's publicity value to the best advantage when it was paraded round the ground floor with a notice telling where he was going and why. On arrival in California Governor Reagan was pictured with the elephant on the lawn of his residence before it was passed over to the Sacramento zoo. Somehow the elephant was poisoned and died, but Harrods sent another one over to replace it. President Reagan's jumbo is still alive and well and has given

198

many happy moments to Sacramento children.

On her return to Spain, Queen Geraldine was forced to sell her villa. Although with the help of King Faisal's gift it was fully paid for, she had to have money to live on as King Leka, whose business connections with Iran had collapsed after the revolution, was no longer able to send his mother a regular allowance. Though she had managed to save a little, all she had was money to last the year.

No property had meant as much to Queen Geraldine as this pretty little villa with its window boxes and small garden that was her very own. There was also another more sinister reason. Tired of curious gapers flocking round the villa, constantly hoping to find out how a queen lives, the police had suggested that for security the Queen should enclose the windows with iron bars. This she could not bear. Dreading the thought of agents and prospective buyers traipsing round her house, she managed to sell it without any intermediaries and has refused to think about it ever again. Driving past it in Madrid last Spring, she stopped the car to look and if she was astonished that bars had in fact now been put on the windows her only remark was: "The yellow rose I planted is doing well."

The Queen moved to an apartment belonging to old friends. Filled with her own furniture it is spacious and elegant with a balcony overlooking a park called "The Playground for Children of the World". From her seventh floor balcony the Queen enjoys watching the tiny dots in red, green and blue anoraks as they play hide-and-seek round a large bronze statue of children holding hands. Next door is the modern church where Queen Geraldine prays. Though a total contrast from the grandeur of the churches in Hungary, and Spain's beautiful old Cathedrals, its simplicity matches her mood today. There among the grey and black praying heads she is anonymous, just another soul seeking comfort in Holy Mass.

Queen Geraldine lives with her sister Virginia, Countess Apponyi, a devoted man-servant José, and two Spanish maids, Maria and Margarita, who come in every so often. It is a modest household by Spanish standards but Queen Geraldine has invested it with her own special elegance. There are no grand parties, but intimate luncheons or bridge evenings with the small and devoted collection of friends surrounding her.

The evenings are never long as she can escape into the two

worlds she enjoys the most . . . science fiction films, or romantic novels which line the corridors of the apartment. England's Barbara Cartland has a whole bookshelf to herself.

We have seen with our own eyes how evil can penetrate mens' minds and take over the world. It was that great Englishman, Edmund Burke, who said: "Evil only flourishes when good men do nothing."

I suppose I am like every other woman in that I enjoy escaping into the world of romance. A good novel takes me away for an hour or so from the problems of this unhappy world today and I come away refreshed.

CHAPTER 22

In the summer of 1978 Queen Geraldine felt uneasy and refused to go to the Costa del Sol in Southern Spain with King Leka and his friends. It was as if the hot summer winds were bringing a warning of something beyond her reach. Something evil.

During the days when she went to the *finca* at Pozuelo de Alarcon to see her son and daughter-in-law they sat together, reminiscing about the past and trying to foresee the future. Spain had been going through a traumatic change from a Dictatorship to a Democratic Monarchy and there were many changes in the air. King Juan Carlos and Queen Sophia had not been to see King Leka for some time whereas before they often exchanged visits, sometimes as often as twice a week, for impromptu supper parties. Both Kings had a technical and military interest in the development of new weapons.

From the contacts that I had in Madrid I knew that it was a critical and tense time as the Socialists were making a great show at the municipal elections. I begged Leka to go and see King Juan Carlos — "Juanito" as he is called in the family. My son is a year and half younger and they had always been the closest of friends.

We had noticed almost every day a helicopter flying over the *finca* and Leka used to say to me, "They are taking photographs again." In November Leka went to see the King and came back totally relaxed. "Everything is all right, Mum." King Juan Carlos had told him that of course he could continue to live in Spain but because of the general unrest there should be no more guerilla training or military presence at the *finca*.

I was still uneasy and the winds in my mind were whipping into a storm. As usual on 28th November, which is Albania's National Day, we sent out our royalist message to the five million Albanian compatriots round the world asking them for unity and never to forget the two million Albanians in Kossova. And as always the message ended "Long live Free Ethnic Albania with Kossova."

The drama began at the *finca* on the night of 17th January 1979. It was nine o'clock and the King was just going to bed when four policemen arrived at the main gate. The Albanian guard informed the King of the arrival of the police from the local village of Pozuelo. They had always been friendly and often went to the office at the *finca* for a drink.

"Your Majesty, we've come on a very difficult mission," were their opening words.

"Why don't you have a drink and tell me about it," the King replied unsuspectingly.

The senior police officer then explained that he had been ordered by the Minister of the Interior to search the house for illegal weapons and for illegal personnel. This in itself was suspicious because it was common knowledge at headquarters that the King had a collection of about one hundred assorted weapons, including antique swords and knives, many of which had been presented by Arab Princes. There were only about forty or fifty modern arms that were used for combat training and arming the ten-man guard. "The only pieces that were not accounted for were some grenade launchers, which were used for training. As that was all we had, the Spanish were suspicious because they thought we were concealing a lot more and wanted to dig up the whole place. You don't want to sit with a cache of arms and explosives in your cellars which could explode at any moment if some idiot dropped a cigarette on top of them and anyway there was no way of concealing a store of weapons in Madrid. Our supporters have weapons throughout Europe and any time we want any, we can get them so why sit on them at the *finca*." The police spokesman then explained to the King: "Knowing your tight security here at the *finca* I offered to come along with my colleagues because the last thing we need is an incident whereby your security personnel might kill our police."

This was perfectly tenable as King Leka insisted that if a policeman, or anyone else, had persisted on entering at that hour the situation could have been serious. "We would not know who they were and the basic reason for having security is to make sure that no one entered unidentified. It is well known to Western Intelligence Sources that Albania is a centre for terrorists and many ETA and Grappo groups are trained in the Balkan countries. The Spanish military intelligence often counted on us to keep them informed as they did not have access to Albania as we had and, what is more, they have not been able to get any useful information out of the country. ETA and Grappo knew of our files, so we had to create our own security system as we suspected that we were one of their prime targets."

Later that night the tension eased when the police assured King Leka that there was no way in which the Ministry would be able "to make us come over the wall." The King did not share their views, however, and pointed out, "If they had been ordered to they would have had to obey and then we would have had a shooting match and it wouldn't have been fun."

King Leka suggested that the police should put their guns away and get in touch with the Minister of the Interior to check that he still held the diplomatic status and extra territorial rights granted him by General Franco. This they did and got the Minister to make the journey to the farm that night to sort things out. The Minister agreed that the King was within his rights in not allowing entry into the *finca* and everyone left quietly around midnight.

> At the beginning of January 1979, the great powers had met at a conference at Guadalupe Island, off the coast of Mexico, and there certain decisions were made. At this conference the Shah of Persia was condemned and it was also at that time that Tito asked Britain to represent him in demands to have my son expelled from Spain.
>
> Shortly after this on 22nd January, King Leka was asked to go to the Ministry of the Interior. He returned to the *finca* devastated and immediately telephoned me. He had been told that he and his family must leave Spain by 1st February.

There were three distinct reasons why King Leka found himself now unacceptable to the Ministry of the Interior as a resident of Spain. The first was his alleged training camp for guerillas, as it was publicly known that there were always as many as twelve young Albanians staying for periods of a few months and then disappearing. The second was the cache of arms that the King had stored at the *finca* in order to protect his records, and the third was the possible threat that ETA and Grappo might make a raid on the *finca* to secure these arms for their own use. If this last were to happen it could result in a shoot-up which in turn could cause an international incident.

On hearing the news from King Leka, Queen Geraldine

immediately decided to make a personal call on as many embassies as possible to ask them to give asylum to her son who was shortly to be without a country. Her first call was to the Jordanian Embassy, knowing the cordial relationship that existed between King Hussein and her son. She was received graciously and assured that the following day a plane would arrive from Jordan to take King Leka, Queen Susan and herself there. Queen Geraldine refused the invitation on the grounds that she felt that she was too old to leave Europe and make a new life in a strange country. Twenty-four hours went by and there was no news of the plane. It was later learned at the Embassy that the Jordanian Airlines plane had been refused permission to land by the Spanish authorities.

As Queen Geraldine called on the various embassies with her appeal for help, she found to her dismay that they were either closed for the weekend or, hardest to bear, she was given a diplomatic rebuff. She called on the Moroccan, Argentine, Saudi Arabian, Brazilian, Jordanian and Chilean embassies. Over several years King Leka had had very good relations with the Moroccan authorities, particularly the military, and he had already learned that he would have all the assurances necessary to go and live in Morocco if he ever decided to leave Spain. When Queen Geraldine called on the Moroccan Embassy she was told that the ambassador was not there. This was not true as she could see through the doors that he was having lunch. In desperation she pleaded with the Chargé d'Affaires to telephone direct to King Hussein and was rebuffed, "Not at the moment but we will let the King know." The Chilean Embassy was more helpful and worked day and night to secure visas and passports but when they finally arrived, the King had left Spain twenty-four hours earlier.

During the negotiations between King Leka and King Juan Carlos, so as not to embarrass the Palace King Simeon of Bulgaria who had been to the Victoria College in Egypt with King Leka, offered to act as intermediary and telephone calls were exchanged almost every hour between the *finca* and the Zarzuela Palace. Remembering those fraught days King Leka recalls: "My brother the King was in a difficult situation and I know it was not his personal decision but, because of our long friendship, I would just once have liked to hear his voice." During the last two days King Simeon spent a great deal of time at the *finca* making telephone calls and discussing with King Leka the latest position. Time was running out . . .

Colonel Charles Inigo Jones takes up the story from the moment when he arrived from London in response to a telephone call from King Leka. They had made many overseas trips together and he was a trusted friend of all the family.

"It was arranged that Terry Colebrook, who took care of King Leka's public relations and lived in the centre of Madrid, should pick me up at the airport. On the way back into Madrid she briefed me about what had happened over the last few days at the *finca* and that frantic efforts were going on to find a country, even if it was only for a few weeks. She explained that visas had to be obtained if the party had to stay a couple of nights in a transit country en route to their final destination. These visas had to cover Leka and Sue, and some of the Albanians who had no passports but only refugee cards issued by the United Nations. In addition there were four or five Shan tribesmen from Northern Thailand, headed by Prince Wong, who had Thai passports. All of this would take time."

When the colonel arrived at Queen Geraldine's house, she filled him in on all the diplomatic activity. They were waiting to hear from Morocco and Jordan who had both been most helpful but as yet no answer had arrived. By the morning of Saturday 27th January, nothing had been done, so a visit had to be paid to the embassies of other countries. On the telephone that night King Leka suggested there should be a meeting at eleven o'clock next morning when everybody would be present at the *finca* to discuss the next move. He had already been in touch with his friends in Rhodesia and they were trying to arrange with their government for at least a temporary home. Though grateful for their help, King Leka felt it was a long way away and was still trying to get refuge in a Middle Eastern country.

"When we arrived at the *finca* next morning the place was buzzing with activity. Packers were in the house sorting out the more important items which were to go into storage, and such things as beds and office furniture which would be sold at a later date. The royal party were to take only their personal clothes with them.

"We went into the house and sat in the chairs in the big drawing room while we had our discussion, but this was soon interrupted by the movers who demanded the chairs and whipped them away for packing. As the day went on it became like a game of musical chairs, until by the end of that first day we were all sitting on rolled up carpets in the middle of the floor."

In the mid-afternoon the doctor was expected to see Queen Susan who was running a temperature and had gone to bed. About five o'clock in the afternoon, one of the guards announced that the doctor had come and Colonel Inigo Jones and Reed Armstrong, a sculptor friend from America, who were in the hall told the visitor that the patient was in the bedroom. As he went along the passage the puzzled man announced that he was a vet and had come to vaccinate the animals before their journey. He was immediately taken to the dogs' room. The real doctor arrived shortly afterwards and said that Queen Susan had to stay in bed and be spared as much strain as possible. There were only forty-eight hours left.

There had been some discussion previously about chartering a yacht. King Leka had asked the Marquess of Bristol about the availability of yachts but he said that his son's boat was somewhere in the Mediterranean and anyway they were having trouble with the skipper. Prince Franz Wilhelm of Prussia (married to the Grand Duchess Maria of Russia) was in Madrid and also contacted various friends to see if a hire was possible. Reed Armstrong did the same at Porto Banus, Marbella, but reported back that all yachts were wintering in Palma and unlikely to be available. Even if the King had found a suitable boat they still had nowhere to go and they would have had to motor in convoy to either Valencia, Barcelona or Porto Banus and this would mean a long trip with all their equipment, men and documents. As this might well have been a target for ETA, the Spanish Government may well have not permitted this move to take place.

The alternative was to find a friendly country, who would be prepared to send an aircraft to pick up the royal party; and if that failed then a plane would have to be chartered.

As it was the winter season it was possible to get airlines who were prepared to offer a plane for a round trip, one day there and one day back, without upsetting their commitments. The main problem was trying to find the money. That evening, King Leka went round to see an old friend, Pepe and asked if he would be prepared to guarantee the cost of the flight. The decision was made when Rhodesia offered to have the royal party for a six-

206

week stay. A call had been put through to Rhodesia to ask if the local Cargoman Airlines would be prepared to fly to somewhere in West Africa to pick up the Madrid party. This would then allow a Spanish aircraft to comply with the forty-eight hour requirements. Cargoman replied promptly that they would do this at no expense to King Leka and they suggested Gabon, as this was a country under the influence of France and therefore would not be expected to put a ban on a Rhodesian plane using their airspace. Most other black African countries would of course have impounded a UDI aircraft.

In the outer office King Leka's Chamberlain, Abedin Mulosmanaj, was sorting out all the papers which had to go with the party. They all had to be very carefully marked as Abedin would not be going with them; he was leaving for New York in three days. For the household side of the packing, with Queen Susan out of action, everybody had their own ideas as to what should be stored, what sold and what taken to Queen Geraldine's house. If one person was called to the telephone someone else would take over giving instructions and cries of, "Where is the china and glass, it should be in the box marked X! I can't find it anywhere!" were heard all over the house.

There was feverish activity in the guards' storeroom and bunk house as the men were sorting out what arms they would carry with them and the King was deciding what presentation weapons should be packed. Some of the swords and daggers were to go into store. Colonel Inigo Jones recalls: "The ammunition was taken out of the cellar and put under guard. I was worried about some of the stuff as it was World War II material and could well be unstable, particularly in the air and in a tropical climate."

Everyone thought that the Spanish Government should pay for the Spantax aircraft to Gabon as King Leka was leaving Spain against his will and only at its request, but when this was put to the Minister he made no suggestions. The discussion was continued at Pepe's house where his wife and two daughters were present. Pepe's family pointed out to their father that as there was so little time why did he not put up the guarantee for the amount so that King Leka could get on with his final plans. This he agreed to do – if necessary.

Everyone was up and about at nine-thirty in the morning, the arrangements were the same as the day before, with Virginia buying food on the way to the *finca*. Sue was in bed and not

207

interested in food and Leka was having breakfast with the men. I wondered how Sue would be able to stand such a long trip but I had underestimated the fibre of Australian girls. Prince Wong went off into the village to get some long grain rice for feeding his men, taking the old Seat car which had no brakes and only worked in two gears. It had been bought to go the two miles into the village with things like the post and needed loving and careful handling if it was to go at all. King Simeon telephoned that he would stay in Madrid as he felt he could be more help there. I sat and counted the hours.

With only forty-eight hours to count-down there was an air of artificial calm. King Leka was dressed in combat gear and fully armed. The Shan tribesmen acted as if it was a Boy Scout summer camp and they must try to show how efficient they were. Colonel Inigo Jones and Reed Armstrong tried to be helpful, but at the same time kept in the background to be available if they were wanted.

It was in the early evening on 30th January that King Leka received a telephone call in his office to say that King Simeon had heard from King Juan Carlos that King Leka was to go ahead with Spantax with the Spanish government footing the bill. As the Ministry did not want any difficulties en route to the airport, nor any newspapermen round the King, an escort would arrive at the *finca* at seven-thirty in the evening. To facilitate departure King Juan Carlos had suggested that they should leave from his own private airport building.

On the last morning it looked as though everything had really fallen into place – the packers had done their job, Queen Susan was slightly better and a few friends had come to say goodbye and drink the royal couple's health in her bedroom. Suddenly old Major Qazim announced that as he had never been in an aeroplane before, he refused to go with the family and would remain in Spain. Although at times he could be a stubborn old man this was a poignant moment because he had been Leka's personal guard from the time he was an infant. Here was another break with the past. It was decided that the Albanian major would stay at the *fina* until such time as it was sold.

Before Queen Geraldine left her home at eight o'clock in the morning to go to the *finca* a friend of the family arrived at her house and pressed into her hand an envelope. It contained a sum of money large enough to enable King Leka to have something to live on for the next few months.

208

Around midday it was announced that one of King Juan Carlos's military equerries had arrived. Everyone was slightly apprehensive but the Spanish general was taken straight to the King Leka's office to be given the Spanish flag which had flown alongside the Royal Standard of Albania. The King held the two furled flags across his heart as he said, "These flags have flown side by side for several years and I want you to accept them in rememberance of a person who loved Spain and never made a single act, a single gesture, a single criticism against Spain." It was a touching moment for both men as the general placed the flags against his own chest.

In the early afternoon King Simeon and Queen Margarita arrived to say goodbye. They had proved to be wonderful friends, so loyal and generous in their practical help. Everyone sat in the porch, on the garden furniture which was to be left behind. Queen Susan, who was now feeling a little better, was dressed in her travelling clothes and King Leka wore an open-necked shirt, blue slacks and a casual coat. Everything else had been put in the van, along with all the less important documents which were going to be shipped to America.

The cars to be used were King Leka's Land Rover, Terry Colebrook's small car, Countess Virginia Apponyi's car, Abedin Mulosmanaj's, the Armstrong's hired car and finally the small broken-down Seat.

As Colonel Inigo Jones remembers, "Luckily for me, Reed Armstrong said to me: 'For heaven's sake don't drive that car to the airport and back to Madrid. You will probably never get there'. It was decided that I should drive the hired car. The guards were allotted to the various vehicles including the van, and each was to carry a weapon. The bigger automatics were concealed in shopping bags from the local supermarket!

"Everybody was tense as we waited for the escort to take us through Madrid. Two large black cars arrived about seven o'clock in the evening, with various security people to escort us. The dogs, and four puppies which arrived at Christmas, were rounded up and put in their kennels; the cat was reluctant to leave Spain and could not be found. It was beginning to get dark and Sue sent people off in all directions to find it. It was eventually found sitting on the roof of the *finca* and it took some time to persuade it to come down and be put in its travelling basket."

At a quarter to eight, the convoy set off. It had been suggested by the security people that the van should go separately as it would hold up the convoy but King Leka was adamant that he wanted it to be in the centre of the vehicles. The security people could not understand his attitude as they were not aware that, apart from the luggage, the van also contained all the King's papers and all the spare weapons and ammunition. It was agreed that the little Seat should set off in advance as it was not reliable and would have to travel more slowly. If it did break down the convoy could pick it up on the way through. The rendezvous was the International Terminal where the royal party was to be given its final directions. In fact the Seat arrived on time, and was sitting outside the terminal. To everyone's horror the police were about to tow it away for unlawful parking and causing an obstruction. This would have been fatal as it contained many things that would have been required on the journey, and also two armed Albanians who did not speak a word of Spanish! The party was finally escorted to the King's terminal where they met in the reception room.

Practical as she is, Terry Colebrook decided to go up to the control tower in case there was any last minute message which was to be passed to the plane. This parting was a sad moment for her as apart from being King Leka's personal assistant for a number of years she was very close to the family.

Mother and son embraced as the engines of the plane warmed up. Queen Geraldine was near collapsing point from the stress of the last days, lack of sleep and not knowing when she would see her son again. "Don't worry Mum. There will be someplace else after Rhodesia," said Leka. But his mother could take no more.

> Can a heart break? I think it is like a violin whose strings are irreparably damaged. I was beyond comforting as someone tried to give me something to drink. Gathering me in her arms Virginia took me to the car where our loyal Minister of Court, Abedin Mulosmanaj, stood silently. There were no words to comfort me.

The aircraft moved away and at the end of the runway was given priority clearance for take off. With gathering speed its lights disappeared into the low winter clouds.

Up in the control tower a message had just come through that clearance had *not* been given for the landing of the Cargoman aircraft in Gabon. Rhodesia therefore suggested that the flight should *not* take off until this was arranged. Unaware, the plane flew on in ignorance of what awaited the royal party at Gabon.

210

CHAPTER 23

The message from Cargoman in Rhodesia was immediately sent on to Tenerife where the plane was to stop over for refuelling, but for some reason it did not arrive there and the plane continued on its way to Gabon.

> When we arrived back at the villa I found some intimate friends who had come to show their sympathy. I served drinks but they saw that I was in such a state that they only stayed ten minutes. After a few hours a doctor was called in to give me an injection to make me sleep.
>
> In the morning the agony returned. I heard that at midnight the police had surrounded the *finca* and made a thorough search of the house and the grounds. All they found was a sad and confused Major Qazim.
>
> I immediately began making a list of all that was necessary to pay off the remaining debts, like my son's overdraft at the bank, the travel agency he used and so on. My head was filled with doubts and queries, but during those days I delved deeply into my mind to make a truthful analysis of my son's life. If ever he needed my help it was now.

In the early morning Queen Geraldine was wakened to be told that a message had arrived from the Spanish ambassador in Gabon to say that the Government there was demanding a vast sum of money and that the plane was being held hostage until there was a settlement.

It was not until many months later that Queen Geraldine learned the details of the traumatic flight to Rhodesia. Although the families corresponded frequently the incident at Gabon was never mentioned. No one was sure that letters would not be censored. One evening an Albanian stood outside the door of her villa in Madrid and said that he had come with a personal message from King Leka for the Queen. Countess Virginia Apponyi tactfully left the room.

He was a strong, forty-year-old man who had suffered

immensely in Albania before he escaped. He had been brutally tortured, imprisoned and condemned to death under the Hoxha régime but had managed to escape to Spain to join King Leka's retinue. Finishing his coffee this Albanian looked at the Queen and said: "I have a long story to tell you. You know what I have gone through in my life. I assure you the fear that I went through when the plane arrived at Gabon was the worst."

The plane had first stopped in Tenerife to refuel and then flown on to Gabon, still unaware that there would be difficulties over the question of outrageous airfield fees. Gabon is a mere dot on the west coast of Africa where a small international airport has been built. As soon as the King's plane arrived it was directed to one side away from the main air terminal. As it was early in the morning everybody wanted to alight. Queen Susan was still running a temperature from her influenza, but needed to get some fresh air and sunshine. The King and Queen were immediately stopped by French Legionnaires who had surrounded the plane. A colonel then stepped forward and asked to speak to the King. Without any formalities he told King Leka that a large sum of money was required for landing fees. As this was not remotely possible the King refused and was told that the plane was to be impounded. King Leka explained that there was no question of the plane being under arrest as it had been chartered by King Juan Carlos and the Spanish Government and he was merely in transit as a plane from Rhodesia was arriving any hour to take the whole party there at the request of the Prime Minister, Mr Ian Smith.

The French colonel listened but was adamant, threatening to surround the whole airport with his troops. By now the sun was beating down on the plane and for those trapped inside without air conditioning it was like a furnace. The colonel made as if to enter the plane but was stopped by the King who firmly said, "Go and tell your President that I accept no illegal menaces and that I will bring out my men and the weapons which I have in the plane. We are quite capable of blowing up the terminal and the jets that are lying around and this will cost your country more than any capture."

This was purely a ruse, as the King was well aware that the President of Gabon might have plans to hand him over to the Albanian Government in Tirana.

By now the King had given orders for all his guards to set out on the aircraft steps all their arms, which included eight machine

212

guns and the grenade launchers, all capable of blowing up the whole airport. Even Queen Susan, her corn-blonde hair glinting in the sun, stood on the top step of the aircraft with her own gun held ready. At that moment they saw a large black car approaching flying the Spanish flag, which drew up alongside the plane. Out stepped the Spanish ambassador who immediately spoke to the King offering shelter for Queen Susan in the embassy. This she refused and the ambassador left promising to get in touch with King Juan Carlos in Madrid.

By now the news of the arrival of the royal plane had spread in the confined Gabon community and the spectators' balcony was filled with people, including diplomats like the Russian Ambassador who was taking a keen interest in the proceedings. Although there was food on the plane, the heat was so great that the King and Queen drank only water.

A second car approached the plane with flags flying which contained a military aide-de-camp who announced, "The President of Gabon invites you to pay a call on him." Both King Leka and Queen Susan immediately checked their guns and the King gave instructions to his Albanian guards in a voice loud enough for everyone to hear, "If we are not back in an hour and a half blow up the plane."

The King and Queen arrived at the governor's house and entered by an underground passage. As they passed from one room to another all the alarms went off, triggered by the metal in the revolvers that the King and Queen were carrying. This fact did not go unnoticed by the equerry who accompanied them. The President received them with formal courtesy apologising and explaining that he had been under pressure all that day not only from Spain, but from France and several Arab countries. All the time the President was speaking, his aide was looking nervously at his watch as the minutes ticked by, apparently too scared to acquaint the President of the instructions King Leka had left behind. Finally with sirens in full blast they left the President's villa and zoomed out to transfer to the Rhodesian plane which had arrived and was standing nearby. It had been twelve hours packed with tension before the plane finally took off at seven in the evening.

The Albanian had finished his story. He and the Queen sat in silence. After he had left, Queen Geraldine began to feel ill. It was a recurrence of the cerebral fever of her youth and she was ill for some weeks.

For King Leka and Queen Susan the story ended with their arrival in Salisbury where they were met by the authorities and made welcome. They were to remain in Rhodesia for over a year before going on to South Africa where they have made their home outside Johannesburg ever since. During her stay in Rhodesia Queen Susan was to lose her third baby – the child that she so desperately wanted to give her husband and Albania, was stillborn.

CHAPTER 24

Queen Geraldine has made two visits to South Africa where King Leka and Queen Susan have been living. Her first trip in 1981 came as a complete surprise when the Albanian community in America sent her a ticket so that she could see her son in his new home, a ranch-style house fifty-two kilometres from Johannesburg. It stands at the end of a long dusty road lined with scrub and thorn trees. The five hundred acres of land are left to nature with chickens, cows and the odd peacock rambling over the dry lawns, scattered shrubs and crumbling outhouses. No one ever enters the property before first being checked by an Albanian guard at the gates who still dreams of the snow capped peaks of his homeland. For Queen Susan the farm is home. The landscape reminds her of the emptiness of her own country and solitude has never worried a girl brought up to station life in the outbacks of Australia. Even that peculiar dry smell that belongs to nowhere else in the world except Africa and the stunted vegetation and thorn bushes is for her reminiscent of Australia.

For Queen Geraldine, it was a time of joy seeing her son in his new surroundings, but also one of great anguish when Queen Susan lost the baby that she was expecting. The two queens had become very close to each other and Queen Geraldine spent two days and nights by Queen Susan's side to share her grief, sleeping on a sofa so as to be at hand whenever she was awake.

Recalling that period, Queen Susan says, "A particularly beautiful quality of my beloved mother-in-law is her unfailing generosity and her very deep spiritual quality which she is able to share without being overbearing. She has a gift to be able to see and assess a person in a positive manner rather than seeing the negative sides. She has not only brought up my husband as a strong believer but has also strengthened my own faith through her example."

There were also many world issues for mother and son to discuss during this visit as it was the time of the revolt in Kossova after Tito's death and the time when an attempt was made to kill

215

the Holy Father, Pope John Paul II. Long into the night they used to sit talking and, with her experience of a lifetime of constant change, and her ability to adapt to whatever situation she finds herself in, Queen Geraldine's advice was invaluable.

During her stay the young King of Zululand invited the Albanian royal family to visit him. The Zulus are a noble race and she was intrigued to see the veneration they have for the mother figure, much as they had in Albania in the old times. At Kruga Park she even saw the elusive white rhino which is said to be an omen of good luck.

Just a year later King Leka wrote to his mother that Queen Susan was expecting a baby. This was her fourth attempt to have a child as she had had two miscarriages and one still-birth. By now she was forty-one years of age and though many women might have given up hope, she was determined to give King Leka the heir that he wanted, just as Queen Geraldine had been to King Zog all those years before.

Even the previous caesarian which she went through alone in Rhodesia as King Leka was away at the time, and the tragedy of the baby girl who was still-born did not take away this determination.

> Exactly a year after my visit to South Africa I managed to save enough money to take a tourist ticket and arrived six weeks before the expected birth of my first grandchild. Sue had been in hospital for two months as an 'at risk' mother and this time they were taking every precaution. She even gave up smoking in the belief that this might have been an added danger. Leka was waiting for me at the airport and looked desperately nervous. "We will leave your baggage at home and then we will go on straight away to see Sue," he said. Thank goodness I insisted on telephoning her as I was feeling exhausted after a sixteen-hour flight. She laughed and said: "No you come tomorrow morning. I am very well and I certainly don't want you to come this evening."
>
> Looking back I ask myself why didn't I buy lots of beautiful baby clothes in Spain as when I arrived and saw that nothing had been arranged I was astonished. Were we all superstitious?

At eight o'clock next morning the telephone rang and it was the hospital to tell King Leka and Queen Geraldine to come quickly. The Sister explained that because Susan had her first child by caesarian the doctor intended to deliver this baby in the same way.

Queen Geraldine and King Leka remained in Queen Susan's airy bedroom in the Johannesburg Clinic while the patient was taken to the operating theatre. They sat and talked catching up on news and trying to look outwardly calm. Within less than an hour she was brought back to her bed still drowsy from the anaesthetic. Then the nurse took King Leka to see his son! The nurse had washed the baby but he was not yet clothed as he was five weeks premature, weighed only 5½ pounds and was going to be put into an incubator.

I waited thanking God with all my heart. I heard Leka simply bounding down the stairs shouting "Mum . . . he is bawling like a sergeant major." I went back with him to admire the beautiful little boy as he lay in his incubator attached to support systems to help him in these first few hours of life. Because he was premature his head was like a skeleton and he had no flesh on his cheeks, but the body was already filled out and he was long and healthy.

For King Leka suddenly the world was filled with wonder and deep satisfaction as he gazed down on his son. It was as if all the harrowing years leading up to this moment no longer mattered. Albania had a Crown Prince and the Zogu dynasty was assured.

When the baby stopped crying, and puckering up its face, Queen Geraldine was able to study the bone structure. The shape was exactly like that of King Zog. The same elongated, elegant forehead and high brow that had given the King such a distinguished and aesthetic profile. Looking at the baby's long limbs she realised, too, that there was every possibility that he would grow to be as tall as his father.

That evening at the farm was a joyous one with telephone calls and telegrams from all over the world. They came from Albanians who had heard the news on their radios, television and in the newspapers. This large global family wanted to share their joy with their King and Queen far away in South Africa. Two families who managed to telephone from Kossova in Yugoslavia were delirious with excitement as they celebrated the birth. King Leka in his no-nonsense way told them, "For God's sake put down the telephone. You are going to be arrested tomorrow morning". All they replied was, "We don't care. We have got a Prince."

The baby was given some resounding names after men who had helped King Leka in the past — Anwar (President Sadat of Egypt), Zog (King Zog I of Albania), Baudouin (King of the Belgians) and Reza (the Shah of Persia). It is expected that when he becomes of age the baby will be known as Zog like his grandfather.

For Queen Geraldine another small Leka was almost like having a child of her own. As Queen Susan says, "Her immense joy at seeing her grandson is still legend at the clinic where he was born. After I brought our son home, our darling Granny was never out of the nursery and the baby's routine did not exist for her. Being a new mother, I felt rather desperate and asked Nanny what I should do. Nanny said, 'Don't worry, madam, all grandmothers act this way, but Queen Geraldine is rather different.' Even at such a young age, the baby's face would light up when he saw Granny. She is a very, very beautiful person, so serene and a really devoted grandmother. Babies sense these things. He can be an absolute beast to me at times but he is always calm with her."

Today he is a strong independent little boy of five. Brought up much as his father was, surrounded by tough Albanian guards, he knows how to take care of himself. "We have already started to teach him how to use his feet and not only his hands. There is none of the Queensberry rules for him," his father says.

Queen Susan believes in the value of home and family and is determined that her son will have a normal family background. He will be sent to a play-group or kindergarten and learn to mix with other children. He will be raised in the Muslim faith in preparation for his eighteenth birthday when he is presented to the Free Albanians of the world. Also in preparation for that day he speaks fluent Albanian. A tough, charming little boy, he looks remarkably like his father did at that age — minus the long curls.

Though she has not even caught a glimpse of Albania, for Queen Susan it is indelibly impressed on her mind that this country is now her home. "Perhaps it was the hardest decision of my life. Australia is something that I love and miss but I've committed myself to our going home one day. Home to Albania."

Christmas 1985 was Prince Leka's first with Queen Geraldine.

Friends say that it was strange to hear this small boy, thousands of miles away from Tirana, speaking in Albanian with his grandmother, and even more so, as they discussed everyday things about South African life. Perhaps he too has a sense of fate like his father King Leka who says: "I have always known what I was destined to do."

Queen Geraldine has no definitive hopes for her future. She is content to live from day to day and despite continuous frail health, she is eternally young in spirit. Her love for her adopted country Albania has never wavered.

My son is maintaining a close watch on the present situation, and should he be able to see an opportunity, knowing him as I do, I believe he will act in the best interests of his people. This, in spite of the fact that some western countries would not like to see a change in Albania as they fear that this would bring about a destabilisation of the Balkans, and thus permit the Soviet Union free entry into the Mediterranean. Here again, the lack of understanding by these countries of the Balkan mentality and situation permits this oppressive, atheist régime to continue in existence.

No matter what these western countries do to maintain the status quo, the natural aspirations of the different ethnic nations that form the Balkan community will eventually bring about the very destabilisation that they fear. Would it not be a far healthier situation to try to work within the parameters of these different ethnic nations and so reach an equitable solution, acceptable to most, and thereby stabilise this highly volatile and dangerous area?

Though my son has been denied the guidance of his father during the last twenty-five years he has not been without friends. Among the greatest influences of his life have been Generalissimo Francisco Franco, King Faisal of Saudi Arabia, whose good advice and deep love for my son put him into the position of being his honorary godfather. His Imperial Majesty the Shah-in-Shah of Iran, Mohamed Reza Pahlavi, President Habib Bourguiba of Tunisia, President Anwar Sadat of Egypt, President John Vorster of South Africa, President Alfredo Stroessner of Paraguay, President Ronald Reagan during his time as Governor of California, His Royal Highness Sheik Zayed Bin Sultan al-Nahyan of the United Arab Emirates, the

219

Right Honourable Julian Amery, the Right Honourable Sir Robert Menzies when he was Prime Minister of Australia and today His Majesty King Hussein of Jordan who is the same age as my son. To all these men I am indebted for their wisdom and friendship over the past difficult years and the help they have given in forming my son's character.

Much of Queen Geraldine's strength stems from her deep faith in God and throughout her life she has used this faith to help other people. Just to be in her presence is an extraordinary experience as she radiates a pure inner serenity and the confidence of a woman to be reckoned with.

Even if I wanted to, I could not live a life of my own. The most beautiful place on earth is worth nothing when you are alone unless you are a completely meditative soul. Apart from my own family I have several million Free Albanians to whom I have also committed my life. I pray for them every day and I will never betray them.

I do not consider myself a brave woman though I have faced many disagreeable situations. The one thing that I cannot tolerate is viciousness in man or woman. I get mesmerised. I am like a rabbit in *Watership Down* – bewildered and numbed.

My whole existence, from early infancy, has been buffeted by the winds of history, which were sometimes tempestuous. Contrary to what some people say, the winds do not only blow from the East, they come from all points of the compass – only their violence varies.